The Tongue of the Fathers

THE MIDDLE AGES SERIES

Ruth Mazo Karras, General Editor
Edward Peters, Founding Editor

A complete list of books in the series
is available from the publisher.

The
Tongue of the Fathers

Gender and Ideology in
Twelfth-Century Latin

Edited by
David Townsend and
Andrew Taylor

PENN

University of Pennsylvania Press

Philadelphia

10 9 8 7 6 5 4 3 2 1

Published by
University of Pennsylvania Press
Philadelphia, Pennsylvania 19104–4011

Library of Congress Cataloging-in-Publication Data
The tongue of the fathers : Gender and Ideology in Twelfth-Century Latin / edited by
David Townsend and Andrew Taylor.
    p.   cm. — (The Middle Ages series)
    Includes bibliographical references and index.
    ISBN 0-8122-3440-5 (cloth : alk. paper)
    1. Latin literature, Medieval and modern—History and criticism.   2. Latin language,
Medieval and modern—Discourse analysis.   3. Civilization, Medieval—12th century.
4. Gender identity in literature.   5. Sex role in literature.   6. Sex in literature.   7. Twelfth
century.   I. Townsend, David, 1955–   .   II. Taylor, Andrew, 1958–   .   III. Series.
PA8035.T66   1998
870.9′35204′0902—dc21   98-9896
                                                                                           CIP

Contents

Introduction

Collections that thematize medieval constructions of gender, sex, and sexuality have become something of a scholarly genre in their own right. Such issues are pervasive in current work on the medieval vernaculars and are increasingly familiar in work by medieval historians.[1] But the study of medieval Latin has remained largely isolated from such developments, bounded in the estimation of both Latinists and vernacularists by its continuing reputation for quintessentially traditional philology. With some notable exceptions (including a recent anthology that also focuses on the Latin tradition, but with attention to periods other than that addressed in the present volume),[2] medieval Latin studies and gender studies continue to whisper to each other through chinks in the wall.

Despite the explosion of commentary on issues of gender in medieval culture, the relatively small community of scholars who focus on Latin texts tends to espouse approaches reflective of the "old" philology—an inclination altogether understandable in light of a necessarily heavy investment in the mastery of a relatively difficult language. At the same time, *users* of medieval Latin in other disciplines often employ medieval Latin texts as foils against which vernacular developments can be represented as culturally innovative. Latin discourse, according to such constructions, endlessly replicates tradition. It upholds a monological and orthodox consensus. It maintains its own authority by the preservation of sameness and the erasure of difference. To enter into this language is, par excellence, to enter into patriarchy. Medieval Latin, in short, is the Tongue of the Fathers.

Such a characterization of medieval Latin does not always represent a failure to attend to the texts' clear assertions of their own intentions: the Latin literary tradition often says as much about itself. Indeed, the very concept of a Latin literary tradition appeals to principles of patriarchal authority that were highly developed and even systematized. *Auctoritas*, that combination of intellectual and moral seriousness that made one an author, belonged to clerics writing in Latin.[3] Stephen Nichols notes the mutually reinforcing circle of moral, grammatical, and social order: "Latin *canon*, derived from Greek *kanon* = *regula*, bore a range of connotations linking literary and linguistic rule governance to religio-political orthodoxy."[4] Latin was indeed admirably suited to serve as an instrument of social control: it was a well regulated and enduring language, access to which was limited almost exclusively to male clerics, but among those same male clerics it was nearly universal throughout Christendom, past and present. This "universal" language, with its substantial vocabulary of abstract terms and its support of extensive hypotaxis, was the ideal instrument for the great medieval systematizations, the encyclopedic codifications of the arts and sciences, theology, canon law, and pastoralia, by which theological and social orthodoxy was imposed upon society as a whole. In contrast to the fluidity and free-play of the vernacular, Latin preserved the judgments of the past in a language ostensibly frozen in time.

This contrast constitutes a central theme in the work of poststructuralist Romance philologists such as Paul Zumthor, Roger Dragonetti, Bernard Cerquiglini, and Alexandre Leupin.[5] Latin enabled the formation of an overwhelming cultural synthesis that encompassed all aspects of social practice, from epistemic organization to the most intimate personal habits. The works of the Church Fathers also offered a comprehensive exegetical code for the interpretation of poetry, one that generated, and continues to generate, interpretations purged of historical dissent and internal contradiction.[6]

The medieval Latin tradition declares a patriarchal mission. This is abundantly clear. But modern scholarship has yet to interrogate the self-declared identity of many Latin texts with anything like the level of aggressive re-visioning that we now expect of Old French or Middle English studies. There is need, in other words, for a gathering of readers that attend to medieval Latin texts with an ear for what reveals itself as problematic in the constitution of Latin as a monologic tongue in unrelenting support of the patriarchy.

The seven chapters in this volume focus on representations and constructions of gender and sexual difference in a range of twelfth-century Latin texts. These texts emerged from centers of cultural prestige and power, and most were authored by men. Two chapters focus on Abelard. The other five examine texts by Heloise, Bernard Silvestris, Hildegard of Bingen, Walter of Châtillon, and Bernard of Clairvaux. This collection, in other words, does not seek primarily to recover marginalized writers. The essays, rather, trace and critique the replication of patriarchy in the quintessentially patriarchal language of medieval high culture. At the same time, they attend to what is problematic in twelfth-century Latin's self-constitution (and in its modern scholarly receptions) as a monologic Tongue of the Fathers. They deal squarely with gender oppression in the discursive economy of the texts and indict it frankly, but they also point to the ideological fissures that admit resistance and heterodoxy within an ostensibly masculinist linguistic and literary tradition. They trace some of the ways in which the Tongue of the Fathers cannot speak without its voice cracking at crucial junctures.

*   *   *

The volume opens with Andrew Taylor's "A Second Ajax: Peter Abelard and the Violence of Dialectic." Taylor points up the tension between the self-presentation of dialectic as an impersonal language of detached truth claims, on the one hand, and on the other the intensely agonistic martial metaphors with which Abelard and his contemporaries describe their disputations. Taylor argues for a sociological analogy between twelfth-century dialectical jargon and other self-contained ideolects by which male homosocial groups seal the bond of their cohesiveness against the uninitiated. The investment of this language in claiming detachment from personal interest and emotion, moreover, is locked in a necessary relation with the apparently contradictory aggression with which Abelard describes his victories and defeats. The claim to detachment and the agonistic metaphor, taken together, point to the originary predicament of patriarchal identity formation, a formation dependent on denial and abnegation for the marks by which the self is identified. The social circumstances under which young men were initiated into Latinity in the period of the rise of the schools were particularly apt for the repudiative division of the self that normative masculine identity requires.

Taylor's chapter sets the stage for later pieces in the volume by delineating forcefully at the outset the fundamentally gendered nature of twelfth-century Latinity, which differed significantly from earlier monastic usage but had not yet evolved into the relentlessly specialized academic subculture of high scholasticism. Some of the later chapters corroborate twelfth-century Latin's patriarchal investment. Others point out the ruptures by which the ideology that sustains that investment succeeds in undermining itself. Nearly all regard the entry into Latinity as tantamount to an entry into patriarchy.

In "*Dominus/Ancilla*: Rhetorical Subjectivity and Sexual Violence in the Letters of Heloise," Marilynn Desmond also addresses issues of linguistic ideological encoding in the same milieu. Complementing Taylor's concentration on public disputation, Desmond focuses on the readerly experience of Heloise herself, whose letters repeat the misogynist gestures of Ovid and other classical authors. Desmond's essay explores how these traditions connect with the moment of eroticized physical violence described by Abelard in the *Historia calamitatum*: the blow he delivers in accordance with his instructions from Heloise's uncle for her punishment. Desmond argues that the pedagogical/erotic violence depicted by Abelard in the *Historia* replicates on the physical level the textual violence of the Latin amatory and rhetorical texts in which Abelard tutored Heloise. Desmond's reading shows us Heloise as neither fully complicit in nor forcefully resistant toward the gendered politics of Ovidian amatory violence.

Alcuin Blamires counterpoints Taylor and Desmond by examining one of Abelard's less read letters to Heloise, which recounts the establishment of female monasticism and enumerates the sources of its authority. While many have dismissed the letter as a dutiful piece of drudgery, Blamires reads it as a committed polemic that uses a range of innovative exegetical maneuvers to challenge contemporary gender assumptions and to provide Heloise with a theoretical basis for her new vocation. Blamires argues that Abelard resists the antifeminist tradition he inherits. He stresses how far Abelard diverges from certain misogynist commonplaces and how radical some of his claims are. Abelard reads the Samaritan woman who meets Christ at the well as providing a biblical precedent for preaching by women when she recognizes him as the Messiah and proclaims him to her people. The anonymous woman who annoints Christ with the contents of an entire alabaster container (Mark 14) assumes a quasi-sacramental authority, so that Christ, the head of the Church, is annointed by a woman, while its member priests are annointed by men. Here, as elsewhere in the letter, Abelard diverges markedly from the main stream of exegesis.

Blamires notes the paradox that Abelard's defense of women anticipates the familiar Lacanian pattern of patriarchal inscription of woman as lack, based as his defense is, in part, on the principle of women's weakness. Men, Abelard insists, are naturally stronger than women, in both mind and body. So Abelard connects the apostles' desertion of Christ to a line from Job: "Pelli meae, consumptis carnibus, adhaesit os meum" (19:20); that is, when the apostles, Christ's flesh, ebbed away, there were left only the women, the skin, to adhere to his body, the foundation of the Church here figured by the bone.

Critics have objected to Abelard's use of women's weakness to demonstrate their spiritual strengths, as if he were structuring his argument in accordance with the pattern of sharp contradiction set out in his *Sic et non*. To be sure, Abelard's insistence on the priority of women's religious accomplishments at times takes on a combative, masculinist cast, characteristic of this master dialectician. But Blamires defends Abelard's use of the "rigid scaffolding of the logic of perfectibility," arguing that without it Abelard would never have been able to push his defense of female authority beyond bland assertions that a few women are distinguished spiritually through special grace. By appealing to the doctrine that weakness will be perfected in strength, Abelard can mediate between the tradition of women's inferiority and the evidence of actual women's powers.

Claire Fanger's "The Formative Feminine and the Immobility of God: Gender and Cosmogony in Bernard Silvestris's *Cosmographia*" takes as its point of departure the often remarked but seldom scrutinized femininity of Bernard's agentive goddesses, Noys, Natura, and Silva. Fanger takes issue with the influential assessments of Ernst Curtius, on the one hand, and of Etienne Gilson, on the other. She demonstrates that Bernard's constructions of gender within divinity are fundamental to his working out of theological problems. The *Cosmographia* is neither "bathed in the atmosphere of a fertility cult" (Curtius) nor unproblematically orthodox beneath a harmless *involucrum* that leaves uncompromised the transcendent truth of normative, and normatively gendered, theology (Gilson). Divine gender for Bernard is, to be sure, not homologous with mundane human gender, Fanger demonstrates, but gendered categories nevertheless lie at the heart of Bernard's speculative theology. Fanger reads the literal level of the allegory—its body, so to speak—as essential. While Bernard's formulations can be (and have been) read as masculinist in their preservation of God's invisible masculine transcendence as First Principle, the God who works in Creation and can be observed there is God as Noys, whose womb is necessary to all possibilities of becoming and plurality. God undeniably has a womb in the *Cosmographia*; but if she also has a phallus, that masculine signifier denotes not so much divine power and activity as stillness and unspeakability.

Joan Ferrante contributes to the literary biography of another of the great twelfth-century cosmographical theologians, Hildegard of Bingen, with a study of her relations with the scribes whom she both commanded and depended upon. Ferrante's "*Scribe quae vides et audis*: Hildegard, Her Language, and Her Secretaries," cleaves closely to the sources to provide a vivid picture of the negotiations of authority and influence implicit in the career of one of the period's most widely influential mystics. Ferrante begins by pointing out that for Hildegard, Latin's status as her medium of communication is not at issue: she appropriates the language unabashedly, straightforwardly abrogating the claims of normative usage and style by appeal to the higher demands of revealed truth. Only at the end of her career does she allow the last of her several male secretaries, Guibert of Gembloux, to "improve" her style, and then only in minor works.

In "Sex and the Single Amazon in Twelfth-Century Latin Epic," David Townsend focuses on a short passage from Walter of Châtillon's *Alexandreis*. Talestris, Queen of the Amazons, visits Alexander with the intention of conceiving a child by him, but on arrival she is disappointed by his unimpressive physical stature. While the passage ostensibly criticizes the "simple savage mind" ("barbara simplicitas") that can only judge on the basis of physical appearances, in various subtle ways it calls Alexander's virility and authority into question. In Townsend's reading the passage's dominant trope is *praeteritio*, which highlights what it purports to conceal. The robes of the Amazons "hide what must be hidden" ("celat celanda"), while Talestris ponders "where the great virtue of the unvanquished prince / might lie concealed," and the juxtaposition does not work to Alexander's advantage. In particular, Townsend contrasts patriarchal constructions of the female body in terms of castration with the text's depiction of the Amazonian body, whose right breast is cauterized in childhood to facilitate use of the bow. In contrast to the patriarchal *metaphor* of "castration," Amazonian society demands a *literal* deprivation, but this deprivation is a mark of power and social inclusion. At the same time, Talestris is capable of nourishing a child with her exposed left breast. This representation of the Amazon challenges notions of the plenitude of the male body. Drawing on Kaja Silverman's analysis of the "dominant fiction" that the penis and the phallus are one, Townsend contends that Talestris displaces the phallus as the mark of binary opposition on which gender is founded. By "juxtaposing the patriarchal imposition of a figurative lack onto the subject with the Amazons' imposition of a literal one, the text problematizes the very notion of 'castration' upon which the dominant fiction depends." For Townsend, Talestris's physical body calls into question the more metaphorically constituted prowess of Alexander, a prowess that attempts to elide an awareness of his less impressive literal stature.

In a chapter on a group of sermons from Bernard of Clairvaux's cycle on the Song of Songs, Bruce Holsinger takes up the connections between gender construction and medieval protocolonialist discourses of the Other to which Townsend's essay alludes, but Holsinger develops the latter theme far more extensively. He exposes Bernard's lethal association of racial figuration, violence, and desire as he traces the connection between the abjection of blackness and the homosocial bonding of monastic and crusading communities in a collective will to die. Taking as his point of departure the words of the Bride, "Nigra sum sed formosa" ("I am black but beautiful"), Bernard develops the theme of blackness as symbol of the earthly body, whose physical mortification is a mark of humility and a promise of redemption. Bodies darkened by beating, like those of St. Paul, and bodies darkened by the sun, like those of the Templars, slough off blackness for whiteness in redemption. Christ is likened to the sun, both darkening the soul with the rays of his love and making the soul appear dark in contrast to his brightness the closer it approaches, so that blackness becomes a symbol of love for Christ and of spiritual advancement.

Holsinger argues for the homoeroticism of Bernard's sermons, in which the Bride becomes a symbol for both the Church at large and the individual Christian who is penetrated by Christ's love, so that male homosocial relations are grounded in the black body of the Bride. Holsinger, however, attributes to these figurations a far-reaching political effect within western Orientalism. He rejects attempts to maintain a separation between, on the one hand, Bernard's self-presentation as a contemplative aloof from the mundane considerations of politics and, on the other, the promulgation of the crusades. Holsinger argues instead for a complex connection between Bernard's extensive exegesis and the discursive strategies by which Eastern and Muslim bodies can be abjected as Other. At the same time that the blackness of the Other is repudiated, the blackness of the believer's postlapsarian body becomes for Bernard the object of homosocial desire for a community of men.

The paradoxical desire for blackness in oneself and one's fellows exists precisely in the relation of that blackness to its eschatological obliteration and replacement by the purity of whiteness. It is not just that Bernard depicts Islam as a discoloration of Christianity and the earthly Jerusalem; the earthly Jerusalem is the imagined site for the union of Christ and his Bride, the new Jerusalem. Here the pious soul can hope for full union with Christ the Bridegroom. In Bernard's writings, crusading, through which the earthly Jerusalem may be recaptured, is, like death, a part of an eroticized trajectory of loss, rapture, and salvation. Bernard's assumption of desire between men linked in longing for sacrifice and purity is inextricably bound up with the sign of pollution inscribed temporarily on the skin of the faithful. Bernard's devotional writing, which circulated widely, thus instilled in Latin Christendom a longing for conquest and a desire to overcome the alterity of ethnic blackness.

∗   ∗   ∗

The following chapters repeatedly reflect a concern for the shaping force of language. To what extent did the privileged *litterati* who are the subjects of these essays manage to control the linguistic patterns that enmeshed them? Did the renewed access to classical and patristic literary models offer them a greater degree of freedom or merely more insidious determinations? Did they speak medieval Latin, or did it speak them?

Traditional readings of the twelfth century were confident that the resurgence of Latinity offered a richer inner life. From C. H. Haskins's classic *The Renaissance of the Twelfth Century* on,[7] the period has been constructed as a precursor of the Italian Quattrocento. The discussion of twelfth-century "humanism" follows this pattern, since the term, borrowed from the historiography of the later Renaissance, links a renewed dedication to classical authors with the beginnings of individualism and a more optimistic view of the human condition.[8] The fullest claim for the role of Latinity in this twelfth-century renaissance has been advanced by Colin Morris: "It may appear at first sight that skillful Latinity is a technical accomplishment which has little connection with individualism or any other view of life, but for men of the age it was an essential preliminary to the imaginative exploration of themselves and the universe."[9] Contrasting the fluent self-expression of Guibert de Nogent, Anselm, and Abelard with Einhard's cumbersome attempt to describe Charlemagne's character by patching together quotations from Suetonius, Morris argues that renewed Latinity was "the indispensable preliminary for the discovery of the individual."[10]

More recent historians have reinforced this picture, while modifying it slightly: although they stress that medieval self-construction differs from modern individualism, they place even greater emphasis on its textual base. Caroline Walker Bynum in "Did the Twelfth Century Discover the Individual?" argues that "The twelfth-century person did not 'find himself' by casting off inhibiting patterns but by adopting appropriate ones."[11] Mary Carruthers claims that the medieval self was "constructed out of bits and pieces of great authors of the past" stored in the memory.[12] By way of illustration, Carruthers offers the speech in which Heloise proclaims her

determination to become a nun, as described in Abelard's *Historia calamitatum*. Instead of using words of her own, Heloise bursts out with the
lines from Lucan's *Pharsalia* in which Pompey's wife, Cornelia, offers to
kill herself to placate the gods after he has suffered a shameful defeat. Carruthers stresses that Heloise "did not 'see herself as' Cornelia in the sense
of acting a role; rather, Cornelia's experience, given voice by Lucan, had
been made hers as well—so much her own that she can use it, even, perhaps, with irony, in such an extreme personal situation."[13] Heloise, in this
analysis, deliberately uses her store of classical poetry to express her inner
feelings; she is a "subject that remembers."[14]

A more fluent Latinity did indeed provide a broader range for personal expression, but the contributors to this volume offer a more cautious assessment of these linguistic developments and the freedoms they
allowed. Heloise's knowledge of classical literature, notably Ovid, Cicero,
Juvenal, and Seneca, was remarkable for a woman of her period, but as
Desmond shows, this knowledge immersed her in a misogynistic tradition
that she did not fully repudiate. As the author of Latin letters, Heloise is
largely constructed by the gendered grammar of violence inherent in the
Latin traditions she has absorbed. Heloise does not simply capitulate to the
Ovidian tradition, but neither, in Desmond's reading, does she struggle
vehemently against it. Blamires, in assessing Abelard's defense of women's
spiritual prerogatives, is more optimistic. He contends that although Abelard was fully imbricated in the patristic tradition that takes the physical
and intellectual weakness of women as a given, he could still launch "raids"
from within this tradition against dominant gender assumptions. Blamires
attributes to Abelard a significant degree of agency. As a means of expressing his empathy for Heloise, Abelard uses dialectical logic, but he is not
completely bound by its limitations: "The strength-in-weakness topos was
an enabling topos."

Although Abelard did not transcend the gender prejudices of his day,
he managed to attack them. Taylor locates Abelard within an equally encompassing tradition, in this case the tradition of dialectical disputation
and the social customs of ritualized male aggression in which Abelard
gained mastery. But Taylor then turns to the one place where Abelard
appears to destabilize this tradition by depicting himself as a dialectical
braggadoccio. Townsend similarily finds that satire destabilizes the gender
roles of the epic tradition, so that the Amazon queen becomes for a moment more authoritative than the great Alexander: the text hints at possibilities of more fluid gender roles that Walter could never assert directly.

"Walter of Châtillon was no feminist," according to Townsend, yet his text subverts the phallocentric authority of Alexander and evokes, if only in passing, the possibilities of discursive and social alternatives in the figure of Talestris. Fanger, in her exploration of the *Cosmographia*'s bold regendering of the divine image, similarly demonstrates how a male author can at least partially escape from the constrictions of the patriarchal symbology with which his speculations originated. Bernard's dependence upon gendered categories to think through the divine nature both privileges the feminine and, at the same time, pries gender loose from divine ontology, relegating it instead to the constructed contingencies of human knowing.

In their explorations of the engendering of the "twelfth-century individual," the contributors show to varying degrees the influence of post-structuralist and postmodernist accounts of the ways in which the human subject is constructed within language.[15] Such accounts draw heavily on Althusser's and Foucault's formulations of how a society can, as a means of ensuring its own continuity, impose upon its members an all-embracing and formative way of seeing the world. But such formulations are not without their dangers: they have been much criticized on the grounds that they obliterate any possibility of resistance.[16] Ideology, as Althusser describes it, seems too pervasive for anyone to stand outside it; power, as Foucault describes it, seems too insidious to resist—such, at least, is the objection. Attention to the ideological power implicit in language runs as a thread through this collection. In following it, the contributors try to steer between a naive optimism about the subject's transcendence of linguistic determination, and a determinism that would dismiss lived experience as a mere epiphenomenon of larger cultural forces.

That most of these chapters corroborate twelfth-century Latinity's replication of masculinist categories of gender and sexual difference will come as small surprise to readers with a background in feminist criticism. The *auctoritas* that accrued to Latin was rooted precisely in its status as a language whose acquisition, chiefly by men, was dependent upon alienation from associations of birth origin and upon bonding with other male pupils in submission to the master and his command of grammar. But in showing how their subject texts play out the relations of patriarchy and Latinity, the following chapters do not simply restate the obvious in regard to a monolithic linguistic tradition. They serve, rather, to illustrate the social specificity of patriarchy's linguistic supports and of the resistances those formations elicit.

Taken together, the essays encourage one to speak of a plurality of twelfth-century Latinities. As the acquisition of Latinity moved increasingly from monastic to other milieux—into the schools and into the courts of aristocratic bishops and secular lords—and as the audience for monastic Latinity came potentially to include these wider readerships, the historical inflections of the language's gendered associations arguably became more various. The jargon of dialectic espoused by Abelard's followers contrasted with the more humanistic literary tradition in which Heloise was so fully steeped. Bernard Silvestris's speculative cosmological poesis, like Hildegard's visions, ventures into allegory in order to supplement the orthodox formulations that the texts are careful not to contradict palpably. At the same time, Bernard's more academic appeal to a broad tradition of previous speculation contrasts with the originality of Hildegard's more phatic pronouncements. Walter of Châtillon's classicizing practice of epic bears an obvious affinity with the literary humanism of Heloise while drawing at times simultaneously upon the speculative traditions of the School of Chartres. Bernard of Clairvaux's ostensibly traditional monastic discourse of devotion proceeds in self-declared contrast to more worldly language, but its performance plays out in full awareness that the linguistic community it purports to address represents only a fraction of its potential audience.

The spaces available for women's agency and voice and for heterodox desire within these Latinities are various, and variously problematic. Nowhere in this volume does the recuperation of such agency occur without the negotiation of significant obstacles. If the homosociality of Taylor's dialectical horde is particularly relentless, the pervasive readerly internalization of misogynist topoi traced by Desmond is particularly insidious. Ferrante's account of Hildegard's relations with her scribes suggests, by contrast, the apogee of what was possible for a woman of substantial authority whose voice relied for its embodiment upon the Tongue of the Fathers. But even Hildegard, despite her scribes' gestures of deference, must negotiate her dependence on them for their control of grammatical correctness, by means of topoi that might suggest instead her marginalization. Fanger shows how a speculative neo-Platonist poetics could begin with the patriarchal assumption of the unknowable First Principle's masculinity but come to reduce that veiled phallic primacy to relative insignificance beside a divine feminine agency. Townsend shows how the representation of the Amazon body effects a kind of discursive guerilla raid upon the militarist trajectory of epic narrative. Perhaps in no other chapter is the paradox of women's agency in the Tongue of the Fathers so heightened as in Blamires's discussion of what he contends are Abelard's radically profeminist exegetical moves to justify the religious life of women—which hinge on the reassertion of women's weakness. In short, this book suggests that resistance to the misogynist and patriarchal ideologies of Latinity articulates itself not as a direct opposition to *auctoritas*, but as a dissipation of its monologic pretensions.

Notes

1. Such collections include Linda Lomperis and Sarah Stanbury, eds., *Feminist Approaches to the Body in Medieval Literature*; Clare A. Lees, ed., *Medieval Masculinities: Regarding Men in the Middle Ages*; Jennifer Carpenter and Sally-Beth MacLean, eds., *Power of the Weak: Studies on Medieval Women*; Jacqueline Murray and Konrad Eisenbichler, eds., *Desire and Discipline: Sex and Sexuality in the Pre-Modern West*; and the growing list of titles in the New Middle Ages series published by Garland.

2. Barbara K. Gold, Paul Allen Miller, and Charles Platter, eds., *Sex and Gender in Medieval and Renaissance Texts: The Latin Tradition*.

3. On the interdependent concepts of authority and authorship, see A. J. Minnis, *Medieval Theory of Authorship: Scholastic Literary Attitudes in the Later Middle Ages*, 10.

4. Stephen G. Nichols, "An Intellectual Anthropology of Marriage in the Middle Ages," 78.

5. Zumthor and Dragonetti conflate under the term *jonglerie* the somewhat disreputable and erotically charged linguistic play of the vernacular *jongleur* with a poststructuralist championing of the play of the signifier and its repudiation of referentiality. See Paul Zumthor, *Essai de poétique médiévale*, trans. Philip Bennett, *Toward a Medieval Poetics* as well as Zumthor's "Jonglerie et langage." See also Roger Dragonetti, "Joufroi, Count of Poitiers and Lord of Cocaigne," esp. 96, an adaptation and translation of a section of *Le gai savoir dans la rhétorique courtoise*. In an analogous manner, Alexandre Leupin conducts his study of medieval poetics under the telling rubric "barbarolexis," the principle by which literature takes the inadequacy of language to name the object of its desire, whether God or sexual climax, and "turns this double lack into the resources of its own production [transforming] a dual impossibility into an affirmation of the desire to write" (*Barbarolexis: Medieval Writing and Sexuality*, trans. Kate M. Cooper, 6). The same spirit informs Bernard Cerquiglini's influential *Éloge de la variante*, which legitimizes the myriad lexical, orthographical and grammatical deviations of the manuscript variants, previously categorized as errors, as a form of linguistic play. The target of this subversion is, at least initially, the grammatical order that the old philologists wished to impose upon the vernacular, but that grammatical order was itself an extension of Latin's grammatical regularity. See Alexandre Leupin, "The Middle Ages, the Other," 28. Leupin himself, it should be noted, extends his study of *barbarolexis* to cover the *Poetria nova* of Geoffrey of Vinsauf and the *De planctu Naturae* of Alan of Lille, but the model clearly valorizes the grammatical disorder characteristic of the vernacular at the expense of the regimentation characteristic of

Latin. By implication, Medieval Latin is thus relegated to the oppressive legacy of "le médiévisme du papa": Zumthor, *Parler du moyen âge*, 31.

6. The most extensive application of patristic exegesis to medieval texts is that of D. W. Robertson, Jr. See in particular *A Preface to Chaucer: Studies in Medieval Perspectives*. For powerful critiques of Robertson's agenda, see David Aers, *Community, Gender, and Individual Identity: English Writing, 1360–1430*, 7; Louise O. Fradenburg, "'Voice Memorial': Loss and Reparation in Chaucer's Poetry"; and Gayle Margherita, "Originary Fantasies and Chaucer's Book of the Duchess."

7. Haskins's *The Renaissance of the Twelfth Century* was first published in 1927 and has been reprinted in several editions.

8. R. W. Southern offers a classic account: "there was . . . in the twelfth and thirteenth centuries a continuous and uninterrupted reassertion of the claims of human dignity. The intellectual enquiries of the period made God, man, and nature intelligible and coherent; the area of the natural world was enlarged at the expense of the supernatural, and the pressure of the unknown which had weighed heavily on many parts of life was lightened" (*Medieval Humanism and Other Studies*, 50).

9. Colin Morris, *The Discovery of the Individual, 1050–1200*, 7.

10. Ibid., 8.

11. Caroline Walker Bynum, *Jesus as Mother: Studies in the Spirituality of the High Middle Ages*, 90.

12. Mary Carruthers, *The Book of Memory: A Study of Memory in Medieval Culture*, 180.

13. Ibid., 179.

14. Ibid., 184.

15. Gabrielle Spiegel offers a general assessment of this "turn to language" in "History, Historicism, and the Social Logic of the Text in the Middle Ages," 74. Spiegel draws on Catherine Belsey's theoretical primer, *Critical Practice*. Those who want a basic introduction might also consult Jane Tompkins, "A Short Course in Post-Structuralism." A useful illustration of the difficulties of understanding the notion of the construction of the subject in language is offered by Laurence Stone, who (erroneously) equates it with the much simpler notion that we all bring to our work a personal perspective or bias. See his "History and Postmodernism, III," esp. 189–90.

16. Alan Sinfield rejects what he has called the "entrapment model" of ideology in favour of one that admits the possibility of the subject's genuine and resistive agency, despite its formation within ideology (*Cultural Politics—Queer Reading*, 26–27). Nancy Partner objects to the "outward move" of cultural poetics, a move "from experience *outwards only* to the group or collective culture," which offers "no concept or premise that could plausibly begin to 'subvert' any of the 'widely shared meanings' whose production, distribution, and enforcement have constructed the human thing which has no self and no personal sexuality" ("No Sex, No Gender," 427). Gabrielle Spiegel remarks, "What gets lost in the concentration on meaning in the place of experience is the sense of social agency, of men and women struggling with the contingencies and complexities of their lives in terms of the fates that history deals them and transforming the worlds they inherit and pass on to future generations" ("History, Historicism, and the Social Logic of the Text," 74).

A Second Ajax

Peter Abelard and the Violence of Dialectic

Andrew Taylor

In Philosophy "so much depends on the nature of the debate. If you're a man, you're expected to do the heavy testosterone thing, right? You're expected to be aggressive, you're expected to handle the put-down, to be able to put down and so on."
— Pat Churchill[1]

At the conclusion of his *Theologia "Summi boni"*, an extensive application of the categories of Porphyry's old logic to the nature of the Trinity, and one of his earliest major theological treatises, Abelard protests that his motives in writing are entirely disinterested:

Hec nos de altissima et incomprehensibili philosophia diuinitatis, coacti frequenter et prouocati ab importunitate infidelium, scribere ausi sumus, nichil asserentes de eis que dicimus, nec veritatem [docere] intendentes, quam neque nos posse scire profitemur. Sed neque hi qui fidem nostram impugnare gloriantur, ueritatem querunt sed pugnam.[2]

(Having been frequently pressed and provoked by the importunities of those lacking faith, I have dared to write this treatment of the most high and incomprehensible philosophy of Divinity, asserting nothing about the truth of what I have written, nor intending to teach the truth, which I acknowledge I am not able to know. But those who glory in impugning my faith seek not the truth but a battle.)

The modesty of the claim is so extreme as to be paradoxical: Abelard writes under the correction of a higher truth, which he admits he cannot know and about which he asserts nothing. In a roughly contemporaneous letter addressed to the bishop of Paris, however, Abelard's personal animus emerges as he blames his opponent, easily identified as the nominalist Roscelin, for "vomiting threats and calumny," while at the same time labeling this opponent "pseudo-dialecticus et pseudo-christianus" and accusing him of detestable heresies.[3]

The language of Abelard's letter contrasts sharply with the impersonal tone of the *Theologia "Summi boni"*, which opens with an almost arithmetical delineation of the various properties that distinguish the three persons of the Trinity. Abelard begins with the theological commonplace that each name of the Trinity is associated with a particular quality: the Father with power, the Son with wisdom, and the Holy Spirit with benignity. He then proceeds, with a logician's clarity, to set out their mutual interconnection:

In his autem tribus, potentia scilicet, sapientia, benignitate, tota boni perfectio consistit, ac parui pendendum est quodlibet horum sine duobus aliis. Qui enim potens est, si id quod potest iuxta modum rationis conducere nescit, exicialis est ac perniciosa eius potentia. Si autem sapiens sit et discretus in agendo, sed minime possit, efficacia caret. Quod si et potens sit et sapiens, sed nequaquam benignus, tanto ad nocendum fit pronior, quanto ex potentia et astutia sua ad efficiendum quod vult est securior; nec spem beneficiorum suorum ceteris prestat, qui benignitatis affectu non commouetur.[4]

(In these three, namely power, wisdom, and goodness, lies all perfection, and no one of them can do much without the other two. If someone is powerful, but does not know how to govern his power according to reason, he has a power that is destructive and pernicious. And if someone is wise and behaves discreetly, but can do little, he is ineffective. But if someone is both powerful and wise but is not good, he will be all the more prone to do harm, the more certain he is of being able to do what he wants because of his power and strength. Nor does anyone who is not moved by a feeling of goodness fulfill the hope of doing good to others.)

In a language purged of all rhetorical figures or personal touches, dialectic presents itself as an innocent tool of theological instruction. Each step follows inevitably. The author is indeed "asserting nothing," as he will claim at the end of the work, but merely tracing out a series of logical relations.

This scientific impersonality of the *Theologia "Summi boni"*, which could be illustrated from almost any passage, is even more pronounced in Abelard's most extensive logical treatise, the *Dialectica*, which survives, with a few lines missing at the beginning, in a single twelfth-century manuscript.[5] What are now the first lines of the *Dialectica* run as follows:

DE DIVISIONE SUBSTANTIARUM

. . . Unde non universaliter in generibus substantiarum accipiendum est, quod ait generalissima substantiarum nomina qualitatem circa substantiam determinare. Quod autem ait primas substantias hoc aliquid significare, idest rem suam ut discretam ab omnibus aliis demonstrare, de omnibus est intelligendum. Cum itaque specialia substantiarum nomina maxime propter qualitates quibus species efficiuntur determinandas inventa sint, propria maxime propter discretionem sunt reperta.

(ON THE DIVISION OF SUBSTANCES

. . . whence, on the matter of the genus of substances, that position which says
that the most general names of substances determine the quality of the substance
should not be universally accepted. On the other hand, the position which says that
primary substances signify this thing, that is, that they point to the thing itself as
discrete from all others, is to be understood of all things. And because the special
names of substances are to be investigated above all, since [they provide] the qualities by which species are made distinct, the proper [or individual names of things]
are to be investigated for the sake of the principle of distinction.)

Here all personality is occluded by the technical jargon of Aristotelian
logical categories: genus, species, substance, and signification, the "hoc
aliquid" and the "rem suam." Controversy, too, retreats before the magisterial phrasing: the positions "which should not be universally accepted"
(non universaliter accipiendum est), as opposed to those "which should be
understood about all things" (de omnibus est intelligendum). Personal involvement is dissolved into a series of passive periphrastic constructions,
whose unspecified obligation encompasses all right-thinking logical men.
It is the conflict between dialectic's self-presentation as disembodied ratio-
nal analysis, on the one hand, and dialectic as a site of masculine aggression, on the other, that I wish to examine.

Abelard and his contemporaries repeatedly describe their debates in
military terms, as clashes of arms, conflicts, or battles, often developing
the metaphor at length. Thus St. Bernard writes of his confrontation with
the Goliardic Abelard:

> Procedit Golias procero corpore, nobili illo suo bellico apparatu circummunitus,
> antecedente quoque ipsum armigero eius Arnaldo de Brixia. . . . Stans ergo Golias
> una cum armigero suo inter utrasque acies, clamat adversus phalangas Israel. . . .
> [C]um omnes fugiant a facie eius, me omnium minimum expetit ad singulare cer-
> tamen. . . . Abnui, tum quia puer sum, et ille vir bellator ab adolescentia, tum
> quia iudicarem indignum rationem fidei humanis committi ratiunculis agitandam,
> quam tam certa ac stabili veritate constet esse subnixam.[6]

(Hulking Golias advances, armed with all his noble warlike gear, while his squire,
Arnold of Brescia, goes before. Golias therefore cries out against the ranks of Israel
as he stands with his squire between the two battle lines. . . . When all fly from his
sight, he challenges me, the weakest of all, to single combat. . . . I refused, not only
because I am a boy and he has been a warrior since his youth, but also because I
judged it unfitting that the grounds of faith should be discussed by human reasoning, when it is agreed that it rests on such a certain and stable truth.)

Similarly, in the *Historia calamitatum* Abelard describes his confrontation
with the man he scornfully refers to as "our teacher," that is, William of
Champeaux, and his pupils as a full-fledged siege:

Statimque ego Meliduno Parisius redii, pacem ab illo ulterius sperans. Sed quia ut diximus locum nostrum ab emulo nostro fecerat occupari, extra civitatem in monte Sancte Genovefe scolarum nostrarum castra posui, quasi eum obsessurus qui locum occupaverat nostrum. Quo audito magister noster statim ad urbem impudenter rediens scolas quas tunc habere poterat et conventiculum fratrum ad pristinum reduxit monasterium, quasi militem suum quem dimiserat ab obsidione nostra liberaturus. . . . Post reditum vero magistri nostri ad urbem, quos conflictus disputationum scolares nostri tam cum ipso quam cum discipulis ejus habuerint, et quos fortuna eventus in his bellis dederit nostris, immo mihi ipsi in eis, te quoque res ipsa dudum edocuit. Illud vero Ajacis, ut temperantius loquar, audacter proferam,

> Si quaeritis hujus
Fortunam pugnae, non sum superatus ab illo.

Quod si ego taceam, res ipsa clamat, et ipsius rei finis indicat.[7]

(I immediately returned from Melun to Paris, hoping for peace from him from then on. But since, as I have said, he had installed a rival in my place there, I set up the camp for my scholars outside the city on Mont St. Geneviève, as if to lay siege to the man who had taken my place. When he heard this, our teacher immediately and shamelessly rushed back to the city, to free from our siege the scholars that he had left, as if they were soldiers whom he had abandoned, and led back the small band of brothers to their original monastery. . . . You have known for a long time about the the conflicts my scholars had both with him and with his disciples after our teacher had returned to the city, and what success fortune gave to our forces (including myself) in these wars. I can refer with some moderation to the line of Ajax, and boldly say:

> If you seek
The result of this battle, I was not conquered by him.

But if I should be silent, the deeds speak for themselves and tell the result of this matter.)

Abelard's depiction of dialectic as a kind of war is no casual trope but reflects an actual transference of social energy, whereby ambitious young men channeled their aggression into the disputation of the schools, just as they might otherwise have channeled it into the regulated warfare of the early tournament, a social mechanism that was expanding at this time.[8] In many ways the groups of students resembled the contemporary war bands of *juvenes* described by Georges Duby.[9] The *juvenes*, the original knights errant, were young warriors who had no land and no immediate prospects and set out to make a name for themselves and win what booty they could. In this quest they wandered freely; indeed, wandering was considered a necessary part of their professional formation, a kind of *studium militiae*.

But they did not wander alone. Rather, they formed into small bands: "More frequently the company collected around a leader who 'retained' the young men, that is who gave them arms and money and guided them towards adventure and its rewards."[10] Much the same could be said of the students who moved from one cathedral school to another in the pursuit of logic. They too were young, ambitious, rowdy, and highly mobile, and they were often united by their loyalty to a charismatic leader who could best all comers in individual combat.[11] They defended their chosen leader aggressively and were not above physically intimidating a rival, as Abelard knew only too well. If their leader were bested once too often, however, they might desert, as so often happened when a stronger champion, such as Abelard, appeared on the scene.

The social parallels between the ritual combat of the young scholars and the combat of young warriors, which have often been noted, are particularly striking if we compare Abelard's early career to that of a champion such as William Marshal, who made his career two generations later.[12] For both Abelard and Marshal, technical proficiency and a series of individual victories brought wealth and an ever increasing following of younger combatants.[13] When Abelard describes how his followers plied him with gifts, how his name was known across Europe, or how he defeated all comers on whatever question they wished to ask, the image he evokes is that of the tourneying hero.

Like these heroes, Abelard was on display, and like the tourneying heroes, the triumphant Abelard was also heavily eroticized.[14] Heloise writes that crowds flocked to catch a glimpse of him when he entered or left a town and that all women were on fire in his presence:

Quis etenim regum aut philosophorum tuam famam exaequare poterat? Quae te regio aut civitas seu villa videre non aestuabat? Quis te rogo in publicum procedentem conspicere non festinabat ac discedentem collo erecto oculis directis non insectabatur? Quae coniugata, quae virgo non concupiscebat absentem et non exardebat in praesentem?[15]

(What king or philosopher could equal your fame? What district, city, or town did not surge forward to see you? Who did not hasten to see you when you appeared in public, and did not strain his head forward and stare after you as you left? What wife, what maid did not yearn for you when you were absent and did not take fire in your presence?)

The careers of both Marshal and Abelard were ultimately crowned with sexual tribute. Marshal benefited from a lucrative marriage when King

Richard gave him one of his wards, the wealthy heiress Isabel de Clare.[16] Abelard, for his part, found that his great reputation made him, at least potentially, irresistible to any woman he might wish to pursue.

Hanc igitur [Heloissam], omnibus circunspectis que amantes allicere solent, commodiorem censui in amorem mihi copulare, et me id facillime credidi posse. Tanti quippe tunc nominis eram et juventutis et forme gratia preminebam, ut quamcunque feminarum nostro dignarer amore nullam vererer repulsam.[17]

(Having considered all the things which normally attract a lover, I selected this woman [Heloise] as the most suitable to take to bed, and I believed I would have no difficulty doing so. At that time my reputation was so great, and I was young and extremely handsome, and did not fear a rebuff from whatever woman I honoured with my love.)

Nor was this love entirely private. Abelard, as Heloise tells us, made her name famous through his songs.[18] Like the lady of the tournament, Heloise becomes the token that reinforces the homosocial bond of the scholarly *comitatus*.[19]

Abelard's critics objected repeatedly to his self-promotion and to dialectic itself, which they condemned as irreverent, jargon-ridden, juvenile logic-chopping.[20] Jocelyn, later bishop of Soissons, was said to have warned a student against Abelard's quibbling and his quarrelsome manner:

Magistrum Petrum . . . disputatorem non esse, sed cavillatorem; et plus vices agere joculatoris quam doctoris, et quod instar Herculis clavam non leviter abjiceret apprehensam, videlicet quod pertinax esset in errore; et quod si secundum se non esset, nunquam acquiesceret veritati.[21]

([He said] Master Peter was not a disputer but a quibbler, and behaved more like a *jongleur* than a doctor, and that just like Hercules, once he had taken up the cudgel, he did not lightly put it down, in other words that he was tenacious when he was wrong; and that if it were not his own position, he would never acknowledge the truth.)

In his *Contra quatuor labyrinthos Franciae* Walter of St. Victor, one of Abelard's most intemperate critics, condemned Abelard as one of the four scholars whose labyrinthine thinking led to heresy.[22] Walter heaps scorn on the scholastic terminology which by claiming that human nature is nothing leads to a heretical rejection of the Incarnation:

Est igitur humanitas que accidentaliter et non substantialiter dicatur? Est et que substantialiter, id est naturaliter sit? Quod si nichil est, nullus homo humanitate homo est. O insania! Dialecticus proponit: omnis homo humanitate homo est. Assumit hereticus: at humanitas nichil est. Diabolus concludit: nichil est ergo omnis homo. Si autem humanitate homo est, omnis homo et humanitas nichil est; ergo omnis homo homo non est. O monstrum![23]

(Is "humanity," therefore, something which is predicated accidentally and not naturally? Or is it something which exists substantially, that is, naturally? Because if "humanity" is nothing, no man is a man because of his humanity. What insanity! The dialectician proposes, "Every man is a man because of his humanity." The heretic adds: "And humanity is nothing." The Devil concludes: "Therefore every man is nothing. If, however, man is man because of his humanity, every man is nothing and his humanity is nothing; therefore, every man is not a man." What a monstrosity.)

For Walter, syllogistic logic and the technical terminology of substance and accident are what build the labyrinth of heretical sophistry.

Others objected to the scope of dialectic. In his *Disputatio adversus Petrum Abaelardum*, William of St. Thierry, a Benedictine abbot with strong Cistercian sympathies, seizes on the very point Abelard makes at the beginning of the *Theologia "Summi boni"*, that dialectic is asserting nothing. William condemns "those academics" who refuse to believe or know anything but insist on "estimating" or reasoning about it ("quorum sententia est nihil credere, nihil scire, sed omnia æstimare") and complains that Abelard "loves to question everything, wishes to dispute everything, equally, whether divine or secular."[24] William particularly objects to Abelard's scholastic language and the expression "videtur nobis" (it seems to us), which Abelard employs when faith alone would guide him better:

Ut nobis, inquit, videtur. Melius ergo ipse aliquid asseret nobis, quam in quo omnes doctores post apostolos convenerunt et consentiunt? Meliusne aliquid ei revelatum est, vel ipse per se adinvenit, quam quod nos docuerunt qui a Domino didicerunt?[25]

("As it seems to us," he says. Does he tell us something that is better than that to which all the doctors of the Church after the Apostles agreed and consented? Is something better revealed to him, or has he found out something better by himself, than that which they have taught us who were taught by God?)

For Bernard of Clairvaux, Abelard's most influential critic, Abelard is a monk "who knows no bounds" and pries into the mysteries of faith,

dum totum quod Deus est humana ratione arbitratur se posse comprehendere. Ascendit usque ad caelos, et descendit usque ad abyssos. Nihil est quod lateat eum, sive in profundum inferni, sive in excelsum supra.[26]

(as long as he thinks that he can understand all that is God by human reason. He ascends to the heavens and descends to the lowest regions. Nothing is hidden from him, whether in the depths of hell or in heaven above).

The fullest account by far of the excess of dialectical argumentation, however, is that of a former pupil of Abelard's, John of Salisbury, in his satire on an academic opponent, disguised under the name "Cornificius."[27] According to John, in the schools where this windy fool first gained his learning, the philosophers "argued interminably over such questions as whether a pig being taken to market is held by the man or the rope."[28] They were swept up in a youthful craze that discarded anything it considered old-fashioned:

Poetae historiographi habebantur infames, et siquis incumbebat laboribus antiquorum, notabatur, et non modo asello Archadiae tardior, sed obtusior plumbo uel lapide omnibus erat in risu. Suis enim aut magistri sui quisque incumbebat inuentis. Nec hoc tamen diu licitum, cum ipsi auditores in breui coerrantium impetu urgerentur, ut et ipsi spretis his quae a doctoribus suis audierant, cuderent et conderent nouas sectas. Fiebant ergo summi repente philosophi. Nam qui illiteratus accesserat, fere non morabatur in scolis ulterius quam eo curriculo temporis quo auium pulli plumescunt. Itaque recentes magistri e scolis, et pulli uolucrum e nidis sicut pari tempore morabantur, sic pariter auolabant.[29]

(Poets who related history were considered reprobate, and if anyone applied himself to studying the ancients, he became a marked man and the laughingstock of all. For he was deemed both slower than a young Arcadian ass, and duller than lead or stone. Everyone enshrined his own and his master's inventions. Yet even this situation could not abide. Students were soon swept along in the current and, like their fellows in error, came to spurn what they had learned from their teachers, and to form and found new sects of their own. Of a sudden, they blossomed forth as great philosphers. Those newly arrived in school, unable to read or write, hardly stayed there any longer than it takes a baby bird to sprout its feathers. Then the new masters, fresh from the schools, and fledglings, just leaving their nests, flew off together, after having stayed about the same length of time in school and the nest.)

John complains of how hastily and with what little expenditure of effort these new doctors acquired their training, and how they despised all that went before them, especially Grammar:

Ecce noua fiebant omnia, innouabatur grammatica, dialectica immutabatur, contemnebatur rethorica, et nouas totius quadruuii uias, euacuatis priorum regulis de ipsis philosophie adytis proferebant.[30]

(Behold, all things were "renovated." Grammar was made over; logic was remodeled; rhetoric was despised. Discarding the rules of their predecessors, they brought forth new methods for the whole Quadrivium from the innermost sanctuaries of philosophy.)

He makes it clear that they did this by employing logical categories.

Solam conuenientiam siue rationem loquebantur, argumentum sonabat in ore omnium, et asinum nominare uel hominem, aut aliquid operum naturae, instar criminis, erat aut ineptum nimis aut rude, et a philosopho alienum. Impossibile credebatur conuenienter et ad rationis normam dicere quicquam aut facere, nisi conuenientis et rationis mentio expressim esset inserta. Sed nec argumentum fieri licitum nisi praemisso nomine argumenti.[31]

(They spoke only of "consistence" or "reason," and the word "argument" was on the lips of all. To mention an "ass," "a man," or any of the works of nature was considered a crime, or improper, crude, and alien to a philosopher. It was deemed impossible to say or do anything "consistently" and "rationally," without expressly mentioning "consistence" and "reason." Not even an argument was admitted unless it was prefaced by its name.)

The result, concludes John, was "a hodge-podge of verbiage" (sartago loquendi). The sheer pace of dialectical disputation is summed up in his claim that arguments were traded so fast one had to bring a bag of beans or peas to act as counters to keep score. Speed, indifference to eloquence or the normal rules of grammar, cavilling, and game-playing: these are the qualities of dialectic as it had come to be practiced. For John they are not inherent vices but excesses, the "sterility" that results when dialectic is separated from other disciplines and pursued without moderation or a genuine desire for knowledge.

John of Salisbury's critique was not directed against Abelard. Abelard himself attacked these men in his *Theologia christiana*, accusing them of disturbing the peace of the Church with their "intolerable verbosity" and of pursuing only their own glory, and insisting that dialectic was not to be confused with "fallacious sophistry" (fallaciam sophisticae).[32] According to John of Salisbury, however, in fighting against this insanity, wiser masters such as Abelard succumbed to it themselves:

Sed et alii uiri amatores litterarum utpote magister Theodoricus artium studiosissimus inuestigator, itidem Willelmus de Conchis grammaticus post Bernardum Carnotensem opulentissimus, et Peripateticus Palatinus qui logicae opinionem praeripuit omnibus coaetaneis suis, adeo ut solus Aristotilis crederetur usus colloquio, se omnes opposuerunt errori, sed nec universi insanientibus resistere potuerunt. Insipientes itaque facti sunt dum insipientiae resistebant, et erronei diutius habiti dum obuiare nitebantur errori. Verumtamen fumus ille cito euanuit . . .[33]

(Others who were lovers of learning set themselves to counteract the error. Among the latter were Master Thierry, a very assiduous investigator of the arts; William of Conches, the most accomplished grammarian since Bernard of Chartres; and the Peripatetic from Pallet [i.e., Abelard], who won such distinction in logic over all his contemporaries that it was thought that he alone really understood Aristotle.

But not even all these scholars were able to cope with the foolish ones. They themsleves became insane while combating insanity and for quite a time floundered in error while trying to correct it. The fog, however, was soon dispelled . . .)

But the fog was not dispelled everywhere. In about the year 1148, after twelve years' absence, John returned to Mont Ste. Geneviève to find that his old friends, Abelard's less prestigious successors, were still engaged in the same arguments:

Inuenti sunt qui fuerant et ubi. Neque enim ad palmum uisi sunt processisse. Ad quaestiones pristinas dirimendas, nec propositiunculam unam adiecerant. Quibus urgebant stimulis, eisdem et ipsi urgebantur. Profecerant in uno dumtaxat, dedidicerant modum, modestiam nesciebant. Adeo quidem, ut de reparatione eorum posset desperari. Expertus itaque sum quod liquido colligi potest, quia sicut dialectica alias expedit disciplinas, sic si sola fuerit iacet exanguis et sterilis, nec ad fructum philosophiae fecundat animam, si aliunde non concipit.[34]

(I found them just as, and where, they were when I had left them. They did not seem to have progressed as much as a hand's span. Not a single tiny [new] proposition had they added toward the solution of the old problems. They themselves remained involved in and occupied with the same questions whereby they used to stir their students. They had changed in but one regard: they had unlearned moderation; they no longer knew restraint. And this was to such an extent that their recovery was a matter of despair. I was accordingly convinced by experience of something which can easily be inferred [by reason]: that just as dialectic expedites other studies, so, if left alone by itself, it lies powerless and sterile. For if it is to fecundate the soul to bear the fruits of philosophy, logic must conceive from an external source.)

John's account of dialectic in the days of Cornificius's youth and in the early days on Mont Ste. Geneviève captures the competitive drive of the young dialectical champions, and although one should distinguish between Abelard's practice and that of his successors, in many ways it confirms the picture Abelard himself offers of his own rise in the *Historia calamitatum*.[35] Logic advanced through aggressive public competition. According to a wise old theologian who allegedly offered guidance to Gerald of Wales when he tired of dialectics:

"Logica tua in qua tantum te torques, quid tibi valebit, nisi socium habeas ad quem disputes, quia dialectica disputatio ad alterum est, nec suffici[e]t ille si impeditor fuerit communis negotii. Oportet ergo judicem adhibere, nec sufficiet unius si forte in partis adversae favorem declinaverit. Turbam ergo convocare oportet et intelligentium ad hoc, ut ars tua utiliter appareat."[36]

(This logic of yours, in which you twist yourself up, what good is it to you unless you have a friend to dispute against, since dialectic is a disputation against someone, nor will he be enough, if he refuses to enter into debate with you. So you will need a judge, nor will one judge be enough, lest he favor the other side. So you will need a crowd, and it will need to be learned, for your art to appear useful.)

This was the social dynamic of the schools.

As a professional discourse, dialectic was certainly well suited to the needs of bright young men in a hurry. Dialectical disputation did not require the extensive rumination and internalization of the Bible and the Fathers that was the heart of monastic *lectio*, nor the extensive familiarity with the classics demanded by the grammarians.[37] In fact, dialectic did not even require that extensive a mastery of Latin grammar, since many of the expressions were used in such a specialized manner that they more or less had to be learned for the discipline. The Latin of medieval students of logic was not entirely reliable either. As Hastings Rashdall notes, "A Statute of Paris makes the ability of the petitioner to state his case before the rector in Latin, 'without any interposition of French words,' a test of his *bona-fide* studentship."[38] For those who only just managed to pass this test, the sparse, linear syntax of a dialectical treatise would have been considerably more congenial than a passage from Virgil.

By concentrating on narrow and highly technical questions such as that of universals, dialectical disputation obviated the need for long linguistic study and allowed for the rapid advancement of the most intelligent, however young or inexperienced, while the development of a specialized technical vocabulary served as a further social bond for its practitioners, a linguistic heraldry. In other words, many of the qualities that gave dialectic its impersonal, scientific feel were in fact highly socially coded, an expression of the aggressive drives and professional needs of the young men who used dialectic to carve out a career.

Abelard first established himself as dialectic's preeminent practitioner, but he then went on, in his logical treatises, to become its preeminent theoretician, and in these treatises Abelard furthered the development of dialect as an artificial and professional language. The sparseness of his style, itself implicitly exclusionary of the mundane and personal, was echoed by a series of theoretical moves through which Abelard severed dialectic from external norms, whether grammatical, physical, ethical, theological, or ontological.

First, with only occasional exceptions, Abelard makes dialectic synonymous with logic, a drastic reduction of its possible scope. Logic is one of the *artes sermocinales*, but Abelard separates it clearly from common linguistic usage and thus from the rules of grammar. Abelard is not hostile to grammar,[39] but he emphasizes repeatedly that the analytical order of logic takes precedence:

Quod autem gramaticorum regulis contrarii videmur, quod multa componimus verba vel substantiva, ut "esse hominem," vel ab aliis quam ab actionibus vel passionibus sumpta, ut "esse album," propter rectam enuntiationum sententiam aperiendam, non abhorreas. Illi enim qui primum discipline gradum tenent, pro capacitate tenerorum multa provectis inquirere aut corrigenda reliquerunt in quibus dialetice [sic] subtilitatem oportet laborare.[40]

(Do not shrink back from me because to reveal the true meaning of a sentence, I seem to go against grammatical rules, and I have put together many verbs or substantives, such as "to be a man," or verbs derived from things other than actions or passions (states of being acted upon), such as "to be white." For those who are on the first stage of a discipline, because of their limited abilities as beginners, have left for those who are more advanced the correction or further inquiry into many things in which the subtlety of dialectic should be used.)

In this respect, Abelard is not alone. As Desmond Henry notes, the work of Anselm of Canterbury "exhibits, quite self-consciously, that artificialization of the Latin language for technical purposes which . . . is characteristic of Scholasticism."[41] Abelard, however, goes further, by confining dialectical conclusions to the order of language alone. Separating logic, as an *ars sermocinalis*, from the sciences, which have as their object how things are, or from ethics, which have as their object how things should be, Abelard effectively limits logic to questions of the legitimate use of analytical categories. In his analysis of such technical problems as the signification of impersonal verbs, for example, Abelard endeavours, as Martin Tweedale puts it, "to disentangle logic from its supposed ontological implications."[42] This is consistent with Abelard's claim in the *Theologia "Summi boni"* that he is asserting nothing.

Abelard's intellectual trajectory, then, is one that involves isolating or delimiting dialectic. Tweedale writes of Abelard's "dereification," that is, his "incessant efforts to show that dialectic and the *artes sermocinales* in general can be developed without their requiring us to believe in the existence of things other than those more or less ordinary ones described by *physica*."[43] The *dicta* of propositions may be true, but they are not things (non sunt essentiae aliquae). As Abelard notes:

Sed opponitur, cum dicta propositionum nil sint, quomodo propter ea contingat propositiones esse veras, quia haec quae nil omnino sunt vel esse possunt, quomodo dici causa possunt? Sed propter patratum furtum homo suspenditur, quod tamen furtum iam nil est, et moritur homo, quia non comedit, et damnatur, quia non bene agit. Non comedere tamen vel non bene agere non sunt essentiae aliquae.[44]

(But it is objected, since the *dicta* of propositions are nothing, how is it that propositions happen to be true on account of them, for how can they be called causes which are completely nothing and which cannot be? But a man is hanged on account of a theft he performed which is now nothing; and a man dies because he does not eat and is damned because he does not act rightly, yet not eating and not acting rightly are not things.)

The point has important repercussions for his philosophical work. A proper understanding of Abelard's position on the ontological status of logical categories—that is, on his position on the ontological status of universals—turns on this very question of the sphere in which logic operates. Abelard is, of course, famous for demolishing the realist position of William of Champeaux and others with the proposition "rem de re predicare monstrum est" (it is absurd to predicate a thing about a thing).[45] Yet he soon abandoned the extreme alternative, the radical nominalism that claims that a universal is a mere vocal sound, and his mature position actually has strong Platonic tendencies. As Tweedale notes: "If we were to treat the *status* and the *dicta* as things, they would be the eternal, necessary realities beloved by all Platonists, which provide whatever intelligibility the world may have. Abelard is not entirely repelled by such a vision."[46] DeRijk clarifies the matter by distinguishing between Abelard's position *as a logician* and his position *as a philosopher*: "Abailard is, as a logician, of the opinion that logic, being an *ars sermocinalis*, is only concerned with *voces* or *sermones*: logical Nominalism. If it had as object *things*, it would not be logic, but physics. Nevertheless he adheres to philosophical Realism."[47] Abelard's position on the question of universals depends on this crucial break between the order of professional disputation and the order of reality.

Logic, for Abelard, offers a master language, one purged of the human imperfections and irrationalities associated with common speech. Logic is equally divorced from questions of ontology, and, thus freed from these responsibilities, it may range broadly, becoming almost a pure intellectual exercise, one that "asserts nothing." It has this freedom precisely because its scope has been so extensively circumscribed. Bernard's criticism that Abelard "thinks that human reason can comprehend all that is God" gets Abelard exactly wrong. Bernard captures the arrogance of dialectic, its free-ranging spirit, its willingness to categorize and schematize the very qualities of the Trinity, but fails to grasp the crucial delimitation that made this freedom defensible.

Twelfth-century dialectic might be seen as just one more instance of a masculine technocratic idiolect. Male cliques often define their membership by technical expertise of a highly specialized nature: computer hackers, stamp collectors, model railway enthusiasts, members of self-styled militia units—all know all there is to be known about a strictly delimited field and share a distinct lexicon in which to display this knowledge. More is at stake in medieval dialectic, however, than just group identification. As Walter J. Ong and Jan Ziolkowski show, the painful business of learning Latin was already a rite of male passage; that is, it was not just a mark of masculinity but part of the process by which masculinity was formed. As in other male rites of passage, the probationer was subject to chastisement at the hands of other men and was isolated from women, particularly his mother.[48] The isolation was built into the language itself. Dialectic as a professional jargon was severed from all mundane contacts and normal communicative functions, so that, as John of Salisbury puts it, it became a matter of shame to talk about a man, or an ass, or any work of nature without supplying the technical terms to classify them in their logical categories.

This process of linguistic isolation follows the recurring pattern by which masculinity is constructed through denial and suppression. Masculinity, as Victor Seidler argues, is "an essentially negative identity learnt through defining itself against emotionality and connectedness."[49] Lynne Segal similarly characterises the authoritarian masculinist identity as one produced through suppression—"the masquerade of power concealing weak and dependent feelings through the assertion of strength"—and exclusion—"the rejection of everything gentle, spontaneous, soft, relaxed, chaotic (seen as intrinsically connected to the body, rather than to the mind)."[50] This separation allows for the essential pose of self-control, the assumption of "a stance of over view" by which "what women have to say is branded with the status of the particular, whilst men offer what they see as an encompassing and objectively-grounded account."[51]

This stance was, and remains, the stance of academic mastery, which offers an all-encompassing account whose objectivity is rooted in personal self-control and a full knowledge of a field. Such mastery is clearly impossible, however, unless this field is strictly circumscribed. The crucial essential relationship between magisterial authority and epistemological limitation is conveyed by a notorious set of verses on the great Platonist and Master of Balliol, Benjamin Jowett:

First come I. My name is J-W-TT.
There's no knowledge but I know it.

I am Master of this College,
What I don't know isn't knowledge.[52]

The theoretical trajectory by which Abelard isolates dialectic and the impersonal language through which he reinforces this isolation are but an extreme case of the general drive of the young scholars to create a world of their own, marked off by the use of a language of their own, in which they can know all that counts as knowledge.

Within the austere depersonalization of Abelard's dialectic, however, there are traces of unease; conflicting strains of self-mockery and sexual braggadocio trouble the impersonal voice. As John Benton notes, "In his *Dialectica* . . . Abelard illustrated the desiderative mood by "Osculetur me amica" . . . and explained the logic of grammar with such sentences as "Petrum diligit sua puella" and "Petrus diligit suam puellam."[53] Benton assumes that Abelard delivered these lines in his lectures "while he was still in a position to joke about it," and it is certainly hard to imagine him delivering them after his castration.[54] Understood in this light, the lines offer a glimpse of Abelard's dramatic oral delivery and give some sense of why Abelard was often stigmatized as a "joculator."[55] Yet the written version of the *Dialectica* is dated by almost all scholars to some period after his castration in 1116.[56] Unless he simply overlooked these lines, Abelard allowed them to stand even when subsequent events made them bitterly ironic. And, at any period, it is suggestive that the references to Abelard and "suam puellam" immediately follow a series that begins "Si aliquis est homo, ipse est risibilis" (If anyone is a man, he is ridiculous).[57]

These conflicting impulses can also be detected in a puzzling allusion in the *Historia calamitatum*. In the account of the first major battle in which he established his control of Paris, Abelard boasts of his victory over William of Champeaux, "non sum superatus ab illo," and compares himself explicitly to Ajax. As most of Abelard's readers would surely have recognized, Abelard here simply repeats a line from *Metamorphoses* (13: 90), which Ajax delivers when contesting with Ulysses for the arms of Achilles. Abelard thus momentarily casts himself in the role of the braggadocio. For D. W. Robertson, Jr., the passage is clearly comic. The mature and pious Abelard recognizes the ridiculousness of his youthful folly: "the military imagery with which Abelard describes his youthful encounters only makes them laughable. . . . Ajax was an early *miles gloriosus* . . . and in associating himself with him, Abelard simply emerges as a 'braggart soldier' of dialectic."[58]

Robertson advances this reading as part of a general argument that attributes to Abelard a wholesale repudiation of his earlier excesses, especially his "sordid affair with Heloise";[59] this reading would attribute to Abelard a no less wholesale repudiation of his linguistic extravagance as a dialectician. But Abelard played the game of dialectic too well, and drew too often on bellicose metaphors, for this moment of self-ironizing to be taken as a total repudiation of his earlier self. There are too many indications in the *Historia* that this folly was not one he had entirely abandoned. Perhaps, as is so often the case, Abelard pretended to an ironic detachment he did not really feel, mocking himself for a braggadocio while still dwelling on his glories and humiliations. Few readers of the *Historia* are left with the impression that Abelard had succeeded in becoming a consistently modest man.

Abelard's recurring depiction of philosophical disputation as battle might be read as an expression of inherent masculine aggression. After all, logical debating does seem to be very much a boys' game. When Pat Churchill suggests that philosophy—that is, the social dynamics of academic philosophizing—offers a chilly climate to women, who are less prepared to do "the heavy testosterone thing," she alludes to the widespread association of aggressive rationalizing with an innate, biologically determined masculine aggression. While few would accept the implicit biological essentialism, many femininst thinkers have expressed deep reservations about the masculinist dynamic that often seems to emerge in academic philosophy and critical theory.[60] The question of what drives the master dialectician is still with us.

The traces of self-mockery and self-doubt in Abelard's writings suggest that in his case the answer cannot be a simple one. That academic disputation in Abelard's day was aggressive is unquestionable. There is, as we have seen, a considerable social reality in Abelard's repeated references to the "wars" of dialectic; dialectic was a form of stylized or ritual combat that could literally drive an opponent into exile. At the same time, rather like the ritualized violence of flyting, the ritualized violence of disputation provided an alternative to actual physical violence.[61] Its practitioners may well have been uneasy on this account. Both Abelard, the eldest son of a minor Breton noble, and Bernard of Clairvaux, whose social status was slightly higher, would normally have been expected to pursue military careers.

Ostensibly, male clerics had renounced both sex and combat, but this renunciation produced deep anxieties. Sexual performance was a crucial element in male sexual identity. As Jo Ann McNamara writes, "Men without women, if deprived of sexuality, came dangerously close to traditional visions of feminity."[62] Combat, a major rite of passage, also played a crucial role in establishing male identity, especially for men in the knightly classes. The repeated recourse by both Abelard and Bernard to the language of war might be read as the testosterone-driven aggression of men who were denied the release of actual physical violence, but it might equally be read as the posturing of men who were ashamed that the life they had chosen as clerics was not aggressive enough. In the latter view, Abelard's bellicose metaphors would offer a rhetorical recuperation of the military career he had abandoned. Similarily, the masculinist language of dialectic may have served to compensate for the anxieties of celibate noncombatants.

The disputations in which Abelard first made his reputation offer an extreme instance of the adversarial method that remains the fundamental paradigm of academic philosophizing in the West.[63] This adversarial method now seems all too obviously characteristic of a specific culture, that male culture that "thrives on argument and prides itself on distinction,"[64] yet to retain its authority the method must claim both objectivity and universality. It cannot afford to reveal itself as a masculine game. Abelard glories in this culture, but he shows as much, and in doing so gives the game away. Whether the figure of Ajax marks aggression, fear, or some combination of the two, he calls into question dialectic's pose of impersonality. Dialectic's claims to impersonal objectivity bear all too strongly the marks of its human proponents.

Notes

1. Quoted in Chris Lehmann, "Pat Churchill, Neurophilosopher," 46.

2. *Petri Abaelardi: Opera theologica III. Theologia "Summi boni", Theologia "Scholarium,"* CCCM 13, 201. Unless otherwise specified, all translations are my own.

3. *Peter Abelard. Letters IX–XIV*, 279–80. On the relation of the text to the controversy between the two men, see the introduction to *Petri Abaelardi: Opera theologica III. Theologia "Summi Boni"*, 39–46.

4. *Theologia "Summi boni"*, 87.

5. *Petrus Abaelardus: Dialectica*, xii–xiv. On the dating of this work, see n. 56 below.

6. *Epistolae*, in *S. Bernardi Opera*, vol. 8, 14. On the symbolic associations of Golias see John F. Benton, "Philology's Search for Abelard in the *Metamorphosis Goliae*," 199–217.

7. *Historia calamitatum*, 66–67. My working assumption is that Abelard did

indeed write the *Historia calamitatum*. While this possibility has been challenged, neither the stylistic differences between the *Historia* and other works by Abelard nor the possible anachronisms are so great that they could not be accounted for by thirteenth-century reworkings. On the other hand, the *Historia* would be difficult to account for as the work of one of Abelard's disciples or his detractors, since it is neither consistently laudatory nor consistently derogatory. The arguments for anachronism were raised by Benton in 1972, but in the light of suggestions made by Chrysogonus, Benton largely abandoned his position in 1980. See John F. Benton and Fiorelli Prosperetti Ercolli, "The Style of the 'Historia Calamitatum': A Preliminary Test of the Authenticity of the Correspondence Attributed to Abelard and Heloise," and the articles by D. E. Luscombe, John F. Benton, Peter Dronke, and Peter von Moos in *Petrus Abaelardus (1079-1142): Person, Werk, und Wirkung*. C. S. Jaeger, "The Prologue to the 'Historia calamitatum' and the 'Authenticity Question'," offers a strong case for authenticity.

8. On the development of the tournament in the early twelfth century, see Maurice Keen, *Chivalry*, 83–84.

9. Georges Duby, *The Chivalrous Society*, trans. Cynthia Postan, 114. Duby himself makes the comparison, n. 9.

10. Ibid., 114.

11. On the wandering of the early scholars, see M. D. Chenu, *Nature, Man, and Society in the Twelfth Century: Essays on New Theological Perspectives in the Latin West*, 270–79.

12. The standard biographies are those of Sidney Painter, *William Marshal: Knight-Errant, Baron, and Regent of England*, and Georges Duby, *William Marshal: The Flower of Chivalry*.

13. Walter J. Ong refers to the medieval curriculum as "a form of ritual male combat centered on disputation" (*Rhetoric, Romance, and Technology: Studies in the Interaction of Expression and Culture*, 17). See also Jody Enders, *Rhetoric and the Origins of Medieval Drama*, 89–96; Martin Grabman, *Die Geschichte der scholastischen Methode*, 2:13–24; and Palémon Glorieux, *La littérature quodlibétique de 1260 à 1320*, 20–24.

14. On the erotic display of the tourneying hero, see Keen, *Chivalry*, 91–94; Helen Solterer, "Figures of Female Militancy in Medieval France," esp. 526–31; and Louise Olga Fradenburg, *City, Marriage, Tournament: Arts of Rule in Late Medieval Scotland*, 209–12.

15. J. T. Muckle, "The Personal Letters between Abelard and Héloïse," 71.

16. Painter, *William Marshal*, 76.

17. Monfrin, *Historia calamitatum*, 71.

18. Muckle, "Personal Letters," 72, cf. Monfrin, *Historia calamitatum*, 73.

19. On this social pattern, see Gayle Rubin, "The Traffic in Women: Notes on the 'Political Economy' of Sex," and Eve Kosofsky Sedgwick, *Between Men: English Literature and Male Homosocial Desire*, 21.

20. Stephen C. Ferruolo provides an excellent guide to the numerous academic factions of the time in *The Origins of the University: The Schools of Paris and Their Critics, 1100-1215*.

21. *Vita B. Gosvini*, ed. R. Gibbon, in *Recueil des historiens des Gaules et de la*

France, vol. 14, ed. Michel-Jean-Joseph Brial; 2nd ed., ed. Léopold Delisle (Paris: Victor Palmé, 1877), 14: 442–43, quoted in Luscombe, *School of Peter Abelard*, 10.

22. William of St. Victor, "Le 'Contra quatuor labyrinthos Franciae' de Gauthier de Saint Victor." On Walter's knowledge of scholastic theology and the texts he criticizes, see P. Glorieux, "Mauvaise action et mauvais travail: Le 'Contra quatuor labyrinthos Franciae,' " and Ferruolo, *The Origins of the University*, 42–43, 328 n. 58.

23. "Contra quatuor labyrinthos Franciae," 223.

24. William of St. Thierry, *Disputatio adversus Petrum Abaelardum*, PL 180, cols. 249, 249–50A. Ferruolo discusses this critique of Abelard in *The Origins of the University*, 72–74.

25. William of St. Thierry, *Disputatio*, cols. 269D-270A.

26. Bernard of Clairvaux, Epistola 191, *Epistolae*, 41.

27. On the general context of the debate, see K. S. B. Keats-Rohan, "John of Salisbury and Education in Twelfth Century Paris from the Account of his *Metalogicon*." L. M. DeRijk believes that "Cornificius" may have been one Gualo of Paris, who was criticized by a contemporary for his "argutias et sophisticas conclusiunculas." See "Some New Evidence on Twelfth Century Logic: Alberic and the School of Mont Ste Geneviève (Montani)," 4–8. J. O. Ward, in "The Date of the Commentary on Cicero's 'De Inventione' by Thierry of Chartres," concludes that the identity of Cornificius is still a mystery.

28. John of Salisbury, *Ioannis Saresberiensis Metalogicon*, lib. 1, cap. 3, p. 10. I have used the translation of Daniel D. McGarry, *The Metalogicon of John of Salisbury*, with occasional modifications.

29. *Metalogicon*, 1.3, pp. 16–17.

30. Ibid., p. 17.

31. Ibid.

32. *Petri Abaelardi: Opera theologica II. Theologia christiana, Theologia scholarium (recensiones breviores) etc.*, III.9.109, p. 199; III.4.41–42, p. 195. J. G. Sikes argues that this critique was directed against Gualo of Paris (*Peter Abailard*, 56).

33. McGarry, *Metalogicon* 1.5, p. 20.

34. Ibid., 2.10, p. 73.

35. The competition among later scholars, may, for example, have been exacerbated by a tightening job market, in which, as Ferruolo claims, "masters competed for students and were willing to adapt their teaching to meet popular demand" (*Origins of the Universities*, 146).

36. Gerald of Wales, *Gemma ecclesiastica*, 350–51. The emendation to "suffici[e]t" is mine.

37. The opposition between the two methods was much discussed in the twelfth century. See Jean Leclercq, *The Love of Learning and the Desire for God: A Study of Monastic Culture*; "S. Bernard et la théologie monastique du XIIe siècle"; and D. E. Luscombe, *School of Peter Abelard*, 111.

38. Hastings Rashdall, *The Universities of Europe in the Middle Ages*, 342.

39. As Martin M. Tweedale notes, "Abelard does not find the grammatical fact of impersonality just another occasion on which dialectic can correct the grammarian" ("Abelard and the Culmination of the Old Logic," 148).

40. DeRijk, *Dialectica*, 140.

41. Desmond Paul Henry, *The Logic of Saint Anselm*, 12.

42. Tweedale, "Abelard and the Culmination of the Old Logic," 155.

43. Ibid., 154.

44. *Peter Abaelards Philosophische Schriften I. Die Logica "Ingredientibus"*, 368–69.

45. David Knowles, *The Evolution of Medieval Thought*, 112.

46. Tweedale, "Abelard and the Culmination of the Old Logic," 156. Cf. the fuller account in his *Abailard on Universals*, esp. 273. The argument that Abelard's position on universals has a Platonizing tendency is suppported by others. Cf. Jean Jolivet, *Arts du langage et théologie chez Abélard*, 353; and Guido Küng, "Abélard et les vues actuelles sur la question des universaux."

47. DeRijk, *Dialectica*, xcviii. DeRijk may slightly overstate the distinction. See W. L. Gombocz, "Abaelardus Bedeutungslehre als Schlüssel zum Universaliens-problem." Although Augustine Thompson sees Abelard's contribution to the universals debate as far less radical than Abelard himself implies, and believes that all that was required was the work of "a clever technician," he nonetheless agrees that what Abelard contributed was a "refinement of terminology" that allowed the question of universals to be distinguished from questions of ontology ("The Debate on Universals before Peter Abelard," 428–29).

48. Jan Ziolkowski, "Cultural Diglossia and the Nature of Medieval Latin Literature"; cf. Ong, *Rhetoric, Romance, and Technology*, 17.

49. Victor J. Seidler, *Rediscovering Masculinity: Reason, Language, and Sexuality*, 7.

50. Lynne Segal, *Slow Motion: Changing Masculinities, Changing Men*, 116, in a discussion of Theodore Adorno, *The Authoritarian Personality*.

51. Seidler, *Rediscovering Masculinity*, 123.

52. John Jones, *Balliol College: A History, 1263–1939*, 221.

53. Benton, "Philology's Search for Abelard," 200, n. 2, quoting *Dialectica*, 151.

54. Ibid., 200. On the dating, see Nicolau d'Olwer, "Sur la date de la *Dialectica* d'Abélard," 382 and DeRijk, *Dialectica*, xxii–xxiii.

55. On the extent to which Abelard developed his thinking in the context of disputation, both with his own students and with opponents, see Luscombe, *School of Peter Abelard*, 5–6.

56. C. Mews, "On Dating the Works of Peter Abelard," dates the *Dialectica* to ca. 1117 and challenges DeRijk's position that the work consists of three recensions, the last one dating from the 1130s (xxii–xxiii). In either case, the issue of why Abelard kept these particular examples remains. Mews also notes further instances of "secular" examples (97, n.7).

57. DeRijk, *Dialectica*, 319.

58. D. W. Robertson, Jr., *Abelard and Heloise*, 112–13.

59. Ibid., xiii.

60. See, for example, Chris Weedon, *Feminist Practice and Poststructuralist Theory*, 12–14; and Ellen Messer-Davidow, "The Philosophical Bases of Feminist Literary Criticisms" and the responses published with the latter.

61. Cf. the argument of Ward Parks that flyting (battlefield abuse) is a mecha-

nism of "reciprocal restraint" that limits casualties and has its roots in "the individual's psychological insecurity" ("Flyting and Fighting: Pathways in the Realization of the Epic Contest," 303). Parks offers further examples of such reciprocal restraint among a variety of species in the introduction to *Verbal Duelling in Heroic Narrative: The Homeric and Old English Traditions*.

62. Jo Ann McNamara, "The *Herrenfrage*: The Restructuring of the Gender System, 1050–1150," 8; cf. Vern L. Bullough, "On Being a Male in the Middle Ages," 41, in the same collection. Nancy Partner similarly states that "medieval society never quite overcame a deep ambivalence to the celibate, constrained, demasculinized male" ("Did Mystics Have Sex?" 303).

63. See Janice Moulton, *The Organization of Language*.

64. Andrea Dworkin, *Pornography: Men Possessing Women*, 127.

Dominus/Ancilla

Rhetorical Subjectivity and Sexual Violence in the Letters of Heloise

Marilynn Desmond

Optimam doloris esse naturam, quod non potest nec qui extenditur magnus esse nec qui est magnus extendi.

It is the excellent nature of pain that it cannot be severe if prolonged, nor prolonged if severe.

—Seneca, Epistle 94

E contra autem per Salomonem dicitur: *Verba sapientium quasi stimuli, et quasi clavi in altum defixi*, qui videlicet vulnera nesciunt palpare, sed pungere.

And moreover, through Solomon it is said: the words of wise men are like stakes, like nails thrust deeply, which clearly do not stroke wounds but pierce them.

—Heloise

In his *Historia calamitatum*, Abelard describes the terms set by Fulbert when he entrusted his niece, Heloise, to Abelard's pedagogical guidance: "ut quotiens mihi a scholis reverso vaccaret, tam in die quam in nocte ei docende operam darem, et eam si neglegentem sentirem vehementer constringerem" (72) (that whatever time I had left, having returned from the schools, I should devote to her instruction by day or by night, and that if I found her to be careless, I should constrain her severely). A violent pedagogy suits Abelard's construction of his sexual desire for Heloise:

Qui cum eam mihi non solum docendam, verum etiam vehementer constringendam traderet, quid aliud agebat quam ut votis meis licentiam penitus daret, et occasionem, etiam si nollemus, offerret, ut quam videlicet blanditiis non possem, minis et verberibus facilius flecterem. . . . Apertis itaque libris, plura de amore quam de lectione verba se ingerebant, plura erant oscula quam sententie; sepius ad sinus quam ad libros reducebantur manus, crebrius oculos amor in se reflectebat

quam lectio in scripturam dirigebat. Quoque minus suspicionis haberemus, ver-
bera quandoque dabat amor, non furor, gratia, non ira, que omnium ungentorum
suavitatem transcenderent.[1] (72–73)

(When he entrusted her to me not only to be taught, but also to be constrained
severely, what else was he doing but giving license to my deep longings, and offer-
ing an opportunity, even if we did not wish it, that if I could not persuade her
through flattery, I might persuade her more easily through threats and blows? And
so, though books lay open, there were more words about love than about reading,
there were more kisses than theses for discussion. Hands were drawn more often
to bosoms than to books, love drew our eyes towards each other more frequently
than it directed them towards the text for reading. Indeed, to attract less suspicion,
I sometimes gave her blows, but out of love, not fury, out of kindness, not anger—
blows that surpassed the sweetness of all ointment.)

As he initiates his affair with his young pupil, Abelard expresses his desire
through the violent eros of pedagogy, and ultimately he claims the erotic
possibilities of violence. He reports that his role as *magister* authorizes
his beating of Heloise, which increases his pleasure as her lover. Such a
construction of desire marks a convergence of the erotic and the violent
traditions of pedagogy in Western culture.

The eros of pedagogy was a given in the classical Mediterranean classroom, but it also had a particular currency within twelfth-century Pla-
tonism. As Leonard Barkan observes, such erotic humanism animated the
twelfth-century classroom: "Not only is the student-teacher relationship
re-investigated (and perhaps re-experienced) in its potential for Socratic
pederasty, but homosexuality is itself understood as homologous to new
practices of rhetoric, grammar, and poetic innovation."[2] In addition, the
magister/discipulus relationship was structured around the threat of corporal punishment, since the *magister* was traditionally given full authority
to discipline his *discipulus*.[3] Desire was elicited as part of the educational
experience and shaped by the erotic violence of traditional pedagogies.
While the same-sex composition of the medieval classroom determined
the homoerotic circulation of institutional eros, Abelard's situation as a
domestic tutor to a female pupil located him within a heterosexual paradigm of pedagogic eros.

Ultimately, this passage enacts an eroticized violence that situates
Heloise as the object of desire precisely because she is the object of violence.[4] Though Abelard reports a mutual pleasure in this sexual performance, he particularly notes his own pleasure: "Et quo me amplius hec
voluptas occupaverat, minus philosophie vaccare poteram" (73) (And the

more these pleasures occupied me, the less time I was able to have for philosophy). Later, in his retrospective description of their affair in his second letter, Abelard essentially repeats this scene of violence, and he suggests that their sexual performances were frequently marked by violence: "Sed et te nolentem et, prout poteras, reluctantem et dissuadentem, quae natura informior eras, saepius minis et flagellis ad consensum trahebam" (89) (But even when you refused, dissuading me as much as you were able in your weaker nature, I would drag you to consent with threats and lashes).

The exchange of letters between Abelard and Heloise acknowledges the significance of violence in their sexual relations, and it likewise enacts a textual and rhetorical play of dominance and submission. As such, the letters exemplify the constitutive features of sadomasochism, generally identified by the "eroticization of relations of domination and submission."[5] Abelard's depiction of his violent sexual performance in these passages is complemented by the submissive, even masochistic subjectivity that animates Heloise's *epistulae*, in which she willingly submits to Abelard's rhetorical violence as it textually reenacts this initial erotic encounter between *magister* and *discipula*. Throughout the correspondence, Heloise performs a submissive role in an erotic dynamic scripted by Ovidian amatory discourse and structured by epistolary rhetoric.

To evoke the category of sadomasochism in relation to Abelard and Heloise is to evoke a complex set of questions about the meaning and values of violence in relation to sexuality. Sadomasochism has been one of the most contested sites of feminist theory; its practices have been the topic of intense scrutiny and debate since it emerged as the flashpoint of the "sex wars" of the eighties to become a case study in performance and sexuality in the cultural-studies contexts of the nineties. Sadomasochism has been repeatedly critiqued for its supposed adherence to patriarchal forms of oppression and violence, yet as Anne McClintock observes, "As theater, S/M borrows its decor, props and costumery (bonds, chains, ropes, blindfolds) and its scenes (bedrooms, kitchens, dungeons, convents, prisons, empire) from everyday cultures of power. At first glance, then, S/M seems a servant of orthodox power. Yet on the contrary, with its exaggerated emphasis on costume and scene, S/M performs social power as *scripted*, and hence as permanently subject to change."[6] Recent feminist writing on sadomasochism emphasizes its status as ritual, negotiation, and performance. In Sue Golding's formulation, sadomasochism works to expose the fact that "the codes of the sexual are both self-evident and completely hidden at exactly the same time."[7] Same-sex sadomasochism, especially among women, has been read for its potential to separate "sexuality from gender and . . . to enact differences in the theater where roles freely circulate," according to Parveen Adams.[8]

Discussions of sadomasochism frequently emphasize the complicity and power of the submissive partner whose participation and pleasure are critical to the intersubjectivity of the performance.[9] Furthermore, the structure of masochistic desire is grounded in a desire for recognition. Jessica Benjamin, for instance, notes that the "fantasy of erotic domination embodies both the desire for independence and the desire for recognition . . . voluntary submission to erotic domination is a paradox in which the individual tries to achieve freedom through slavery, release through submission to control."[10] Abelard's *Historia calamitatum* represents Heloise as a submissive *discipula* and masochistic lover, roles Heloise later performs in her letters. The narrative of sadomasochism in the correspondence has a textual lineage in its connection to Ovidian amatory discourse. In addition to such intertextuality, the letters are shaped by the prescriptive tradition of the *ars dictaminis*, a hierarchical encoding of textual communication that reiterates the power relations of amatory discourse. The same-sex pedagogical practices and the traditions of Latin readership likewise situated Heloise within particular disciplines that might ostensibly separate sexuality from gender and make legible the codes of the sexual. Thus, the intertextual theatrics of this rhetorical performance of domination and submission suggest that the ultimate meanings of Heloise's submissive eroticism are rooted in the gendered traditions of learning and readership as much as in the paradoxes of heterosexual power relations.

The *puella* Abelard selected for his amorous script was not a blank canvas, but a woman known for her extensive learning and knowledge of classical Latin texts. Indeed, Barbara Newman observes, "It is likely that Heloise had read both Ovid and Jerome, as well as Seneca, Lucan, Cicero, and a variety of ecclesiastical authors, before she ever laid eyes on Abelard."[11] Peter Dronke has demonstrated the significance of the *Heroides* to Heloise's epistolary performance of desire, and he points to Heloise's adaptations and citations of, as well as allusions to, Ovidian texts.[12] Heloise's extraordinary level of schooling and skill enabled Abelard's erotic enterprise, as he himself notes: "Tanto autem facilius hanc mihi puellam consensuram credidi, quanto amplius eam litterarum scientiam et habere et diligere noveram" (71) (Moreover, I believed that this girl would consent all the more easily to me as much as she was known to have and to esteem knowledge of letters). Abelard here assumes that erudition in a woman is less likely to shape her as an autonomous, independent subject than to make her submissive to the advances of her *magister*. Heloise's literacy and extensive experience with the Latin textual tradition—especially the Latin amatory tradition represented by the Ovidian *corpus*—developed her awareness of her part in this erotic encounter. The female reader of Ovidian amatory discourse is situated as the object of eroticized violence in an elaborate power play in which she could only acquire power through submission. For a learned woman like Heloise, the rhetorical eros of classical Latin poetry was easily transferred into the eroticized violence of her affair with her *magister*.

Throughout the citations of Heloise's statements in the *Historia calamitatum* and the epistles signed by Heloise, we find significant traces of her extensive reading in classical Latin texts.[13] For the anomalous learned woman of the twelfth century, the experience of Latin language and literature would encourage a highly gendered reading. As Walter Ong notes, Latin was not only an entirely learned language, but a language deployed by men in homosocial contexts: "the monopoly which Latin exercised in formal education combined with the structure of society in the West . . . to give the language its strangest characteristic. It was a sexually specialized language, used almost exclusively for communication between male and male."[14]

The woman reader and writer of Latin in the twelfth century inhabited a masculine linguistic and textual tradition animated throughout by unquestioned assumptions regarding male privilege; such assumptions are routinely expressed as misogyny in the poetic tradition and misogamy in ecclesiastical writings.[15] Furthermore, the twelfth-century tradition of the *ars dictaminis* requires quotations from textual authorities as a display of epistolary artistry that connects the writing of letters to the study of grammar.[16] Heloise's subject position as a letter writer thereby necessitates her extensive citation practices, and the process of citation causes her to quote the misogynous authority of classical and biblical material, as in her letter's citation from Ecclesiastes: "et inveni amariorem morte mulierem, quae laqueus venatorum est, et sagena cor eius; vincula enim sunt manus eius"(79) (I found that woman was more bitter than death: she is a hunter's net, and her heart a snare, and her hands are chains). Heloise cites but never interrogates such statements not only because she has been so effectively interpellated into a masculine language and discourse as a reader of Latin texts, but also because any recognition and authority she might claim as an anomalous woman writer of letters depends entirely on her rhetorical deployment of textual authority through citation. Heloise exemplifies the construction of the female reader as an "immasculated" reader, in Judith Fetterley's terms: "As readers and teachers and scholars, women are taught to think as men, to identify with a male point of view, and to accept as normal and legitimate a male system of values, one of whose central principles is misogyny."[17] Her unquestioning rehearsal of classical misogyny and ecclesiastical misogamy testifies to the extraordinary linguistic mastery she has achieved.

In addition to her citations of Cicero, Juvenal, and Seneca, Heloise appears to be especially well read in Ovid. In a discussion of the "literary and intellectual partnership" of Abelard and Heloise, Dronke places Ovid "among those texts that both he and she cite oftenest, and cite at times in such unexpected contexts that it gives the impression of spontaneous recollection."[18] Ovid's *Ars amatoria* appears to be a text that Abelard and Heloise both knew well. Heloise, for instance, cites *Ars amatoria* 1 in her third letter to Abelard, which discusses the adaptation of the Benedictine rule for women. In this passage, she quotes at length from Ovid as an authority on banquets and wine drinking as causes of fornication. Such a highly incongruous citation of a secular Latin authority in a discussion of the religious life of women points to the sort of spontaneous recall posited by Dronke; Heloise would appear to know her *Ars* almost by heart. As *magister*, Abelard most likely would have known the *Ars*, given its centrality in the twelfth-century Latin curriculum.[19] Both Abelard and Heloise speak of desire in language that echoes Ovidian amatory precepts; while those precepts are codified by the lessons of the *Ars amatoria*, they are evident as well throughout the Ovidian corpus, in texts such as the *Amores*, the *Remedia amoris*, and the *Heroides*.[20]

Ovid's *Ars amatoria* presents itself as a handbook for a predatory male sexuality within a hierarchical dynamic that emphasizes the sexual pursuit and domination of women. Most notably, the *Ars* includes moments that normalize and eroticize male violence against women. The first two books of the *Ars* are a treatise on desire narrated by a *praeceptor amoris*; these books constitute a pedagogical manual designed to teach the male heterosexual subject how to acquire and manipulate the female object of desire. The *praeceptor* asserts his pedagogical authority in military language, and he sees the performance of heterosexual desire as a rhetorical strategy that empowers the male subject in his amatory conquest: "qui noua nunc primum miles in arma uenis" 1.36 (you who as a soldier enter into new battles now for the first time). The third and last book of the *Ars* instructs the female reader in her heterosexual obligations; while it purports to "arm the women against the men," it does not situate the woman reader as an equal match to the male lover. The *praeceptor* works instead to tutor the woman reader in the art of being the object of male desire. The *praeceptor* instructs his female reader in the categories of grooming and cosmetics, demeanor and manners, as well as personal hygiene. He likewise discusses appropriate sexual responses for the female lover, who is encouraged to discipline her appetite for food and drink, as well as her emotions, and to respond in a calculated fashion to male advances, even to the extent of faking orgasms: "Tu quoque, cui Veneris sensum natura negauit, / dulcia mendaci gaudia finge sono" 3.797–8 (and you to whom nature has denied the feeling of sexual love, feign sweet joy with counterfeit sounds). The coy and calculating female—if she learns the lessons of the *praeceptor*— might be able to manipulate her male suitors; her *ars*, however, depends entirely on her responses to sexual advances made by men. As the *praeceptor* puts it, "efficite (et facile est) ut nos credamus amari" (3.673) (Make us believe we are loved—and it is easy). Just as the first two books of the *Ars* tutor the male reader in the pleasures of effectively deployed dominance and violence, *Ars amatoria* 3 tutors the female reader in the erotics of submission, a power play she may be able to manipulate to her advantage.

Abelard also would appear to have learned his Ovidian lessons well: when he speaks of having his way with Heloise, he connects rhetoric and violence as the constitutive features of eros: "ut quam videlicet blanditiis non possem, minis et verberibus facilius flecterem" (That her whom I could not persuade through flattery, I might persuade more easily with threats and blows). In the *Ars*, the *praeceptor* speaks of *blanditia* as the basic skill that a male lover might effectively employ to initiate his affair: "cera tuae primum conscia mentis eat; / blanditias ferat illa tuas imitataque amantem / uerba" (1.438–40) (Let a wax tablet go forth as a witness to your thinking; it would bear your flatteries and words that imitate a lover). The *praeceptor amoris* likewise encourages his disciple to use force—indeed to rape—his *puella*:

uim licet appelles: grata est uis ista puellis;
    quod iuuat, inuitae saepe dedisse uolunt.
quaecumque est Veneris subita uiolata rapina,
    gaudet, et improbitas muneris instar habet. (1.673–76)

(Suppose you to entreat with violence; such violence is pleasing to women; what they wish, they wish to have given unwillingly. Whoever is violated by a sudden act of sexual violence is pleased, and she considers the audacity to be a gift.)

In his statement that he might deploy *blanditia* followed by force, Abelard as *magister* echoes the erotic and pedagogic authority of the Ovidian *praeceptor*. Thus Heloise as a pupil encounters a *magister* armed with an Ovidian amatory arsenal—both the rhetoric and the violence associated with erotic dominance. As a reader of Ovid herself, she had absorbed the disciplinary lesson of the amatory treatise: that for the woman reader as object of desire, violence and forcible sex are erotic, and eros is rhetorically constructed.

Heloise's pregnancy and Abelard's castration illustrate the limits of the Ovidian script in the ambient world of twelfth-century Paris. Heloise's pregnancy brings their private, sexual activities under the scrutiny of social authority and eventually leads to Abelard's castration and their entrance into religious life.[21] It exposes an aporia in the *Ars* for these two Ovidian lovers—that for women, the performance of heterosexual desire carries reproductive consequences and the resulting biological risks of childbirth. Ovid's *Ars* offers no advice on contraception, nor on managing the social complications of reproduction. As their experience forcefully demonstrates to Abelard and Heloise, reproduction is a social act subject to the surveillance of a patrilineal regime, so that Fulbert, Heloise's uncle, owns the reproductive rights of his unmarried niece. Since the *Ars* scripts heterosexual desire without mentioning reproduction, their readerly experiences of Ovidian desire as an entirely private intersubjective experience did not provide them with effective rhetorical responses to the public consequences of Heloise's pregnancy. In the *Historia calamitatum*, Abelard expresses dismay at their predicament "quanta contritione super afflictione puelle sum afflictus!" (74) (How greatly I was agitated with grief over the suffering of the girl!) Abelard reports that Heloise rejoices to be pregnant; Heloise, however, never mentions her pregnancy nor their child in her letters to Abelard, a silence that reflects the Ovidian silence regarding reproduction.

Heloise's pregnancy makes public their private desires and their secret marriage fails to legitimize her pregnancy. The process of subjecting their private world to public scrutiny results in further violence that eventually destabilizes Abelard's identity. As Abelard relates in the *Historia*, Fulbert publicizes the "secret" marriage of Abelard and Heloise. When Heloise denies the marriage and attempts to privatize her desire, Fulbert becomes violent towards her: "Unde vehementer ille commotus crebris eam contumeliis afficiebat" (79) (Then in his violent agitation he repeatedly hurled abuse at her). Abelard intervenes to remove Heloise from Fulbert's power, and once Heloise has been installed in the convent, Abelard becomes an object of violence in her place when Fulbert has him castrated as a punishment that publicly marks him as abject. Abelard's castration occurs as the result of this circulation of violence, which is intended to police private desires so that they serve the reproductive goals of a patrilineal, patriarchal social order. Women are the conventional targets of such violence, and Abelard becomes a target through substitution; once the object of such patriarchal violence, Abelard considers himself to have undergone a change in his gendered identity.

Abelard narrates his castration as a transformation of his identity: he calls himself a "monstrous spectacle" (omnibus monstruosum spectaculum futurus, 80) and comments that the Old Testament forbids eunuchs to enter churches, since they are considered unclean—*immundus*—the same term used to describe menstruating women excluded from the temple in the pollution laws of Leviticus 15:20. Abelard claims that castration frees him from sexual desire and thereby releases him from fleshly temptations and the attractions of the world; though rendered abject and monstrous, as a eunuch he ultimately acquires greater potential for spiritual transcendence. Peggy Kamuf, in describing Abelard's status, notes that "the power conferred by the phallus is in its absence represented by the impotent delegate. Dissociated from the ambiguity of its own potency, the sex of the master, by means of this representation, operates as an unequivocal sign of a legitimate right to power."[22] In renouncing his previous position as subject of male heterosexual desire, Abelard assumes that his status depends on the phallic authority conferred on him through his possession of a penis and testicles. Deprived of these "parts of his body" and their fetish value in the heterosexual paradigm, he renounces claims to the particular form of phallic sexuality authorized and performed within a heterosexual paradigm. While Abelard sees his castration as an event that reconfigures his phallic authority into more spiritual values by altering his anatomy, Heloise's desire is not constructed solely around Abelard's anatomy, and his castration does not substantially reconfigure her desire for him. The rhetorical structure of their epistolary desire exemplifies their conflicting views of his masculinity.

The construction of desire between Abelard and Heloise was never limited to the physical performance of desire nor ever wholly dependent on the intact phallic masculinity of Abelard, a fact that Abelard overlooks after his castration, though Heloise insists upon it throughout her first two letters. Ovid's poetry repeatedly emphasizes the erotic value of letters, and from the start of their affair, Abelard saw the exchange of letters as an erotic act. In the *Historia* he praises Heloise's learning, not only because it would make her more responsive to his advances, but also because it would enable the epistolary eroticism that he considers a significant component of a sexual relationship: "nosque etiam absentes scriptis internuntiis invicem liceret presentare et pleraque audacius scribere quam colloqui" (71) (and indeed, when apart, we would be allowed to be present through written mediators, and to write many things more boldly than we could speak them). The exchange of letters starts at the very beginning of their affair and persists intermittently throughout their lives; their letters represent a rhetorical shaping of desire that enacts a textual eros as a supplement to their physical performance of sexuality at the beginning of their relationship, and that textually substitutes for the (hetero)sexual act after Abelard's castration. Abelard's castration re-situates the desire of both letter writers, and the physical violence of their early sexual encounter is later re-enacted in the rhetorical violence Heloise reads in Abelard's epistles. Though scholars such as Barbara Newman and Martin Irvine, among others, have read Heloise as a repressed woman,[23] her epistles point to a sustained eroticism that is repeatedly expressed and thereby performed rather than repressed.

Heloise's letters testify to her persistent desire for an eroticized, textualized relationship with Abelard despite his castration, and her letters eventually function to recognize Abelard's phallic authority in spiritual matters as a consequence of his anatomical lack. In her unwavering recognition of Abelard as phallic and powerful, Heloise performs the conventional role of the female heterosexual subject in the libidinal economy of Western culture. As Kaja Silverman has demonstrated, the female subject is historically expected to deny the psychic reality of male castration and thereby uphold a construction of masculinity that supports the "dominant fiction." Silverman asserts, "the 'ideal' female subject refuses to recognize male lack, and that disavowal and fetishism provide important mechanisms for effecting this refusal. Indeed, traditional masculinity emerges there as a fetish for covering over the castration upon which male subjectivity is grounded."[24]

In her letters, Heloise sees Abelard with her "imagination rather than her eyes," as Silverman defines the task of the female in the heterosexual matrix. Language is the conventional mechanism for maintaining phallic identification, and Heloise finds in the rhetorical formulas of the *ars dictaminis* the linguistic fetish for her imaginative refusal of Abelard's castration. Her first letter to Abelard scripts her subject position in the rhetorical paradigms of the salutation, in keeping with the precepts of the *ars dictiminis*, which recognize rank in the grammatical placement of names: "Domino suo immo patri, coniugi suo immo fratri, ancilla sua immo filia, ipsius uxor immo soror, Abaelardo Heloisa" (68) (To her master, indeed her father, to her husband, indeed her brother, from his slave/servant, indeed his daughter, the wife of him, indeed sister, to Abelard, Heloise). The rhetorical structure of the *epistula* shapes desire around the *dominus/ancilla* hierarchy, which subsumes the other hierarchical relationships acknowledged here: father/daughter, husband/wife, brother/sister.[25] The father/daughter pair of the first phrase is expanded in the second. Within this context, the initial category of the salutation—*dominus*—inscribes Abelard's phallic masculinity; the second phrase of the salutation offers the alternatives of *coniunx* and *frater* as substitutes that vary the role of the dominant term and yet maintain the inherent inequality, since brother and sister, like husband and wife, represent a gendered hierarchy. Heloise's epistolary eroticism rehearses—indeed, by its repetitions fetishizes—a rhetoric of dominance and submission in which the masculine term occupies the position of power; Heloise later insists on the rhetoric of hierarchy as part of a proper salutation, as we shall see.

Heloise's first letter to Abelard directly equates letter writing and desire. The entire letter develops her complaint that Abelard has not written to her since his castration, thirteen years earlier, though he did compose a long *epistula consolationis* to a male friend. Heloise's complaint is designed to claim Abelard's attention for the heterosexual desire her letter enacts in opposition to the homosocial world rhetorically figured by the *Historia* as a letter addressed to a male friend in need of consolation. She complains bitterly throughout the letter: "non . . . fluctuantem me et iam diutino moerore confectam vel sermone praesentem vel epistola absentem consolari tentaveris" (70) (nor . . . did you try to console me, wavering and already consumed with a long lasting sorrow, neither with a word in your presence nor a letter in your absence). In this passage, she goes on to invoke their marriage bond (nuptialis foedere sacramenti) and to express the status of her enduring desire: "immoderato amore complexa sum" (I have been embraced by an excessive love).

The entire letter is aimed at provoking an epistolary response from Abelard; Heloise reminds him that before his castration, he wrote frequent letters to her at the start of their affair; she insists on the efficacy of letters by citing an authoritative passage from Seneca regarding the potential of letters to bring separated people together. Heloise's letter demands that Abelard address a letter to Heloise and thereby provide the erotic recognition that marked her submissive role in their relationship. Heloise directly equates Abelard's epistolary silence with his castration, which marked the end of his desire, and she begs him to send her a letter:

Concupiscentia te mihi potius quam amicitia sociavit, libidinis ardor potius quam amor. Ubi igitur quod desiderabas cessavit quicquid propter hoc exhibebas pariter evanuit. . . .Dum tui praesentia fraudor verborum saltem votis quorum tibi copia est tuae mihi imaginis praesenta dulcedinem.(72)

(Lust rather than friendship joined you to me, the ardor of desire rather than love. Thus when what you desired ceased, whatever you displayed disappeared as well. . . . While I am cheated of your presence, at least promise me through your words, of which you have plenty, the sweet presence of your image.)

Heloise's appeal acknowledges that the performance of desire is textual as much as physical, and letters as a transcription of language appear to be one option for her erotic experience. In a similar vein, she asserts that Abelard's poetic gifts and his ability to compose love songs are one significant component of his attraction for her.

Heloise describes Abelard's sweeping power as though her identity depended entirely on her emotional submission to him: "Solus quippe es qui me contristare, qui me laetificare seu consolari valeas" (70) (In fact, it is you alone who have the power to sadden me, to cheer me or console me). In this first letter, she represents Abelard as her *dominus* in her declaration that if Augustus as emperor offered her the magnificence of an imperial marriage, she would rather be a *meretrix* than *imperatrix*: "carius mihi et dignius videretur tua dici meretrix quam illius imperatrix" (71) (More dear and more worthy would it seem to be called your *meretrix* than the empress of that one). The word *meretrix* evokes the erotic world of amatory adventures outside of marriage—the world of courtesans, mistresses, and concubines of Terence, Plautus, and above all Ovid. Ovid uses the term with some frequency in his amatory poetry, and the object of desire in the *Ars* is implicitly a *meretrix*.[26] The term *meretrix* situates Heloise in a socially abject yet exotic position outside of marriage; Heloise revels in the Ovidian eroticism of this language in her rhetorically playful embellishment on the terms *concubina* and *scortus*.

In her letter, Heloise takes linguistic and erotic pleasure in the epistolary contract, since it allows her to rehearse her masochistic subject-position as *ancilla* to his *dominus*: she exists only through Abelard, and she has denied herself all pleasure in accordance with his will ("Omnes denique mihi voluptates interdixi ut tuae parerem voluntati," 73). Yet she revels in the power she attains through such submissive gestures. As Claire Nouvet

notes, "this apparent self-humiliation in fact reverses the master/slave relation, for it puts the master in the position of debtor. . . . The whore is the
true master of a master who precisely could not be master without her."[27]

Heloise composed her first letter after Abelard's castration had transformed his erotic violence into indifference. In the face of his indifference,
she writes to ask for recognition in the form of a letter addressed to her as
his *ancilla*. Her subject-position as *ancilla* in her letter textualizes her status
as an abject or discarded lover who has relinquished her entire self into the
control of her *dominus*, and she rhetorically performs this role, repeatedly
and excessively: "Non enim mecum animus sed tecum erat. Sed et nunc
maxime si tecum non est, nusquam est" (73) (My heart was not with me
but with you. But especially even now, if it is not with you, it is nowhere).
Her submissive desires in the face of Abelard's rhetorical silence after his
castration are an attempt to sustain her submissive pleasure in a violent
eros during their initial performance of desire before Abelard's castration.
The rhetorical scripting of desire made possible by the *artes*—the *Ars amatoria* and the *ars dictaminis*—creates and sustains an intersubjectivity in
which Heloise seeks recognition through the rhetoric of submission.

Heloise's first letter characterizes Abelard's epistolary indifference as
a form of rhetorical violence, an abusive gesture of psychic denial as dam-
aging as physical abuse, and one which causes her to suffer exceedingly.
Helen Solterer asserts the significance of the medieval investment in an
"analogy between words and physical blows. In a preprint society such as
the medieval world, this link was acutely felt, and with it the fundamental
connection between words and actions."[28] Both Abelard and Heloise consider verbal abuse and rhetorical violence to be more painful than physical
abuse. For Heloise, the rhetoric of Abelard's *Historia* situates her as a discarded and even abject lover; her exquisite descriptions of suffering in her
first letter create a space in which she might pleasure in this pain. Like the
beatings and sexual violence she experienced from Abelard as his student
lover, the rhetorical violence of his *Historia* allows her to experience identity through suffering his indifference. In response to the implicit violence
of Abelard's rhetorical indifference, and as a dedicated reader of Seneca,
Heloise cultivates a language of endurance and pain often rhetorically self-
conscious of its status as performance.

Abelard responds to Heloise by sending her an *epistula*, yet he implicitly refuses her desire for submission in his saluation, which denies his
role as *dominus*: "Heloisae, dilectissimae sorori suae in Christo, Abaelardus, frater eius in ipso" (73) (To Heloise, his most beloved sister in Christ;

from Abelard, her brother in Christ). This refusal elicits Heloise's extensive critique of his deviation from the rhetorical expectations of the *ars*:

Miror, unice meus, quod praeter consuetudinem epistolarum, immo contra ipsum
ordinem naturalem rerum, in ipsa fronte salutationis epistolaris me tibi praeponere
praesumpsisti, feminam videlicet viro, uxorem marito, ancillam domino, monia-
lem monacho et sacerdoti diaconissam, abbati abbatissam. Rectus quippe ordo est
et honestus, ut qui superiores vel ad pares scribunt, eorum quibus scribunt nomina
suis anteponant. Sin autem ad inferiores, praecedunt scriptionis ordine qui praecedunt rerum dignitate. (77)

(I am astonished, my one and only, that contravening the custom of letters, or
rather against the natural order itself, you have presumed to place me before you
at the front of the salutation of the letter, that is, the woman before the man, the
wife before the husband, the servant before the lord, nun before monk, deaconess
before priest, and abbess before abbot. It is the correct and proper order that they
who write to their superiors or equals place the names of those they address before
their own names. But if they write to inferiors, they who go before in dignity go
before in the order of writing.)

In her desire to be rhetorically situated as Abelard's inferior, Heloise reiterates in her second letter her need for recognition as the submissive partner
in their relationship. Thus she asserts that Abelard should not praise her
("Quiesce, obsecro, a laude mea," 82). In Heloise's terms, the *ars dictaminis*, which reflects the "natural order," justifies the terms of her desire:
rhetoric and nature script her subject position and her desire.

Heloise's second letter is structured by her complaint that the language of Abelard's letter has caused her, and her community of nuns, considerable pain and anxiety. His intimations of mortality are experienced as
violence and rhetorically expressed as such in Heloise's metaphorical prose:
"parce unicae saltem tuae huiusmodi scilicet supersedendo verbis quibus
tamquam gladiis mortis nostras transverberas animas ut quod mortem
praevenit ipsa morte gravius sit" (78) (At least spare your one and only
by omitting words of this sort, for with them, as with lethal swords, you
thrust through our souls, so that what comes before death is worse than
death itself). She depicts her suffering in graphic language drawn from the
classical idiom of her textual training when she describe's Fortune's blows:

. . . plenam in me pharetram exhausit ut frustra iam alii bella eius formident. Nec,
si ei adhuc telum aliquod superesset, locum in me vulneris inveniret. Unum inter
tot vulnera metuit ne morte supplicia finiam. (78)

(She has emptied a full quiver into me so that others fear the hostilities of that one
in vain. If she had one spear left, she would not find a place in me for a wound. She
only fears that among so many wounds, I might end my sufferings in death.)

As Peter Dronke comments in reference to Heloise's use of the metaphor of the erotic wound, "In the Ovidian language of love, love is an inflicted wound that only the beloved can heal."[29] Heloise's exuberant use of metaphor and mythical personification to express the painful experience of reading Abelard's letter suggests a readerly pleasure in his rhetorical violence. She engages in an animated response to the discourse that she finds painful, since that very discourse offers her a recognition that acknowledges her needs and desires.

Although Heloise's first letter was shaped by her insistent pleas for a response from Abelard that would simultaneously recognize her as *ancilla*, her second letter is marked by an exquisite expression of her erotic desires as memory of their earlier sexual performance: "Hoc autem in me stimulos carnis haec incentiva libidinis ipse iuvenilis fervor aetatis, et iucundissimarum experientia voluptatum plurimum accendunt" (81) (The same youthful fervor and the experience of the most delightful pleasures kindle greatly in me the goading of the flesh and the incentives of desire). She claims to be the cause of Abelard's sufferings and insistently expresses her desire to be the one who suffers. The rhetoric of Heloise's second letter is a sustained expression of pain and pleasure as well as the painful memory of pleasure:

In tantum vero illae, quas pariter exercuimus, amantium voluptates dulces mihi fuerunt ut nec displicere mihi, nec vix a memoria labi possint. Quocumque loco me vertam, semper se oculis meis cum suis ingerunt desideriis. Nec etiam dormienti suis illusionibus parcunt. . . . Nec solum quae egimus, sed loca pariter et tempora in quibus haec egimus, ita tecum nostro infixa sunt animo, ut in ipsis omnia tecum agam, nec dormiens etiam ab his quiescam. (80–81)

(Truly, so sweet were the pleasures of lovers to me that they cannot displease me nor be loosened from memory. To whatever place I turn, always they put themselves before my eyes with their desires nor do they spare me their illusions in sleep. . . . Not only the things we did but the places and times in which we did them are fixed in our heart with you, so that I do all things in those places with you, nor in sleeping am I spared these things.)

In describing her autoerotic experiences, Heloise paradoxically notes that the *voluptates* of lovers never fail to please her, yet she uses a biblical citation to lament the misery of her corporeal captivity (Romans 7:24: "Infelix ego homo. . ."). This is a highly sexual passage, and Heloise produces it as an autoerotic performance of desire as substantial as her previous heterosexual experiences with Abelard, an interpretation that is consistent with the "ethic of intention." As Heloise defines the ethic of intention in her first letter, the spirit in which deeds are performed constitutes their meaning. Abelard elaborates explicitly on this premise in his *Ethica*: "Non itaque concupiscere mulierem sed concupiscentiae consentire peccatum est, nec uoluntas concubitus sed uoluntatis consensus dampnabilis est" (So sin is not lusting for a woman but consenting to lust; the consent of the will is damnable, but not the will for intercourse).[30] Heloise consents to the intense performance of desire in which her memory of Abelard participates in the autoerotic act with her. The passage depicts her persistent performance of sexual desire in intense and fulfilling terms: "ut in ipsis omnia tecum agam." Although this passage is often considered proof of Heloise's repression, Heloise describes a powerful autoerotic experience, not a repression of sexual experience. Indeed, Heloise's sexuality causes her dismay precisely because it is not repressed and thereby constitutes a transgression of *castitas* and *virtus*, the privileged categories of Christian doctrine.[31] She categorizes her autoerotic sexual experiences as sex acts to which she continues to consent:

Quo modo etiam poenitentia peccatorum dicitur, quantacumque sit corporis afflictio, si mens adhuc ipsam peccandi retinet voluntatem, et pristinis aestuat desideriis? Facile quidem est quemlibet confitendo peccata seipsum accusare, aut etiam in exteriori satisfactione corpus affligere. Difficillimum vero est a desideriis maximarum voluptatum avellere animum. (80)

(How is it called repentance for sins, however much it is an affliction of the body, if the mind retains the very will toward sinning, and burns with former desires? It is an easy thing for anyone to accuse oneself of sins in confession, or even to strike the body in order to make exterior satisfaction; but it is most difficult to turn the mind away from the desire for the greatest of pleasures.)

Heloise's powerful conviction that she should repent for her performance of these "greatest of pleasures" demonstrates her conviction that these sexual experiences are sex acts, not fantasies.

Heloise's letters inscribe and enact a sexuality defined by the masochistic subjectivity of her relationship with Abelard, a dynamic that persists long after his castration, their separation, and her entry into a religious life. The pedagogical and religious institutions as well as the rhetorical practices of her day likewise required of the learned woman a passionate submission to authority, however violent. The relationship of Abelard and Heloise as it emerges from their letters demonstrates the cultural contexts for this engendering of rhetoric and rhetorical structuring of gender. As an "immasculated" woman learned in elite Latin textual cultures who employs the prescriptive rhetoric of the *ars dictaminis*, Heloise has been constructed to cite misogynist texts and to express a cultural hatred and fear of woman. On the other hand, Abelard's masculine privilege as a powerful *magister* is initially compromised by his castration, but paradoxically, the less "masculine" he is on a corporeal level, the more authority he gains in spiritual stature, so that he interprets his castration as his salvation. Heloise, the "immasculated" woman, and Abelard, the emasculated man, enact a rhetoric of dominance and submission in their correspondence that is ultimately structured by the social inequities of the religious and secular institutions of their day: no matter how learned, Heloise can never earn the status or privileges of masculinity, yet Abelard's compromised "masculinity" only increases his claim on privilege, authority, and power.

The physical and rhetorical violence of the correspondence is paradigmatic of the pervasive violence against women that animates the discourses of Western culture. As Christine Froula identifies the vulnerability of the woman reader, "Metaphysically, the woman reader of a literary tradition that inscribes violence against women is an abused daughter. Like physical abuse, literary violence against women works to privilege the cultural father's voice and story over those of women, the cultural daughters, and indeed to silence women's voices."[32] Heloise's voice, so rhetorically effective in its deployment of the Latin sentence for elaboration and stylistic emphasis, is not silenced, yet her extraordinary skill in Latin prose and her brilliant reputation in Latin scholarship served to enable her subjugation within the heterosexual paradigm of violence that equated learning with erotic submission and self-hatred for the female reader and writer of Latin as the tongue of the Fathers.

Heloise's letters constitute a rhetorical eroticism of domination and submission within a heterosexual paradigm shaped by a recognizably sadomasochistic script. As a script, however, sadomasochism is not limited to a heterosexual performance, nor is the female limited to the masochistic role.[33] If sadomasochism functions as a parody of power relations and the gendered assignment of dominance and submission, Heloise's superb rhetorical skill invites an interpretive understanding of violence against women in the Latin literary tradition as the product of pedagogic, erotic, and literary discourses. And the very theatricality of these discourses reveals the codes of the sexual and the assignment of gender to be open to reinterpretation and reinvention. In the very excess in which Heloise revels in the sadomasochism of the Ovidian script, we see literary sadomasochism itself as a parodic script that exposes not only the violence of the Latin literary tradition but also the rhetorical and linguistic basis of violence itself.

Notes

1. I use the following editions: *Historia calamitatum*, ed. Jacques Monfrin; J. T. Muckle, "The Personal Letters between Abelard and Heloise" and "The Letter of Heloise on the Religious Life and Abelard's First Reply"; Ovid, *Amores, Medicamina faciei femineae, Ars amatoria, Remedia amoris*, ed. E. J. Kenny; translations are my own.

2. Leonard Barkan, *Transuming Passion: Ganymede and the Erotics of Humanism*, 48–49.

3. On corporal punishment in the classical era, see Stanley F. Bonner, *Education in Ancient Rome from the Elder Cato to the Younger Pliny*, 143–45; for the medieval era, see Pierre Riché, *Les écoles et l'enseignement dans l'Occident chrétien de la fin du Ve siècle au milieu du XIe siècle*, 208–9; James J. Murphy, "The Teaching of Latin as a Second Language in the Twelfth Century"; and Cora E. Lutz, *Schoolmasters of the Tenth Century*, 75–86.

4. Catherine Brown comments specifically on this scene: "Such violence resists interpretation as a powerful man's abuse of a helpless woman. Abelard's introduction of the erotic scene leads one to expect this, but the *Historia* delivers something more disturbing because less easily explained: a passionate relation mutually constructed through mutual violence to pleasurable ends" ("*Muliebriter*: Doing Gender in the Letters of Heloise," 30).

5. Sandra Lee Bartky, *Femininity and Dominations: Studies in the Phenomenology of Oppression*, 47. For a survey of the "sex wars" see Ruby B. Rich, "Feminism and Sexuality in the 1980's"; see also Carla Freccero, "Notes of a Post-Sex Wars Theorizer." For recent studies of sadomasochism as performance, see Anne McClintock, "Maid to Order: Commercial S/M and Gender Power," and Chantal Nadeau, "Girls on a Wired Screen: Cavini's Cinema and Lesbian S/M." For a statement of the position against sadomasochism, see Sheila Jeffreys, "Sadomasochism: The Erotic Cult of Fascism." Peggy Kamuf reads the erotic violence in these letters as a destabilizing threat to Abelard's mastery; her model does not allow for the theatrics of sadomasochism, whereby both partners in the erotic exchange of violence have a degree of power and the ultimate mastery of Abelard is thereby questioned. The erotics of violence and masochism also works to fix the poles of the power dynamic, and in the case of twelfth-century institutions of heterosexuality, they replicate the gendered power relations of the ambient culture. See Peggy Kamuf, *Fictions of Feminine Desire: Disclosures of Heloise*, 1–43.

6. McClintock, "Maid to Order," 208.

7. Sue Golding, "Sexual Manners," 62.

8. Parveen Adams, "Of Female Bondage," 264.

9. See Pat Califia, "The Limits of the S/M Relationship" and "Feminism and Sadomasochism"; and Susan Farr, "The Art of Discipline: Creating Erotic Dramas of Play and Power."

10. Jessica Benjamin, *The Bonds of Love: Psychoanalysis, Feminism, and the Problem of Domination*, 52.

11. Barbara Newman, "Authority, Authenticity, and the Repression of Heloise," 69. On the education of Heloise, see Joan M. Ferrante, "The Education

of Women in the Middle Ages in Theory, Fact, and Fantasy," 19–22; on Heloise's citations of classical material, see Helen C. R. Laurie, *The Making of Romance: Three Studies*, 96–118. On the significance of Heloise's reading of Seneca, see Martin Irvine, "Heloise and the Gendering of the Literate Subject." On Heloise and Augustine, see Nancy A. Jones, "By Woman's Tears Redeemed: Female Lament in St. Augustine's *Confessions* and the Correspondence of Abelard and Heloise." On Heloise and the discourse of monasticism, see Linda Georgianna, "Any Corner of Heaven: Heloise's Critique of Monasticism."

12. Peter Dronke, *Women Writers of the Middle Ages*, 107–39.

13. On the issues surrounding the authenticity of Heloise's letters, Barbara Newman comments that the letters "could have been preserved only at the Paraclete, where it was Heloise and not Abelard who had leisure to put them in publishable form" ("Authority," 55). Given her control over the letters as a collection, it is reasonable to assume that Heloise saw the *Historia* as a relatively accurate transcription of her statements and positions.

14. Walter J. Ong, "Latin and the Social Fabric," 211. See also his *Orality and Literacy: The Technologizing of the Word*, 112–15; "Rhetoric and the Origins of Consciousness"; and "Latin Language Study as a Renaissance Puberty Rite." On the role of Latin literacy in the various formations of medieval cultures, see R. I. Moore, *The Formation of a Persecuting Society: Power and Deviance in Western Europe, 950–1250*, 124–53. For a discussion of the implications of the homosocial construction of Latin readership, see Desmond, *Reading Dido: Gender, Textuality, and the Medieval Aeneid*, 7–15.

15. See Katharina Wilson and Elizabeth Makowski, *Wikked Wives and the Woes of Marriage: Misogamous Literature from Juvenal to Chaucer*. For a sympathetic assessment of Abelard's placement within misogyny and misogamy, see Mary Martin McLaughlin, "Peter Abelard and the Dignity of Women: Twelfth Century 'Feminism' in Theory and Practice."

16. Martin Carmargo, *Ars dictaminis, ars dictandi*, 56. On the relationship between letter writing and textual authority, see R. W. Southern, *Medieval Humanism and Other Studies*, 86, who suggests that the "act of writing a letter was an exercise in a learned science." On the relationship between the reading of classical epistles, the *ars dictaminis*, and the circulation of personal love letters in the eleventh and twelfth centuries, see Giles Constable, *Letters and Letter Collections*, 26–56 and *The Letters of Peter the Venerable*, 1–12. Peter Dronke places the Abelard-Heloise correspondence in the context of similar letter collections in "Abelard and Heloise in Medieval Testimonies," 25–26.

17. Judith Fetterley, *The Resisting Reader: A Feminist Approach to American Fiction*, 12.

18. Dronke, *Women Writers*, 112.

19. On the importance of the *Ars amatoria* in the medieval classroom, see Ralph Hexter, *Ovid and Medieval Schooling*, 23–25; see also John Baldwin, *The Language of Sex: Five Voices from Northern France Around 1200*, 20–23.

20. The *Ars amatoria* itself codifies attitudes towards sexuality that are found throughout the Ovidian corpus, so that every aspect of sexuality in the Ovidian idiom of the correspondence has a multitextual set of possibilities. Abelard and Heloise may use constructs to express desire that are drawn more generally from

their experiences with the entire Ovidian corpus; nonetheless, those constructs can be traced as well to the *Ars amatoria*.

21. For a general discussion of public and private in the letters of Heloise, see Glenda McLeod, "'Wholly Guilty, Wholly Innocent': Self-Definition in Heloise's Letters to Abelard."

22. Kamuf, *Fictions*, 43. For a psychoanalytic discussion of castration in relation to Abelard, see Jean-Charles Huchet, "La voix d'Héloïse."

23. See Newman, "Authority," and Irvine, "Heloise and the Gendering of the Literate Subject." For a discussion of sublimation as an explanation of Heloise's dedication to learning, see Nancy F. Partner, "No Sex, No Gender," 433–39.

24. Kaja Silverman, *Male Subjectivity at the Margins*, 47.

25. For a discussion of the *salutatio* as the unit of the *ars dictaminis* that expresses social hierarchy, see Carmargo, *Ars dictaminis*, 22.

26. "Non mihi, sacrilegas meretricum ut persequar artes,/ cum totidem linguis sint satis ora decem" (*Ars* 1. 435–6)(Not ten mouths, nor as many tongues would be enough for me to tell the profane arts of the meretrix). Ovid employs *meretrix* to denote the female lover in the following poems: *Amores* 1.10.21; 1.15.18; 3.14.9; *Heroides* 15.63.

27. Claire Nouvet, "The Discourse of the 'Whore': An Economy of Sacrifice," 761.

28. Helen Solterer, *The Master and Minerva: Disputing Women in Medieval French Culture*, 11.

29. Dronke, *Women Writers*, 115.

30. Text and translation from *Peter Abelard's Ethics*, ed. and trans. D. E. Luscombe, 14–15. For a discussion of the "ethic of intention" as a philosophical category elaborated by Abelard, see Mary Martin McLaughlin, "Abelard as Autobiographer: The Motives and Meaning of His 'Story of Calamities,'" 485. As Chris Ferguson notes, "Abelard composed the *Ethica* (c. 1135–39) not long after the *Historia calamitatum* c. 1132, and likely was working on the *Ethica* while also composing the *Historia calamitatum*" ("Autobiography as Therapy: Guibert de Nogent, Peter Abelard, and the Making of Medieval Autobiography,"). Although Abelard is historically credited with the concept of the "ethic of intention," it is significant that both Abelard and Heloise seem to share a philosophical command of the concept, and it emerges in both the letters and his treatise at roughly the same time. As Peter Dronke notes in another context, "the parallels between Heloise's third letter and contributions to the *Problemata*, and works of Abelard's such as the *Sic et Non* and the *Ethica*, may be better explicable in terms of Abelard's and Heloise's shared pursuit of certain problems than in terms of her slavishly repeating things he had already set down in written form" (*Women Writers*, 112).

31. Martin Irvine generally characterizes the desire in the correspondence as repressed, and he sees this passage as emblematic of Heloise's "unfulfilled desire" ("Heloise and the Gendering of the Literate Subject," 105).

32. Christine Froula, "The Daughter's Seduction: Sexual Violence and Literary History," 633.

33. For a fuller discussion of masochism, see Gilles Deleuze, *Coldness and Cruelty*; and Jean Laplanche, *Life and Death in Psychoanalysis*, 85–102.

Caput a femina, membra a viris

Gender Polemic in Abelard's Letter "On the Authority and Dignity of the Nun's Profession"

Alcuin Blamires

The correspondence between Heloise and Abelard as collected in manuscripts circulating in the later Middle Ages has the character of a three-act drama: act 1, the *Historia calamitatum*, Abelard's account of his misfortunes and defense of his career; act 2, the "Personal Letters" (as their editor termed them), which were prompted by Heloise's reading of the *Historia* and led up to an epistolary crisis when Abelard forbade her to speak more of their love; and act 3, the "Letters of Direction," a title popularized by translator Betty Radice in acknowledgment that here Heloise asks for, and receives, advice from Abelard in his capacity as spiritual director to her and the other nuns of the Paraclete.[1] The impression of a sharp break between acts 2 and 3 is hard to avoid, since Heloise herself at this point states that she has "set the bridle of [Abelard's] injunction" on her words[2] and hopes to displace her emotional turmoil by resorting to that area of communication "in matters pertaining to God," to which Abelard had wanted to restrict their correspondence since his first reply.[3]

While generations have been enthralled by acts 1 and 2 of this drama, most have been reluctant to sit through act 3's prospective lapse (as Barbara Newman has put it) "from titillation into tedium."[4] In any case, those reliant on translation do not know how much "tedium" they are missing.[5] Abelard's fulfillment in letter 7 of Heloise's request to know "unde sanctimonialium ordo coeperit, et quae nostrae sit professionis auctoritas" (how the order of nuns began and what authority there is for this profession) is consigned to three pages of summary by Radice on the grounds that it is "prolix and not very logical in the arrangement of [its] many examples."[6] To me this seems a pity, not because the length or coherence should be defended to the death but because readers are thereby denied the chance to see how Abelard here conducts some of the period's most exciting revisionist raids on dominant gender assumptions. Moreover, the letter (more, I believe, than the Rule for female religious that follows it in some manuscripts)[7] constitutes a logical consummation of their correspondence hitherto—Abelard's attempt, at last, to respond to Heloise with the empathy for which she has so yearned. I will return to this claim at the end of this chapter, but one aspect of it must be broached immediately if we are to understand the implicit point of Heloise's question, and thereby of Abelard's coded reply.

It is easy to mistake Heloise's question about the beginnings of the *ordo sanctimonialium* and the *auctoritas* of the conventual profession for a gesture of resignation, maintaining communication with Abelard at the cost of setting him a dutifully learned question devoid of personal nuance. But I believe that the topic is dynamically related to the couple's past and present situation. The key is Heloise's lack of what Abelard had successfully constituted for himself: a historically resonant identity matching his sense of his own powers.

Abelard had been well versed in the ancient and patristic topos of the unattached, undistracted philosopher before he wrote the *Historia*.[8] But by the time of the *Historia*, after the crises in his career that it records, he was ruminating rather obsessively on the ancient pedigree and the proper context of the true Christian thinker's lifestyle.[9] He felt that prior to his affair with Heloise he had uniquely actualized the role of *philosophus* by a habit of constant study that excluded worldly socializing, and even more by living in an "entirely continent" way.[10] But the implication of the affair was that he fell behind the philosophers;[11] he became an anti-model, of one distracted by *voluptas* from *philosophia* into mental *perturbatio*.[12] According to his account, Heloise herself contributed to this analysis, attempting to dissuade him from marriage when their affair became public by rehearsing the incompatibility of domesticity with the *condicio philosophorum*, which requires flight from the world.[13]

Continuing to report—or embroider, or gloss—her argument, Abelard declares that the true monk is a descendant of the asocial philosophers of antiquity: "quod nunc igitur apud nos amore Dei sustinent qui vere *monachi* dicuntur, hoc, desiderio philosophiae, qui nobiles in gentibus exstiterunt philosophi" (this is the practice today through love of God of those among us who truly deserve the name of monks, as it was of distinguished philosophers among the pagans in their pursuit of philosophy).[14] Equally, a modern monk can trace his lineage back through John the Baptist to the Old Testament—to the "filii prophetarum" (sons of prophets) in 4 Kings 6: 1–4, whom "the Old Testament calls monks, as St. Jerome bears witness." These "monks" suggested to Elisha that they should go to the Jordan and cut wood there to build themselves shelters in the wild.[15]

Not surprisingly, when Abelard retreated to the abbey of St. Denis after his relationship with Heloise culminated in his castration, he found consolation in the supposition that God had freed him from distractions of world and flesh so that he could become "nec tam mundi quam Dei vere philosophus" (a true philosopher not of the world but of God).[16] The logical extension of all this was personal philosophical solitude in the wilderness, precisely what Abelard subsequently sought to achieve beside the Ardusson River in Troyes by constructing a rudimentary oratory, later the site of the hermit-school community he was to name the Paraclete. He expressly connects this venture with the philosopher-monk topos as before,[17] harping on those "sons of the prophets" who built huts by the Jordan, as his own disciples built them by the Ardusson.[18] The concept remained deeply important to him. He was still citing (from another Jerome epistle) the Jordan hut builders as the *principes* (leaders) of the monastic calling in the Rule he compiled for Heloise, which constitutes letter 8.[19]

Abelard, then, could supply himself with valuable *principes* or originary antecedents as he struggled to adapt his self-image from a scholastic to a monastic—preferably maverick monastic—calling. But where did this leave Heloise? She was a formidable scholar in her own right.[20] In fact, even her request for Abelard to write about the origins of nuns is itself introduced with a sophisticated allusion to one of those Jerome epistles of which they both had close knowledge. Abelard can help dispel her passionate grief, she says, by filling her mind with a new preoccupation as one nail drives out another, "ut enim insertum clavum alius expellit."[21] Tracing this nail metaphor to Cicero, the editor prevents us from appreciating how incisively Heloise has actually borrowed it from Jerome, who applies it to the difficulty a monk may experience in driving out burning desire ("flammam . . . carnis"), unless one can substitute a more transcendent love.[22] However, even supposing a conventual context able to sustain the intellectual qualities shown here, there was no foundational genealogy comparable to that which Abelard had constructed to link a highly educated nun with august *female* philosophical-monastic forbears.[23] And that was why, if her husband would not respond to her emotionally, the next best thing was to challenge him (albeit strategically on behalf of "all" the Paraclete nuns) to console her by formulating an originary *auctoritas* for the identity as nun into which he had rushed her at their crisis.[24]

That he understood her absolutely is proved both by some features of letter 7 now to be considered and by the way he concludes it: trusting that he has not only dealt with the *auctoritas* of her calling, but also commended its *propria dignitas* (particular dignity) and its *excellentia* so that she may embrace it the more zealously.[25] He, as *philosophus*, could never ultimately be short of *propria dignitas*; culture was littered with famous male antecedents. Letter 7 is all about recovering and inventing the dignity of a professional genealogy for her, and thence arise its power and its radicalism in terms of gender issues.

Having retrieved the challenge to which the letter responds, we now need to survey what precedents and arguments it offers, attending particularly to strategies of gender polemic that those arguments adopt. This will provide a context for discussion of some particularly striking examples of polemic and for attendant questions about Abelard's standpoint. In concluding, I will suggest how the strategies deployed in the letter express the "empathy" that I am attributing to it.

Abelard was not writing in a vacuum, of course. Scattered across medieval religious culture were strands of pro-female or anti-misogynist discourse appropriate to his purpose.[26] As he developed these strands, he seems to have had in mind broadly four emphases that they might promote, Parity, Priority, Exclusivity, and Supremacy: Parity, because it was important to establish that the female religious profession developed on an equal footing with that of men; Priority, because both a nun's *dignitas* and her *auctoritas* would be reinforced wherever women could be shown to have preceded men in key aspects of religious life (the "women did it first" argument); the Exclusivity of specific practices, achievements, or rewards associated with female but not male religious (the "men never did this" argument) categorically enhanced the profession to which Heloise belonged; and Supremacy lay especially in instances of female triumph (despite the "weakness" attributed to the sex) where males proved inadequate in situations of crisis.[27] The reader will quickly detect from the following synopsis how often Abelard invokes Parity, Priority, Exclusivity, and Supremacy.

Christ, he argues, gave *auctoritas* for "monkhood" to men and women alike when he traveled preaching with the twelve and with several women, who dedicated their own possessions to his subsistence.[28] The special devotion of the women was emphasized when they anointed him. Only women anointed the living Christ. Exclusive in every sense (as I shall later emphasize), this anointing was the sole item that Christ personally nominated for inclusion in the gospels. Then, at his passion, the male disciples—even Peter the *apostolorum princeps*[29]—signally failed to stand by their Lord. In contrast, the women showed extreme fidelity and resolve; accordingly they were rewarded (Priority) with the first sight of Christ resurrected. He greeted them in a manner he had prohibited (Exclusivity) to the male disciples,[30] and it was from the women (Priority again) that the men had to "learn" what they were to preach of the Resurrection.[31]

Abelard now goes forward from the gospel evidence, using sources in Eusebius's *Ecclesiastical History* to argue that in the nascent church women and men alike developed the embryonic monastic life, especially those reported by Philo who lived by Lake Mareotis, including "mulieres . . . seniores virgines . . . propter amorem philosophiae spontanea voluntate nuptiis abstinentes" (voluntarily abstaining from marriage for love of philosophy).[32] He concludes—as do some recent scholars, but against the trend of medieval thinking—that in early Christianity women were not *disiunctas* (distinguished) from men "in his quae ad Deum pertinent" (in what pertains to God).[33]

Returning from the nascent church to Old Testament prefigurations, Abelard unexpectedly claims that since daughters as well as sons of Aaron were mentioned as recipients of the Israelites' offerings, women must have shared the office of Levi, and their religion was not separate from the *clericorum ordine*.[34] The later shared terminology of *diaconissae/diaconi* is taken to confirm that there were in effect "Levite-esses" (further reinforcing Parity) alongside the priestly Levites. Moreover the vigil kept by women at the doors of the Tabernacle while men slept signifies a criticism (Supremacy) of the negligence of male priests. Belonging to that line of women was Anna, who "departed not from the temple," addressed the infant Christ there alongside Simeon, and preached publicly about him. Luke seems to commend her continence and prophecy more than Simeon's and offers no suggestion, Abelard notes, that Simeon "preached" to others (Exclusivity again). We might observe *en passant* that Abelard's great mentor, the third-century exegete Origen, specifically argued that Anna's public speaking (Vulgate *loquebatur omnibus*) did *not* constitute public preaching. Origen, no less than those challenging heterodox views soon after Abelard's time, wanted to crush any suggestion that scripture authorized women to preach.[35]

From Anna the widow, the *De auctoritate sanctimonialium* moves on to stress the elaborate concern for the institution of religious widows and deaconesses in the Pauline epistles—far exceeding any apostolic detail on behalf of male bishops or deacons.[36] Abelard had already likened Heloise to the Pauline widows in letter 5,[37] and he became so attached to the term *diaconissa* that he persisted in substituting it for *abbatissa* throughout his Rule for nuns.[38] In the present context he takes the possibilities of a female diaconate so far as to cite a view that the reference in Romans to Phoebe *in ministerio ecclesiae* amounts to apostolic authority that women may be ordained.[39] As for consecrated virginity in the developing church, Abelard notes its claim to Exclusivity in its privilege of being conferred only by bishops at particular feasts: mere monks can be consecrated any time, by an ordinary abbot.[40]

Abelard proceeds to argue woman's supremacy in religious life on the basis that God favors her virtue, bestowing grace on her "weakness" so that the "last becomes first." The supremacy accorded woman's virtue is seen in Deborah, victorious "viris deficientibus" (while men failed); and in Judith, whose single-handed exploit against massed enemies overshadows David's combat with but one Goliath. Such solo heroines put so-called masculine toughness to shame. Likewise the *constantia* of the mother celebrated in the second book of Machabees (7: 1–42) deeply shames modern monkish gluttony when one recalls that she lost the lives of seven sons, and her own, rather than eat proscribed meat. In the *fortitudo* of Jephtha's daughter may be found another instance of shaming supremacy. Refusing to deny a father's vow even though it required her death, she puts St. Peter in his place with his craven denial of Christ.[41]

The ultimate gift of grace was for woman to bear Christ. Supremacy here features in a perhaps unexpected way: in the deduction that Christ thereby honored the female genitalia by his parturition more than he subsequently honored the male's by his circumcision. Then, at the Visitation, woman achieved another "first." While high priest Zacharias said nothing, his wife Elizabeth *nuntiavit* (prophesied) Christ's conception, exceeding the Baptist's prophecies in that the Baptist only uttered them after, but she before, the Nativity. Just how far woman outstrips man in this domain of prophecy is finally confirmed by the range of the Sibyl's foreknowledge of Christ, so complete as to cover the descent to hell, which not even Isaiah, nor even the evangelists, could anticipate.

Abelard is particularly struck, as will be explained shortly, by the divine *gratia* manifest in the Samaritan woman with whom Christ conversed by the well. The abundance of *gratia* showered upon women is otherwise exemplified in Christ's miracles of healing performed predominantly for them, and in miraculous conversions of prostitutes—Mary Magdalene and Mary the Egyptian—which witness the force of Matthew's dictum that "meretrices praecedunt vos in regnum Dei" (prostitutes enter the kingdom of heaven before you).[42]

Chastity on the other hand (Abelard's final theme) is a perfection "rare among men, frequent among women." It was honored in St. Agatha when she miraculously protected a crowd of pagans from Etna's fire beneath her veil. One does not hear, adds Abelard impishly, of any monk's hood which ever wrought such a thing. But the chief thrust of the argument here is to assert that the *forma* and *dignitas* of Heloise's profession is underwritten by a comparable *institutio* of a kind of consecrated chastity in pagan times that was elaborately protected by law. Just as Abelard, therefore, can track role models in antiquity, so can Heloise. Admittedly, the ancient *praerogativa* of vestal virginity is not strictly relevant to her, but Abelard is careful also to report from yet another context in Jerome the Roman respect for women who, like Heloise, honored Juno in being *univirae* (one-husband wives); he connects *univirae* with *monachae* (monkesses) because etymologically *monachus* means *solitarius* (alone).[43]

It remains for Abelard to recall the special solicitude shown by the Fathers for women, above all by Jerome, who incurred suspicion by associating with Paula and Eustochium as he himself had incurred it when he tried to assist Heloise in her early days at the Paraclete. (Moreover, Jerome wrote voluminously for his female protégées while, on the other hand—Exclusivity extending even to patristic letter-writing—leaving requests from the venerable Augustine unanswered.) If there is a characteristic Abelardian self-defensiveness in the precedent of the great *doctor* calumniated for consorting with women, we should also notice how pointedly he juxtaposes it with Christ's familiarity, in defiance of pharisaical objection, with the *beata meretrix*.[44] Is Abelard recalling Heloise's spectacular earlier assertion that she would rather be his whore, his *meretrix*, than the wife of an emperor?[45] Is he paying her the compliment of pursuing her own self-description and identifying for that, too, a reassuring antecedent?[46] Whether as *univira* or Pauline "widow" on one hand or as *meretrix* on the other, woman's—or Heloise's—preeminence seems to be assured; we recall that "meretrices praecedunt . . . in regnum Dei." In the letter as a whole the nun's (Heloise's) moral, monastic, and intellectual inheritance is vouchsafed by examples ranging from Miriam and Anna to Paula, Mary Magdalene, Phoebe the deaconess, and the women who shared a philosophical life of meditation on the shores of Lake Mareotis.

I hope I am guilty of representing the *De auctoritate sanctimonialium*

as a more urgent piece than it is sometimes reckoned to be. Christopher
Brooke dismisses it as conscientious hack work, claiming that "Abelard
dutifully did what he was told, dug out all he could from the New Testament and the early fathers about the devout life of widows and nuns,
and lots of good commendable references to holy women."[47] Abelard's
pro-female epistle seems to me, on the contrary, to be not drudgery but
committed polemic. It is the very combativeness, found here as in other
works analyzed by Andrew Taylor in the present volume, that leads to
potentially off-putting features, particularly the strident (and perhaps in
its competitive ethos, paradoxically the masculinist) insistence on things
women did "first" or on things that "we do not find ascribed to any male."
To object to this, however, would be to slight the urgency of the quest
for female innovation and priority, still of concern to Christine de Pizan
so much later in the *Cité des dames*.[48] Moreover, it took Abelard's peculiar
combative nerve to demote celebrated males to secondariness on a scale so
massively disdainful as to include David the conqueror of Goliath, Isaiah
the archprophet, John the Baptist, St. Peter "Prince of Apostles," all the
other male disciples, and even—because women's claims on Jerome's time
were greater than his—St. Augustine.

The letter is packed with creative exegesis. Sometimes it is creative in
the sense applicable in "creative accountancy." An instance of this would
be the way Abelard uses an incidental reference to Aaron's "daughters" in
the Book of Numbers to invent a category of priestesses (*Levitae*), opti-
mistically suppressing the seven other references to "Aaron and [only] his
sons" that immediately surround it.[49] Yet this argument is but an aside in
Abelard's radical and cogent case for the evolutionary significance of the
early religious widowhood and female diaconate which the Church had
done its best to obscure by the twelfth century but which feminist theology has lately recuperated.[50] Just how radical his pro-female stance could
be, and how little he deserves to be thought a weary essayist clocking up
commendable references to holy women, may most clearly be seen if we
ponder his discussions of, respectively, the Samaritan woman, the anointing of Christ, and Christ's female followers at the time of the Passion.

In John 4: 1–42 Jesus sits by a well and, while the male disciples go to
buy meat, asks a woman of Samaria for drink. She wonders at such a request from a Jew. In response Jesus hints at his identity and at the "living
water" he might give. He pretends to bid her "call her husband," yet reveals that (though she has had five husbands) she is not now married. She
recognizes him as a prophet, and Jesus confirms that he is the Messiah

whose coming she knows of. On their return the disciples are surprised to find him talking with this woman, but he further surprises them by refusing their meat and referring instead to metaphorical meat. Meanwhile, the Samaritan woman has urged the nearby city dwellers to come out to Christ: many of them "believed in him, for the word of the woman giving testimony" (4: 39); others believe "not for [her] saying" (4: 42) but after they have heard Jesus in person.

Abelard's enthusiastic response to the Samaritan woman distinguishes itself from the back-handed compliments conferred on her by Augustine and Jerome.[51] He would have found a mildly more positive account in Origen,[52] but his enthusiasm is most closely anticipated in Chrysostom's commentary. Here the emphasis is comprehensively positive, highlighting the woman's intelligently probing curiosity, her readiness to learn, her prudence, and her exemplary zeal and wisdom as she eagerly takes up the evangelists' function ("evangelistarum officio fungitur") and performs it with "magnam sapientiam" (judicious tact).[53]

One detail in particular suggests to me that this account has contributed to the *De auctoritate sanctimonialium*: the strategy of comparing the Samaritan woman advantageously with Nicodemus. Both Abelard and Chrysostom disparage Nicodemus for failing to make any apostolic use of insights gained from his own conversation with Christ, which is reported earlier (John 3:1–15).[54] In general, Abelard not only matches but surpasses Chrysostom's enthusiasm. He presents the Samaritan as one enjoying a remarkably privileged familiar conversation with Christ and goes on to highlight her missionary function. She was filled with the spirit of prophecy, "spiritu prophetiae repletam."[55] In going to summon forth the people of the city, she achieved another women's Exclusive, since Christ elsewhere forbade his disciples to enter any Samaritan city—a second detail borrowed, but improved, from Chrysostom.[56] She was in fact a proto-preacher, "praecurrens et civitati nuntians eius adventum" (running before and announcing his coming to her city), and "quae audierat praedicans" (preaching those things that she had heard).[57] It was with her that Christ's preaching among the gentiles began.

Again, we should not miss the polemical note in Abelard's unembarrassed regard for a woman's preaching. But beyond this, he goes on to offer a lyrical profeminist theory about the meaning of Jesus's "thirst" at the well. He interprets the thirst as a special yearning for all women's salvation, and connects it with the spiritual "meat" that, Jesus explains to the disciples, means doing the will of his father. In asking the woman for

drink, according to Abelard, "huic praecipue siti suae per salutem feminarum satisfieri velle se insinuat" (Jesus suggests that he wishes to quench
his thirst principally for the salvation of women).[58] This striking exegesis
probably combines an idea from Chrysostom, who speaks of Christ's hunger (or *desiderium*) for humankind's salvation,[59] with Augustine's suggestion that Christ "thirsted" to develop and to "drink" the woman's faith.[60]

There was little else for Abelard to build on in Augustine's interpretation. Augustine, to be sure, commends the woman for running to spread
the word (*evangelizare*).[61] But by the time he concedes this, he has comprehensively undermined her autonomy in the matter by urging a metaphorical significance in Jesus's bidding: "Go, call thy husband" (4:16). Her
five previous husbands are the five senses that lead to understanding. As
the woman reaches recognition of the Messiah, she is in effect "calling her
husband" (her understanding) who is "the head of the woman": so it is
her understanding/"husband" which then acknowledges Christ as "head of
man."[62] By this recourse to the classic biblical gender paradigm whereby
male or husband is "head" of the woman or wife, Augustine has strategically emptied the Samaritan woman of independent judgment. That
which, in her, leads her to acknowledge Christ turns out to be an inner
impulse that is gendered as quintessentially masculine.

Such gender structuring, implicitly rejected by Abelard in the case of
the Samaritan woman,[63] is explicitly and even (by the standards of his day)
outrageously flouted in his discussion of the women's anointings of Christ,
which dominates the beginning of the *De auctoritate sanctimonialium*. Evi-
dently these anointings are, for him, the very foundation of the *dignitas*,
the *praerogativa* of women, for they establish women in an extraordinary
position of quasi-sacramental authority over Christ himself.

Abelard's emphasis falls chiefly on the unnamed woman who anoints
Jesus's head, breaking open a whole alabaster container in the extremity of
her fervor.[64] The key to the immense significance Abelard assigns to this,
beyond its expression of *devotio feminarum*, lies in the interpretation of the
action as a fulfilment of the prophecy in Daniel 9: 24:

Septuaginta hebdomades abbreviatae sunt super populum tuum et super urbem
sanctam tuam, ut consummetur praevaricatio, et finem accipiat peccatum, et deleatur iniquitas, et adducatur iustitia sempiterna, et impleatur visio et prophetia, et
ungatur Sanctus sanctorum.

(Seventy weeks are shortened upon thy people, and upon thy holy city, that transgression may be finished, and sin may have an end, and iniquity may be abolished;
and everlasting justice may be brought; and vision and prophecy may be fulfilled;
and the saint of saints may be anointed.)

In letter 7, Christ is this saint of saints: "ecce enim sanctum sanctorum mulier inungit" (behold, a woman anoints the saint of saints).[65] Not merely does she proclaim him Christ by her action, but also "quasi corporalibus sacramentis eum in regem et sacerdotem consecrans Christum, id est, unctum, corporaliter ipsum efficeret" (it is as though with bodily sacraments she *consecrates* him King and Priest; that is, she *makes* him, bodily, "the anointed one", which is what "Christ" means).[66]

All other priorities and supremacies in the letter pale by comparison with what is asserted on this basis. The implications are portentous. First, even though males subsequently gained a prerogative over sacraments of unction such as anointing priests and kings, a woman anointed—consecrated—Christ, the very origin of the Church. Second, where men were to anoint as a symbolic act, woman consecrated Christ not metaphorically but actually. Third, Christ refused to accept kingship from men—indeed fled from those who offered it: but he accepted both kingship (a heavenly kingship) and priesthood from women in accepting the double anointings, head and feet. Fourth, Joseph of Arimathea and Nicodemus anointed Christ's *dead* body with preservative ointments, prefiguring his body's incorruptibility, but the two anointings of his live body were by women.

Crowning the wholesale disruption of conventional medieval gender hierarchy implicit here is Abelard's defiant reversal of the most potent paradigm of all: "Christus ipse a muliere, Christiani a viris inunguntur; caput ipsum, scilicet, a femina, membra a viris" (Christ himself by a woman, Christians by men are anointed. The head by a woman, the limbs by men).[67] Woman, not man, links with "head" at a formative moment in Christ's mission. By comparison, the male hegemony over sacraments such as ordination and coronation in the entire history of the Church is secondary, for men can but anoint "the limbs."

The radicalism of the power claimed for woman in the episode is enhanced when one realizes that nothing so ambitious emerges from the homilies and *vitae* concerning St. Mary Magdalene that were circulating during the twelfth century. Their stress is on the intimacy of the anointing; or, if ritual implications are acknowledged, they are attenuated or diffused, partly because the preferred typology involves not the stark passage in Daniel but the bride/*sponsa* of Canticles, herself a mere figure for the Church in relation to Christ.[68] Formulations I have seen so far do not remotely approximate the absolute sacramental primacy derived from the episode by Abelard.

The letter's third striking example of gender polemic is the account of Christ's women followers at his death. The contrast between the disciples' cowardice and the women's loyalty is of course unavoidable in the Gospels, but it is not often as satirically etched as by Abelard. He mocks the males with their laudatory titles "Apostle Beloved of the Lord," "Prince of the Apostles," even as he describes how they melted away. He enhances the steadfastness of the women by systematic use of a masculine-nuanced vocabulary of toughness, which implicitly exposes the fraudulence of conventional medieval wisdom about woman's "instability." The "undaunted" women "stood firm"; they "staunchly" remained close to the sepulchre; their "perseverance and steadfastness" everywhere contrasted sharply with the disciples' *defectus*; in brief, the disciples were all promises and words, whereas the women proved their love by deeds.[69]

A bizarre exegetical centrepiece in this narrative of male disgrace is the suggestion that it was prophesied in Job's anguished cry, "Pelli meae, consumptis carnibus, adhaesit os meum" (the flesh being consumed, my bone hath cleaved to my skin, 19: 20). The connection with the Passion is worked out as follows. The "bone" constitutes the strength of the body, and so signifies Christ's body, foundation of the church. The "flesh" is within the skin, and corresponds to the apostles, whose business was "inward food" (the soul). That leaves the "skin," the outer covering, to symbolize the women who "procured things needful for the body."[70] Job's torment is a prefigurement because at Christ's death his "flesh" (disciples) ebbed away so that the "skin" (women) "stuck" to the bone—their Lord.

As gender polemic, this obviously takes away with one hand what it grants with the other. The women's staunch, undeviating, courageous loyalty is enhanced, yet simultaneously it is predicated on an analogy that insists on their normative preoccupation with bodily externals instead of the soul, which is the province of the male disciples. What is therefore notable here is that while the symbolism appropriately challenges convention in one respect by designating the male disciples—with their carnal instinct for self-preservation—as flesh (contrast St. Gregory's terse formula "Eua uelut caro . . . Adam uelut spiritus" [Eve representing the flesh. . . Adam representing the spirit][71]), Abelard nevertheless contrives to salvage the association between males and spirituality or the soul. He even reinforces the contradiction in the very process of trying to justify the flesh/skin symbolism:

Sunt et viri naturaliter tam mente quam corpore feminis fortiores. Unde et merito per carnem, quae vicinior est ossi, virilis natura; per pellem muliebris infirmitas designatur.[72]

(Men are naturally stronger than women in both mind and body. So the manly nature is rightly indicated by "flesh," nearer to the bone; womanly weakness is indicated by "skin.")

What can one say about this appeal to "manly strength" even amidst Abelard's powerful demonstration of its utter inapplicability to the circumstances surrounding the crucifixion? The question is the more acute because the passage just quoted is Abelard's addition to his source for this exegesis, Gregory's *Moralia in Job*.[73]

Gregory's analysis is, in fact, a miniature *locus classicus* for a defense of women founded on their courage during the crucifixion, and the immense popularity of the *Moralia* during the Middle Ages would explain why the *topos* featured so frequently in debates about women.[74] Gregory expounds the equation of bone/*fortitudo*/Christ/church; the equation of flesh with the disciples, who "infirma sapuerunt" (discovered their weaknesses) during the Passion; and the equation of skin/exteriority with the women, who served the lord with "exterioribus ministeriis." But it is notable that Gregory's use of the concept of *infirmitas* is confined to the disciples. Abelard, in his more extended analysis, struggles to re-gender *infirmitas* as female. Why, in an epistle commendatory to women, does he want to do this?

In answering that question we come to a celebrated crux in Abelard's gender theory.[75] It seems that perhaps more than any other medieval writer he took to heart the notion that it was women who fulfilled Christ's reassurance, reported by St. Paul when he found himself assailed by the "sting of the flesh," that through grace, strength might be made perfect in weakness: "Sufficit tibi gratia mea; nam virtus in infirmitate perficitur" (2 Cor. 12:9). For Abelard, as Heloise agreed and as was almost universally the case in his time, it was axiomatic that woman is *infirmior* (weaker).[76] However, Christ's comment seemed to hold out a unique advantage of perfectibility precisely through *infirmitas*. The *De auctoritate sanctimonialium* pursues a lexical connection with St. Paul's earlier suggestion that in the case of the human body, "weaker" limbs (gendered female by Abelard) are treated with a kind of compensatory honor:

Sed multo magis quae videntur membra corporis infirmiora esse necessariora sunt, et quae putamus, ignobiliora membra esse corporis his abundantiorum honorem circumdamus et quae inhonesta nostra sunt abundantiorem honestatem habent. Honesta autem nostra nullius egent. Sed Deus temperavit corpus ei cui deerat, abundantiorem tribuendo honorem.

(Much more those members of the body which seem to be more feeble are more necessary: and those members of the body which we think to be less honourable, upon
these we bestow more abundant honour; and our uncomely parts have more abundant comeliness. For our comely parts have no need: but God hath tempered the
body together, having given more abundant honour to that part which lacked.)[77]

In identifying women with "weaker," "uncomely" parts of the body—indeed (uncannily anticipating modern hypotheses about male inscription
of the female as lack) with a part of the body which *deerat* (lacked)—Abelard's profeminine stance may seem to collapse. The reader's instinct will
be to protest: with friends like that, who needs enemies? Women, having
earlier in the letter appropriated the status of head rather than limbs, *caput*
as against *membra*, now dwindle to the status of *ignobilia membra*.

It is tempting to wonder whether, in Mary McLaughlin's striking
formulation, Abelard was trapped in a *sic et non* of ambivalently profeminist and antifeminist impulses.[78] McLaughlin herself believed that "this
ambivalence finds its resolution in [Abelard's] expansion of the vision of
Christ's companionship with women."[79] The present discussion has amply
corroborated that view, but I would wish to underline how the Abelardian resolution *depended* on a prior attribution of weakness to women.
McLaughlin herself observes that an example of negative comment on
woman found elsewhere in Abelard in his exposition of Genesis is "in no
way incompatible with his argument for her dignity in the order of grace,"
because it "accounted for the initial weakness of that nature which was to
be transformed by grace."[80] Trying to mediate between a received tradition of woman's inferiority and contradictory evidence of her powers, he
perceived how absolutely the latter might be predicated upon the former
through the doctrine of *infirmitas* perfected in strength.[81] Abelard persis-
tently asserts the operation of that principle in the letter. Woman's *fortitudo*
is magnificently shown in example after example. That her "weakness" is
perfected *as strength* is the point of his expansion of the commentary on
Job. Her weakness and her strength become symbiotic. It is therefore precisely because she is a "weak member" of the Christian body that she
achieves the special dignity of consecrating the "head" of that body.

There is, of course, something exasperatingly impenetrable about the
way in which this logic systematically stands the misogynistic topos of
weakness on its head so that it becomes pro-female. Our instinct as readers
is to try to expose the contradictions inherent in the process. By this approach, intimated by McLaughlin and developed by Sister Prudence Allen,
it is possible to unpack two Abelardian views of women: one according to

the order of nature, and another according to the order of grace. On the basis of such a distinction an inconsistency could be pinpointed between, on the one hand, the enhancement of woman as anointress of "the Head" (in the order of grace) and, on the other, the support given by Abelard's Rule for formal male authority over a convent on the conventional basis that (in the order of nature) "the head of the woman is always the man."[82]

Scrutinized in this way, Abelard can be shown to exemplify both sides of the medieval debate about women, as I have shown elsewhere.[83] Yet because Abelard's point is precisely that every defect attributed to women merely enables further triumph through grace, he eludes the reader intent on chipping away at his profeminism. Andrea Nye (though without reference to the *De auctoritate sanctimonialium*) has recently characterized his thought as rigid and oppositional and compared it unfavorably with Heloise's flexible and affectively responsive thinking. "Heloise's thought," she suggests, "has the flowing quality that Abelard found so dangerous in the female tongue."[84] Nye's argument is provoked partly by the way a passage early in the Rule exhorts nuns to silence on the grounds that a woman's "softness of body" gives her tongue particular flexibility, and "the more mobile and given to words it is," the more it becomes "the seedbed of all evil."[85]

Two responses might be offered here: one from Abelard, and another on his behalf. The one from Abelard would be his own emotional appreciation of women in whom grace wrought remarkable speech: Anna, Elizabeth, the Samaritan woman converting townsfolk by preaching what she had heard (the tongue, as it were, made perfect in weakness). From Nye's point of view, this response would still carry the taint of suspect ratiocination. So a second response that seems worth making on Abelard's behalf is that without the rigid scaffolding of the logic of perfectibility, he would hardly have had the language (and probably even he would not have had the nerve) to mount such a profeminine discourse. The strength-in-weakness topos was an enabling topos. Although no predecessor saw such vistas in it, the tenacity of Abelard's logic enabled him to do something more substantial with the topos than refer *en passant* to a few famous females as "exceptions by special grace."

It is not a matter of claiming that Abelard transcended all sorts of gender prejudices of his day. For example, whatever his talk of woman's equality of "clerical" function in the early church, his Rule insists that neither the Sacristan nor any of the sisters must touch the altar vessels or altar cloths (except when asked to wash them!).[86] In actuality, he could hardly say otherwise in view of canon law on such a matter.[87] The point is not that Abelard could not everywhere sustain the profeminine campaign he mounted in letter 7, but rather that he was able and willing to mount such a daring campaign on that scale at all.

It might be objected that private correspondence is not very daring, but this letter is a self-consciously rhetorical piece: at one stage it inscribes an audience of brethren and fellow monks, "O fratres et commonachi," who are rebuked for gluttony.[88] The letter was therefore not intended, ultimately, for Heloise's ears only. However, it was for her ears initially, and in concluding I should like to return to the nature of its celebration of her and to the earlier claim that it represents a consummation of their correspondence.

Heloise had reacted sharply to the *Historia calamitatum* because in it Abelard seemed so oblivious to the immense debt of assurance she felt he owed her as founder of her community at the Paraclete and as husband, but above all as the person whom she had always, as was well known, given a love beyond all bounds (". . . eo te magis mihi obnoxium, quo te semper ut omnibus patet immoderato amore complexa sum").[89] She pointedly reminds him that amidst the trauma of separation, she received from him nothing like those numerous careful treatises written by the Fathers for the *doctrina*, *exhortatio*, and *consolatio* of holy women. When Abelard replies that he has not written her a *consolatio* because her *prudentia* seems to make that superfluous, she protests that his confidence in her strength is unfounded. She explicitly adds that she does not *want* anodynes about virtue perfected in weakness. "Nolo, me ad virtutem exhortans, et ad pugnam provocans, dicas: 'Nam virtus in infirmitate perficitur.'"[90] When, therefore, Abelard subsequently founds the *De auctoritate sanctimonialium* precisely upon that text, how can he think that he is repaying his "debt" to her?

I believe that the conclusion of letter 7 answers this question by simultaneously invoking the treatises addressed to women by Fathers such as Ambrose and Jerome and distancing itself from them. They are invoked personally in that an awareness of a personal "debt" to Heloise is indeed acknowledged, albeit obliquely, by Abelard's allusion to a sermon that he (mistakenly) supposes to have been written by Jerome for Paula or Eustochium. Abelard quotes pseudo-Jerome's observation that a request cannot be refused when one is "bound by the profound love" (nimia vestra devinctus dilectione) of the one asking it.[91] Indirect and coded though this is, it is a moment when Abelard finally acknowledges the "debt" he owes Heloise for her boundless love.

But this is not all. Abelard continues to invoke the treatises of the Fathers, underlining the risks to their reputations run by the authors (especially Jerome) when they assisted holy women. This, of course, is a defensive maneuver designed to buttress Abelard's letter against calumny: a reminder that egotism shadows much that he writes. Yet he also *distances* himself from the comparable efforts of these, his models, in one crucial particular. He draws attention to the fact that Jerome showers flattering rhetoric upon Paula, quoting an extravagant claim that if all his limbs were tongues, and every joint of his body had a voice, he could not utter words worthy of her. Abelard comments drily, "in earum laudibus aliquatenus veritatis tramitem excedere videatur" (in their [women's] praise he appears to go some way beyond the bounds of truth).[92] More gobbets of *adulatio* are quoted from a letter to Demetrias, and to this he finally adds that another sort of extravagance is represented by Ambrose's *consolatio* to the sisters of the dead Emperor Valentinian, promising their brother's salvation.

To Heloise, Abelard is saying, "Do you want *those* kinds of spurious consolation?" He cannot ultimately allay any of her fears about her own salvation. Nor will he emulate Jerome in flattering her. (Praise and flattery, after all, had been a subject of subtle debate between them, extending even to such finer nuances as the detection of refusals to be flattered that smack of self-flattery.[93]) But within those limits "debts" have at least partially been discharged. What he has offered has a claim to be more than conventional consolation, more than superficial tribute. Abelard believed that their new relationship did not admit of formal epistolary avowals of intimate obligation; but, for him to offer a historically authenticated profile of Heloise's profession, suffused with the achievements of women, exploratory of ancient precedent, and rooted in a near visionary view of woman's consecratory relation to Christ, was no small gesture of his personal responsibility to her. There is nothing in Jerome's encomiastic flourishes to match the degree of empathy Abelard here seeks, once and for all, to show Heloise.[94]

Notes

1. Editions referred to are J. T. Muckle, ed., "Abelard's Letter of Consolation to a Friend (*Historia calamitatum*)" (hereafter Muckle 1950); "The Personal Letters Between Abelard and Heloise," (hereafter Muckle 1953); "The Letter of Heloise on the Religious Life and Abelard's First Reply" (hereafter Muckle 1955); and T. P. McLaughlin, ed., "Abelard's Rule for Religious Women." The translations referred to are Betty Radice, *The Letters of Abelard and Heloise* (hereafter Radice) and for

the letter *De auctoritate vel dignitate ordinis sanctimonialium*, C. K. Scott Moncrieff, *The Letters of Abelard and Heloise* (hereafter Scott Moncrieff). The numbering of the letters is something of a headache. I have followed the increasingly prevalent practice (though not adopted by Radice) of numbering the *Historia* as the first letter, so that Heloise's response to it is letter 2, et seq. The letters incorporated in the Muckle and McLaughlin editions are those that existed as a corpus in a number of manuscripts from the thirteenth century onwards. Other "uncollected" letters are described in David Luscombe, "From Paris to the Paraclete: The Correspondence of Abelard and Heloise."

2. ". . . verbis etiam immoderati doloris tuae frenum impositum est iussionis" (Muckle 1955: 241; Radice: 159). Abelard had asked her to rid herself of her bitterness of heart: "Hanc amaritudinem. . . depone" (Muckle 1953: 87; Radice: 145).

3. "Sin autem humilitati tuae aliter videtur, et in iis etiam quae ad Deum pertinent magisterio nostro atque scriptis indiges, super his quae velis scribe mihi ut ad ipsam rescribam" (Muckle 1953: 73; Radice: 119). I consider the correspondence essentially authentic. A long and diversionary debate about the status of the letters has been decided, in my view, in favor of authenticity by three contributions especially: Peter Dronke, "Abelard and Heloise in Medieval Testimonies," originally published separately by Glasgow University Press (1976) and now reprinted in his *Intellectuals and Poets in Medieval Europe*; Luscombe, "From Paris to the Paraclete"; and most definitively, Barbara Newman, "Authority, Authenticity, and the Repression of Heloise."

4. Barbara Newman, "Flaws in the Golden Bowl," 111. Letter 6, Heloise's request for a female Rule, is receiving increasing attention: see Linda Georgianna, "Any Corner of Heaven." The glowing exception to the neglect of letter 7 is Mary M. McLaughlin, "Peter Abelard and the Dignity of Women," a seminal work to which I am extensively indebted.

5. Scott Moncrieff's translation does not appear to be widely known. Parts of the letter are translated, with comment, in Blamires et al., eds., *Woman Defamed and Woman Defended*, 232–36.

6. Muckle 1955: 242; Radice: 159, 180.

7. McLaughlin, "Abelard's Rule," 241, indicates that the Rule is complete in only one of the manuscripts; two manuscripts have about two-thirds of the text, and four have only the introduction.

8. Muckle 1950: 174. The *Theologia* can be dated to 1122–25; see Mary M. McLaughlin, "Abelard as Autobiographer," 477–78, 480. The relevant passages are in *Theologia* 2: 94–106; see esp. PL 22, cols. 1187ff.

9. McLaughlin highlights Abelard's concern with his intellectual and spiritual vocation (especially when he set up the Paraclete) and the function of the *Historia* as a whole in "justifying and preparing the way for his new vocation" as monk-philosopher ("Abelard as Autobiographer," 472, 477, 485).

10. "antea vixeram continentissime"; "frequentatione nobilium feminarum studii scholaris assiduitate revocabar"; "continentiae meae fama praeterita" (Muckle 1950: 182–83; Radice: 65–67).

11. "amplius a philosophis et divinis immunditia vitae recedebam" (Muckle 1950: 182; Radice: 65).

12. Muckle 1950: 184; Radice: 68.

13. Muckle 1950: 187; Radice: 71–72.

14. Muckle 1950: 187; Radice: 72.

15. "Apud Iudaeos . . . filii prophetarum, Heliae vel Helisaei sectatores, quos, beato attestante Hieronymo, monachos legimus in veteri Testamento" (Muckle 1950: 187; Radice: 72); and Jerome, Letter 125: 7, *Ad Rusticum*, PL 22, col. 1076: "Filii prophetarum (quos monachos in veteri Testamento legimus) aedificabant sibi casulas propter fluenta Jordanis, et turbis urbium derelictis, polenta et herbis agrestibus victitabant."

16. Muckle 1950: 191; Radice: 77.

17. Muckle 1950: 199–200; Radice: 89–90.

18. McLaughlin suggests that "only in the idyllic 'solitude' of the Paraclete, removed yet not wholly isolated from the pressures of the larger world, had he been successful in reconciling his intellectual aspirations with his . . . sense of spiritual vocation," and that the Paraclete venture enabled him to unite "the noble anachoresis of Plato and his followers with the world-renouncing zeal of Jewish and early Christian ascetics" ("Abelard as Autobiographer," 477, 480). More pragmatically, justifications for an eremitical existence were necessary to Abelard at this time in defense of his flight from the monastery of St. Denis. The venture also reflects the separatism demonstrated by Robert d'Arbrissel at Fontevrault.

19. "Nos autem habeamus propositi nostri principes Paulos, Antonios, Hilariones, Macharium et, ut ad scripturarum materiam redeam, noster princeps Elias, Eliseus, duces prophetarum, qui habitabant in agris et solitudine et faciebant sibi tabernacula praeter fluenta Jordanis" (McLaughlin, "Abelard's Rule," 248; Radice: 192, from Jerome, letter 58: 5, *Ad Paulinum*, PL 22, col. 582).

20. Newman, "Authority," 128–29, 148–50. See also Joan Ferrante, "The Education of Women in the Middle Ages," 19–20.

21. Muckle 1955: 242; Radice: 159.

22. "Philosophi saeculi solent amorem veterem amore novo, quasi clavum clavo expellere: . . . nos amore virtutum, vitia superemus" (Jerome, letter 125: 14, *Ad Rusticum*, PL 22, col. 1080). This source (though not its ulterior point) is mentioned by Georgianna ("Any Corner of Heaven," 231) in the course of her full discussion of the opening of letter 6.

23. Newman interestingly speculates that for Heloise, as much as for Abelard, "the classical *otium philosophicum* exerted a strong attraction" ("Authority," 150).

24. My diagnosis of a deeply personal motivation for Heloise's request differs from that of McLaughlin, who believes that it arises from Heloise's perception of the "ambiguous status" of the female monastic life, in that theoretically "nuns were laywomen living a religious life"—an ambiguity underlined by the period's enthusiastic female response to the call to the *vita apostolica* ("Peter Abelard and the Dignity of Women," 294). Georgianna connects Heloise's request with controversy over varying interpretations of the Benedictine Rule ("Any Corner of Heaven," 231–32). Unfortunately, Catherine Brown overlooks the request in her absorbing exploration of a "deployment of cultural masks of 'the feminine'" by Heloise ("*Muliebriter*: Doing Gender in the Letters of Heloise," 42).

25. Muckle 1955: 281; Scott Moncrieff: 175. This concluding passage validates

the manuscript title *De auctoritate vel dignitate ordinis sanctimonialium*, which was adopted by Muckle in his edition of the letter (1955: 253), though he had earlier (1950: 164–65) referred to it as the *De origine sanctimonialium*. For convenience (while retaining the important focus on female *auctoritas*) this essay will abbreviate the manuscript title to *De auctoritate sanctimonialium*.

26. See Blamires, *Woman Defamed and Woman Defended*, esp. 228–32 for a translation of "De matrona" by Marbod of Rennes (ca. 1035–1123). For a survey of profeminine polemic of the Middle Ages see Blamires, *The Case for Women in Medieval Culture*.

27. This had a long history in relation to scriptural figures such as Deborah, whose role as prophet and judge was often supposed an exemplary rebuke to the "effeminacy" of men in her time (see Alcuin Blamires and C. W. Marx, "Woman Not to Preach," 54.

28. ". . . quae proprias etiam facultates in quotidianam eius alimoniam dicarant" (Muckle 1955: 254; Scott Moncrieff: 132), alluding to Luke 8: 1–3, a passage that Abelard several times recalled in the context of Augustine's introduction of it into his *De opere monachorum* (PL 40, col. 552), probably because of the authority this gave for his own association with Heloise (see Muckle 1950: 207; Radice: 99–100).

29. Muckle 1955: 256; Scott Moncrieff: 136.

30. Muckle 1955: 258; Scott Moncrieff: 139; alluding rather ingeniously to Christ's instruction "neminem per viam salutaveritis" (salute no man by the way) at Luke 10: 4.

31. ". . . ut per eas apostoli primum addiscerent quod toti mundo postmodum praedicarent" (Muckle 1955: 258; Scott Moncrieff: 139).

32. Muckle 1955: 260; Scott Moncrieff: 143. Eusebius claimed as Christian a pre-Christian monastic community of *therapeutae* and *therapeutrides* described in Philo's *De vita contemplativa*. Eusebius founds the claim especially on Philo's statement that women belonged to this community "and that most of them are aged virgins who kept their chastity from no compulsion . . . but rather from voluntary opinion, from zeal and yearning for wisdom" (*Ecclesiastical History* 2: 17; see also 1: 147–55, esp. 153).

33. Muckle 1955: 261; Scott Moncrieff: 143.

34. Muckle 1955: 261–62; Scott Moncrieff: 145.

35. See Alcuin Blamires, "Women and Preaching in Medieval Orthodoxy, Heresy, and Saints' Lives." Origen argued against Montanists in his commentary on 1 Corinthians that "it was not in an assembly [i.e., not contravening St. Paul's restrictions] that Anna spoke out" (Greek text in Claude Jenkins, "Origen on 1 Corinthians," pt. 4, *Journal of Theological Studies* 10 (1909): 42). Anna was one of two precedents cited by the Waldensians (ca. 1190) to justify women's preaching, according to Bernard of Fontcaude in *Adversus Waldensium sectam liber* 8: 6–7. He countered that neither prophesying nor "speaking" is synonymous with preaching (PL 204, col. 827).

36. Muckle 1955: 264; Scott Moncrieff: 149–50.

37. Muckle 1953: 83; Radice: 138.

38. "diaconissam, quam nunc abbatissam nominant" (McLaughlin, "Abe-

lard's Rule," 252; Radice: 199). In the diaconate (Greek *diakonos*, "servant") Abelard saw an ideal of authority-as-service suited to a monastic context. On deaconesses and abbesses, see further McLaughlin, "Peter Abelard and the Dignity of Women," 299 nn. 33–34 and 304 n. 52.

39. "Hic locus, inquit, apostolica auctoritate docet etiam feminas in ministerio Ecclesiae constitui" (attributing this to a commentary by Claudius) (Muckle 1955: 265; Scott Moncrieff: 150; and Rom. 16:2).

40. This "privilege" is emphasized at the beginning of the pseudo-Jerome treatise *Virginitatis laus*, PL 30, col. 163.

41. Jephtha's daughter was a favorite theme with Abelard; McLaughlin ("Peter Abelard and the Dignity of Women," 312–13) suggests that Abelard sees this heroine as a role model for Heloise.

42. Muckle 1955: 274; Scott Moncrieff: 166; Matt. 21:31.

43. Muckle 1955: 276; Scott Moncrieff: 168. In discussing Galatians 6:10 in the third book of *Commentariorum in Epistolam ad Galatas libri tres*, Jerome protests that pagan morality often exceeds that of Christians, "in quorum condemnationem habet et Juno univiras, et Vesta virgines, et alia idola continentes" (PL 26, col. 433). Newman argues that "Heloise fulfilled to perfection the classical ideal of the *univira*" ("Authority," 151). The *monachus, id est solitarius* point is echoed in McLaughlin, "Abelard's Rule," 248; Radice: 192, and comes from Jerome, letter 58:5, PL 22, col. 582.

44. Muckle 1955: 280; Scott Moncrieff: 174; and the *peccatrix* of Luke 7: 39.

45. Muckle 1953: 71; Radice: 114.

46. Heloise's point is that a *meretrix* is less meretricious than a wife who marries for money or status, a point intricately analyzed by Claire Nouvet, "The Discourse of the 'Whore': An Economy of Sacrifice." See also Andrea Nye, "A Woman's Thought or a Man's Discipline?" 14; and Peggy Kamuf, *Fictions of Feminine Desire*, 15–16.

47. Christopher Brooke, *The Medieval Idea of Marriage*, 117.

48. See Christine de Pizan, *The Book of the City of Ladies* 1:33.1–1:41.3, pp. 70–85. Women's ability to innovate is part of Christine's wider concern with female *auctoritas*. See also Maureen Quilligan, *The Allegory of Female Authority*, and Blamires, *The Case for Women in Medieval Culture*, chap. 8.

49. Confusingly, *Levitae* could mean "deacons" in the Middle Ages (see Revised Medieval Latin Word List), but the context makes clear that Abelard is envisaging *Levitae* as female Levites. He argues that we speak of deaconesses and deacons "ac si in utrisque tribum Levi et quasi Levitas agnoscamus" (as though in these we recognise severally the tribe of Levi and female Levites) (Muckle 1955: 262; Scott Moncrieff: 145). Aaron is told that the first fruits are given to himself "et filiis ac filiabus tuis" (and to your sons and daughters) in Numbers 18:11 and 19, but verses 1, 2, 7, 8, 9, 21, and 23 of the same chapter assign only Aaron and his sons to the sanctuary and priesthood; see also Exodus 30:30.

50. See Elizabeth Schüssler Fiorenza, *In Memory of Her*. The continuities discerned by Abelard, linking temple door keepers to widows and deaconesses, and deaconesses to abesses, seem to be corroborated in Jean Daniélou, *The Ministry of Women in the Early Church*, 17, 22–24, 31.

51. Augustine's interpretation is discussed below. Jerome's comment is in letter 125, *Ad Rusticum* (one of Abelard's favorite sources on monastic life): "Quid Samaritana vilius? Non solum ipsa credidit, et post sex viros unum invenit Dominum, Messiamque cognovit ad fontem, quem in Templo Judaeorum populus [*populos* in PL] ignorabat: sed et auctor fit salutis multorum, et Apostolis ementibus cibos, esurientem reficit, lassumque sustentat" (PL 22, col. 1073). (What could be of less worth than the woman of Samaria? Yet not only did she herself believe, and after her six husbands find one Lord, not only did she recognize at the well the Messiah whom the Jews failed to recognize in the temple; she brought salvation to many, and while the Apostles were buying food she comforted him who was hungry and weary) (*Selected Letters of St. Jerome*, 399).

52. Origen commends the woman for eagerness and acknowledges that Jesus "uses her as an apostle to the people in the city" so that she becomes the *principium* for their belief. But he also describes her as a "femella . . . quae facile decipi posset" (mere gullible woman) and underlines the negative implication of verse 42, which disparages the contribution of her words (*Commentary on John*, PG 14, cols. 447, 450, 495; trans. Harold Smith, *Ante-Nicene Exegesis of the Gospels*, 2: 94–95, 116).

53. Even the negative implication of verse 42 is erased so as to enhance her dignity: "discipuli magistram superarunt" (the students overshot their instructress). References are to the medieval Latin version of John Chrysostom, *Homiliae in Joannem*, 31–35, PG 59, cols. 175–200, esp. 185, 193, 198. Translations of the Latin are my own, but for an English translation of Chrysostom's Greek text, see "Homilies on the Gospel of St. John and the Epistle to the Hebrews," in *Select Library of the Nicene and Post-Nicene Fathers*, 14: 106–23, esp. 113, 118, 122.

54. "Statimque mulier credidit, multo sapientior Nicodemo; nec modo sapientior, sed et fortior. Ille namque multis auditis hujusmodi, nec alium quempiam advocavit, neque ipse fiduciam habuit: haec vero apostolico fungitur officio" (Chrysostom, *In Joannem* 32, PG 59, col. 184) (The woman immediately believed, being much wiser than Nicodemus—in fact, not only wiser but also more forceful. For whereas Nicodemus, after hearing numerous similar things, neither summoned anyone nor had secure faith, she actually took up the role of an apostle). For further contrasts, see Hom. 33. Compare Abelard, *De auctoritate sanctimonialium*, "Legimus et familiare colloquium cum Nicodemo illo Iudaeorum principe Dominum habuisse quo illum quoque ad se occulte venientem de salute sua ipse instruxerit, sed illius colloquii non tantum hunc fructum esse consecutum. Hanc quippe Samaritanam et spiritu prophetiae repletam esse tunc constat quo videlicet Christum et ad Iudaeos iam venisse et ad gentes venturum esse professa est" (Muckle 1955: 273). In John 3: 1–15 Nicodemus comes to Jesus by night and prompts a discourse on Christian rebirth. The Nicodemus/Samaritan woman juxtapositon has been seen as part of a larger design of male-female complementarity in John's gospel by Schüssler Fiorenza, *In Memory of Her*, 326.

55. Muckle 1955: 273; Scott Moncrieff: 163.

56. Muckle 1955: 273; Scott Moncrieff: 164, alluding to Christ's instruction in Matt. 10: 5: "in civitates Samaritanorum ne intraveritis." Contrast Chrysostom: "Vide quomodo declaret mulierem. . . egressam esse ex civitate . . . ne quis diceret ipsum transgredi praeceptum suum, cum vetaret in civitatem ingredi Samaritano-

rum" (*In Joannem* 31, PG 59, col. 180) (See how he declares that the woman *came out* . . . so that Christ could not be said to transgress his own command prohibiting his disciples from entering any Samaritan city).

57. Muckle 1955: 273; Scott Moncrieff: 164.

58. Muckle 1955: 273; Scott Moncrieff: 163.

59. "Ut enim nos cibum, ita ille nostram salutem desiderat" (Chrysostom, *In Joannem* 34, PG 59, col. 194).

60. "Ut fidem in ea operaretur, et fidem ejus biberet" (Augustine, *In Joannis evangelium*, Tractatus 15: 31, PL 35, col. 1521).

61. Augustine, *In Joannis* 15: 30, PL 35, cols. 1520–21.

62. "*Voca*, inquit, *virum tuum*: adhibe intellectum per quem docearis, quo regaris.' Ergo constitue animam excepto intellectu tanquam feminam: intellectum autem habere, tanquam virum. . . . Loquebatur caput viri cum femina, et non aderat vir" ("Call your husband," says Jesus: "bring here understanding," through which you can be taught and by which you can be ruled. Read the soul which is without understanding as the woman, and possession of understanding as having a husband. . . . The "head" of man was speaking to the woman; but no "husband" was present) (Augustine, *In Joannis Evangelium* 15: 19, PL 35, col. 1517; my translation).

63. Indicative of the wide circulation of Augustine's interpretation of the husband as "understanding" is its appearance in the *Glossa ordinaria* on John 4:16 (PL 114, col. 372). The *Glossa*'s commentary on the Samaritan woman is briefly contrasted with Abelard's in Joan Ferrante, *Woman as Image in Medieval Literature*, 23.

64. This version occurs in Mark 14: 3–9 and Matt. 26: 6–13, but Abelard also has in mind Luke 7: 36–50 and John 12:1–7, where the feet of Jesus are anointed (by a sinful woman in the former; but by Martha's sister Mary in the latter).

65. Muckle 1955: 254; Scott Moncrieff: 133.

66. Ibid. The interpretation is repeated in Abelard's Sermon 11, PL 178, col. 455.

67. Muckle 1955: 255; Scott Moncrieff: 133. For discussion of the gendered hierarchy that Abelard upsets here, see Blamires, "Paradox in the Medieval Gender Doctrine of Head and Body."

68. ". . . sacri liquoris effluentiam, usque ad frontem, et tempora, colli quoque confinia, delicatissimis digitis suis, ut balsamita nobilis, accuratissime dilatavit. Complevit itaque, Maria, operibus piae devotionis, quod rex Salomon in persona ejus, olim cecinerat in Canticis amoris: *Dum esset in accubitu suo nardus mea dedit odorem suum*" (*Vita beatae Mariae Magdalenae*, 18; PL 112 cols. 457–58) (She skillfully spread the consecrated perfume over his forehead and temples, his neck, and adjacent areas, as though it were the unction of nobility. In this way, Mary fulfilled the work of religious devotion that Solomon in his person once sang of in the Song of Love: "While he was on his couch, my nard gave forth its fragrance") (*The Life of Saint Mary Magdalene and of her Sister Saint Martha*, 55–56). Later in the *Vita* she epitomizes the Christian who graduates from clinging to the feet of Christ's humanity to embracing the head of his divinity (PL 112, col. 1480; Mycoff, 80). For Abelard's contemporary Honorius of Autun, the anointing signified that the Church would come to Christ with the fragrance of virtue (*De sancta Maria Magdalena*, PL 172, col. 981).

69. Muckle 1955: 256–57; Scott Moncrieff: 135–37.

70. The reference is probably to the women's role in providing sustenance; see n. 28 above.

71. From Gregory's answer to the ninth question of Augustine of Canterbury, in *Bede's Ecclesiastical History of the English People*, 100–101. For stimulating reassessments of such symbolism, see *Feminist Approaches to the Body in Medieval Literature*, ed. Linda Lomperis and Sarah Stanbury.

72. Muckle 1955: 257; Scott Moncrieff: 137.

73. Gregory the Great, *Moralia* 49.33, PL 75, col. 1068. An abbreviated version of the Job interpretation is applied specifically to Mary Magdalene's loyalty to Christ in the sermon *In veneratione sanctae Mariae Magdalenae* attributed to Odo of Cluny (d. 942): "Quasi enim consumptis carnibus pellis ossi adhaeret, quando, discipulis fugientibus, beata Maria Magdalene cum Domino perseveravit" (PL 133, col. 718).

74. See examples from *The Southern Passion* and from Christine de Pizan in Blamires, *Woman Defamed and Woman Defended* (245, 284); further discussion of this *topos* can be found in Blamires, *The Case for Women in Medieval Culture*, chap. 5. Heloise herself knew the *Moralia* (see letter 4 in Muckle 1953: 80; Radice: 132).

75. McLaughlin, "Peter Abelard and the Dignity of Women," 329; Prudence Allen, *The Concept of Woman*, 278.

76. For Heloise on feminine weakness, see Muckle 1953: 70, 81; 1955: 244–45; and Radice: 111, 133, 162–64.

77. Muckle 1955: 268, quoting 1 Cor. 12: 22–24; and Scott Moncrieff: 155.

78. The description is offered, with guarded support, in McLaughlin, "Peter Abelard and the Dignity of Women," 294, 320, and echoed by Allen, *Concept of Woman*, 278–79.

79. McLaughlin, "Peter Abelard and the Dignity of Women," 320.

80. Ibid., 308.

81. Among others who disseminated the theory of women's strength-in-weakness in the twelfth century was Hildegard of Bingen; see Barbara Newman, "Divine Power Made Perfect in Weakness."

82. McLaughlin, "Abelard's Rule," 258; Radice: 210.

83. Blamires, *Woman Defamed and Woman Defended*, 90–91, 232–36.

84. Nye, "A Woman's Thought," 13.

85. McLaughlin, "Abelard's Rule," 245–46; Radice: 188–89.

86. McLaughlin, "Abelard's Rule," 260; Radice: 214.

87. See, for example, Burchard of Worms, *Decretorum Libri XX* 8: 84: "Femina non det poenitentiam, nec corporale cum oblatione, nec calicem super altare ponat" (PL 140, col. 808).

88. Muckle 1955: 269; Scott Moncrieff: 158.

89. Muckle 1953: 69–70; Radice: 111–13.

90. Muckle 1953: 82; Radice: 135.

91. Muckle 1955: 279; Scott Moncrieff: 172; pseudo-Jerome, Epistola IX, "Ad Paulam et Eustochium," PL 30, col. 122.

92. Muckle 1955: 279; Scott Moncrieff: 173.

93. See especially Heloise's second letter (Muckle 1953: 82; Radice: 134–35)

and Abelard's reply (Muckle 1953: 87; Radice: 143–44). Once again, much of the framework comes from Jerome; especially from the warnings about *vana gloria* in *Ad Eustochium* (Letter 22: 27, PL 22, cols. 412–13).

94. I should like to thank Andrew Taylor, David Townsend, David Klausner, the Social Science and Humanities Research Council of Canada, and the Pantyfedwen Committee of the University of Wales Lampeter for enabling me to contribute to this volume by presenting a version of this chapter at the University of Toronto.

The Formative Feminine and the Immobility of God

Gender and Cosmogony in Bernard Silvestris's *Cosmographia*

Claire Fanger

The crafty penis fights against Lachesis,
Rejoins the thread Fate's hand has severed through.
The blood flows down to kidneys from the head
And there achieves the form of pallid sperm;
And Nature molds the liquid with such skill
That grandsires in similitude return. . . .
World needs no members but the human state
requires them; they must be supplied by Physis:
The head's melodic ears, its wakeful eyes,
And feet for going, hands to form and shape.
      —Bernard Silvestris, *Cosmographia* [1]

I have argued . . . that, for instance, within the sex/gender distinction, sex poses as "the real" and the "factic," the material or corporeal ground upon which gender operates as an act of cultural *inscription*. . . . The "real" and the "sexually factic" are phantasmatic constructions—illusions of substance—that bodies are compelled to approximate, but never can. What, then, enables the exposure of the rift between the phantasmatic and the real whereby the real admits itself as phantasmatic?
      —Judith Butler, *Gender Trouble* [2]

Intelligible Sexes and Unintelligible Divinities: Posing the Questions

Written in the mid-twelfth century, Bernard Silvestris's Platonic creation myth *Cosmographia* is in two parts: the first, or "Megacosmos," tells of the construction and ordering of the great world by Noys, also called

God's Mind, Intellect, Providence, Will, and Second Self. The second, or "Microcosmos," is the complex narrative of the construction of Man, the great World's microcosm, by the daughters of Noys. Let us begin *in medias res*, or indeed rather near to the end of things, by observing that the first created human being described in the closing lines of the *Cosmographia*, quoted above, clearly possesses male genitalia. Yet if the penis, in being shown to be created before the feminine genitalia, is valorized by its priority, it is nevertheless valorized only in the context of the human condition. On the one hand it is said to be the penis specifically that "fights against Lachesis," carrying on the primary work of reproduction and perpetuating the human race (the womb is not mentioned at all); but, on the other hand, it is pointed out (echoing *Timaeus* 33C–34A and 44D and E) that World (the macrocosm, the form prior to humanity, which humanity reflects) has no need of *any* limbs—thus, the masculine member, like the other bodily extremities, has no universal analogue (nor, so far as may be deduced from the *Cosmographia*, any divine one).

Bernard does not get so far as describing the first created woman, and we do not know in the terms of his myth how she might have been formed or represented. Yet if Femina as such is absent from Bernard's work, it may be remarked that there is no dearth of feminine sexual organs. The womb is frequently mentioned as a divine attribute shared by the three formative goddesses in the *Cosmographia*: Silva, Natura, and Noys. Womb figures as a certain generative aspect of the divine—an aspect that often seems to be represented as ontologically prior to the masculinity that it forms or engenders. Certainly this much may be said: it is feminine Silva who, with the help of feminine Noys, engenders masculine World; feminine Physis who, with the help of other feminine deities, constructs the physical body of masculine Homo. Within the time span outlined in the *Cosmographia*, we do not witness the construction of a human woman, yet all of the formative, active, and generative divinity that we have been allowed to see manifests itself as feminine.

I bring this up at the outset in order to gesture toward a problematic complexity of gender representation in Bernard's myth—a complexity that has yet to receive the attention it deserves. In the passage from *Gender Trouble* quoted in my epigraph, Butler puts a question to her audience: "What, then, enables the exposure of the rift between the phantasmatic and the real whereby the real admits itself as phantasmatic?" One may answer that the attribution of female body parts to immaterial divine beings exposes such a rift—or at the very least, may be used to expose such a rift if we put the right questions to it. For if there can be such a thing as divine gender, in what does it *really* consist? In Bernard's Platonic context, should the human penis be seen as more or less phantasmatic than the divine womb? Put another way, why did the womb seem to Bernard the most appropriate figure for divine production and reproduction? Does the presence of feminine sexual organs in the divine realm imply, in some sense, somewhere else in the divine realm, a masculine alternative? And if so, then where does the phallus of God lie hid? (Or if God hasn't got one, then why not?)

These questions are in part disingenuous; I do think there is more going on in the *Cosmographia* than the focus on the presence or absence of a divine phallus allows one to grasp. Nevertheless, I wanted to begin by emphasizing how deeply issues of gendered embodiment are implicated in Bernard's lofty abstractions, in his considerations of the relations between divinity and the world.

My epigraphs place a quotation from Judith Butler in apposition to an extract from Bernard Silvestris in order to allow the play of certain resonances in both writings which seemed to me of interest. Butler's terms of reference are, of course, different from Bernard's, but similarities can be found in the way both allow us a glimpse beyond the corporeal ground of sex. In the writing of both we are encouraged to conceive of gender, even sex itself, not merely as something understood, but as something by which we understand.

In Butler's view, gender is best conceived as a matter of praxis; gender is, as she puts it, performative. In the arguments that Butler refutes, biological "sex" is somewhat dangerously seen as the real or solid ground underlying the more phantasmatic (and in principle escapable) cultural construction of "gender." But "sex" itself, Butler argues, is constituted in discourse as a form of knowledge. It derives its cultural power from an assumed reality of being that is supposed to underlie it and to be separable from the cultural knowledge that overlays it, but in fact is not.[3] If Butler's position is that "sex," too, is knowledge, this is not to deny that biological sex is "real"; it merely makes it possible to identify our "knowledge" of "sex" as a political force because of the ways it appears to be ontological when it is in fact epistemological.

Exposing the rift between the phantasmatic and the real is not merely a matter of exposing what is false or misconstructed in the presumed object of knowledge, but also, to follow Butler's own practice, of tracing what knowledge *does*, or is made to do: it is a matter of examing the uses to which knowledge is put. In the *Cosmographia* we are able to examine a very specific use of knowledge in an allegory about the construction of the world. Bernard makes a direct link between knowledge and gender through this allegory: Noys is God's Mind, Wisdom, and Intellect. She is also feminine, and her gender, as I will argue, is crucial to the framework of Bernard's thought. In this chapter I would like to explore both what the connection between divine femininity and divine intellect meant to Bernard, and also what it might mean to us. I aim first and foremost for a clear reading of the *Cosmographia* that will emphasize issues of gender in the work that have so far tended to be either ignored or oversimplified—sometimes disastrously—by previous commentators. Beyond this, however, I would like to open out Bernard's writing so that it can engage with our modern conversation about gender and knowledge a little more freely. One reason for the resonance between Bernard's words and those of Judith Butler is that Butler's arguments in one aspect represent a recent development of a centuries-old conversation about Rhetoric and Truth—a conversation in which Bernard Silvestris, from another place and time, is also taking part.

Divine Ideas: Scholarly Apprehensions of Noys's Gender

Modern readings of the *Cosmographia* have been marked not so much by controversy over Noys's gender (though there is some of that, too) as controversy about its importance. The textual evidence is clear enough: Noys is attended everywhere by feminine pronouns and adjectival forms. At the same time, however, it is reasserted at many points that Noys is a unity with God, that they are of one mind and coeternal: Noys is referred to as "imago nescio dicam an vultus, patris imagine consignatus" (an image, or rather a face stamped with the image of the Father—"Megacosmos" iv.5). Is her femininity, then, integral to Bernard's philosophical purpose, or is it mere window dressing, a traditional attribute of Sapiential figures but nothing more? To some, Noys's femininity has appeared an unconvincing attribute. Linda Lomperis remarked as recently as 1988 that "throughout most of the *Cosmographia* Noys's female status seems secondary, seems, in fact, to be suppressed by her constant and close association with God. . . . It therefore seems appropriate to say that although Noys may walk like a woman, she certainly talks like a man."[4]

In a work like the *Cosmographia* it would be curious if anything as foregrounded as Noys's gender should be found entirely insignificant; yet it has proven oddly difficult to see just what its significance is. The question of the femininity of Noys has in the past been entwined with the question of the extent to which the *Cosmographia* should be read as a relatively orthodox Christian work, or whether it in fact represents a fundamentally pagan perspective. E. R. Curtius makes one such argument for the importance of the feminine principle in the *Cosmographia*.[5] Perhaps predictably, Curtius's most extreme statements are the ones most often quoted: "Bernard," he writes, "represents a pagan Humanism which eliminates everything Christian except for a few ultimate essentials. . . . The whole [of the *Cosmographia*] is bathed in the atmosphere of a fertility cult, in which religion and sexuality mingle."[6] Curtius here refutes a reading by Etienne Gilson, who in an attempt to rescue the poem from previous charges of paganism placed it in the tradition of hexameral literature and read Noys (against the textual evidence, but not for the first time)[7] as masculine, and argued for an identity of Noys with the Logos.[8] The *Cosmographia*'s most notable modern commentators thus set up between them an interesting duality of readings: either the work represented a fundamentally Christian handling of creation in the hexameral tradition, with Noys appearing as masculine Christ, or the work has little about it that is Christian, and the feminine Noys is a pagan fertility goddess.

Neither of these readings reflects with complete accuracy the Noys of Bernard's text, as subsequent readers were quick to point out. Yet it was Gilson whose opinion was to be most influential, in the sense that his representation of the work's Christianity has been accepted as the more fundamentally accurate. Other deficiencies of Gilson's reading have since been corrected; it is no longer possible to read Noys as masculine, though her christological affiliations continue to be argued.[9] In an important 1948 article, Theodore Silverstein pinpointed Noys's most important antecedents: she is, he asserted, a composite of Minerva and the female figure of Sapientia in the Solomonic literature of the Bible.[10] Silverstein thus insisted on Noys's femininity without deeply analyzing it. But in asserting Noys's Sapiential sources, Silverstein did succeed in demonstrating that Noys could be traced to a figure at once female and a traditional—if slightly esoteric—part of Christian mythology (in other words, that she could actually be Christian without being masculine, a point that seems to have taken a surprisingly long time to make). Brian Stock, in the only book length-study of the *Cosmographia*, allows that Curtius, Gilson, and Silverstein all provide useful clues to Noys's meaning,[11] but he does not comment on the discrepancies of gender between them or the overall significance of Noys's gender in the *Cosmographia*.[12] More recently, Winthrop

Wetherbee[13] and Peter Dronke[14] have contributed important insights to the study of the *Cosmographia*. Dronke makes the stronger case of the two for Noys's important femininity, emphasizing the work's rhetorical voluptuousness in a manner mildly reminiscent of Curtius and reading the work with his usual sensitivity, but he ultimately gives scant attention to gender in its philosophical aspect as a means of codification.

The most recent writer to comment at any length on the subject of gender in the *Cosmographia* is Jean Jolivet in his article "Les principes féminins dans la *Cosmographia* de Bernard Silvestre."[15] To the critical conversation about the *Cosmographia*, Jolivet adds the enticing suggestion that Gramision (or "Granusion," as the word was rendered prior to Dronke's edition)—the earthly paradise in which Man is constructed by Physis—in fact represents the womb, or even the feminine genitalia.[16] Jolivet also once again refutes Gilson's reading of Noys as masculine, writing that "in all the narratives in which she is implicated, in all the discourses where she is addressed, her femininity is more or less explicitly present, and inversely there is nothing to indicate a masculine character in her."[17] But Jolivet addresses her significance in the work as a whole only briefly. His view is that "Bernard presents us with an absolute First Principle which surpasses all distinction of sex, and an exclusively feminine series of originary figures" whose reproduction "presupposes no masculine element."[18]

The implications of Noys as an exemplar of divine Femininity cannot adequately be unfolded without considering briefly the extent to which Jolivet is correct in asserting that the proliferation of goddesses in the *Cosmographia* "presupposes no masculine element"—whether, indeed, the Prima Usia surpasses (or suppresses) sex distinction entirely.[19]

Blinded by the Light: Evidence of Divine Masculinity in the *Cosmographia*

Certainly it appears to be so. It is true that where Tugaton is mentioned, it is defended from speculations about gender as it is defended from all other speculations: Tugaton ("the Good" in Greek) is the "inaccessible light," which "quia lumen se defendit a lumine, splendorem ex se videas caliginem peperisse" (because the light guards itself from the eye [or guards itself by means of light], it might seem to you that its splendor begot darkness from itself—"Microcosmos" v.3). But there do exist hints elsewhere in the work that this light may mean more than it speaks. Very bright lights are often masculine, associated with great power and the capacity to fertilize. There is Sol, for example—

Inter Oiarsas Geniosque celestes quos eterna sapientia mundano vel decori vel regimini deputavit, Sol—illustrior lumine, presentior viribus, augustior maiestate, mens mundi, rerum fomes sensificus, virtus siderum, mundanusque oculus tam splendoris quam caloris inmensitate—perfuderat universa. ("Microcosmos" v.13)

(Among the celestial Geniuses and Oyarses which eternal Wisdom destined to be classed as Glory or Rule of the World, Sol, brighter in light, more present in powers, more august in majesty, Worldly mind, sensitizing tinder of things, power of the stars, and eye of the World, infused the universe with an immensity both of splendor and of heat.)

The Sun, in keeping with his mythological character, is of course masculine—the "infusing" of the world with splendor and heat. Yet Sol, as worldly mind and eye, may be seen to refer as much through mentality to Noys as through fire to Tugaton. The worldly genders, even where humanity or animality is not in question, are subordinated to, and not precise analogues of, the divine ones.

A more explicit identification of fire or light with the power to impregnate comes in Bernard's description of the ethereal fire that surrounds the cosmic orb:

Quicquid enim ad essentiam sui generis promotione succedit, ex celo—tanquam ex deo vite—subsistentie sue causas suscipit et naturam. . . . Ignis namque ethereus, sociabilis et maritus, gremio Telluris coniugis affusus, generationem rerum publicam, quam de calore suo producit ad vitam, eam inferioribus elementis comodat nutriendam. ("Megacosmos" iv.1–2)

(Whatever succeeds in the promotion to being of its own race takes its nature and causes from heaven, as if from the God of life. . . . For the ethereal fire, sociable and husbandly, having been shed into the lap of his wife Tellus, supplies the common generation of things, which he leads forth to life from his own heat so that it may be fostered among the lower elements.)

Here, more than in the description of Sol, the fire is identified both with divinity and seed. Yet the homely images effectively obviate any strong comparison between the etherial fire and the Inaccessible Light; the impregnation of Tellus is different, an act more animal and less austere than any we are able to imagine between Noys and Tugaton, the Will and Goodness of God.

Beyond a general association between bright light and the fertilitizing power of seed, suggestions of a masculine character in Tugaton or the Prima Usia are quite difficult to find. The fact that Noys "divine voluntatis semper est pregnans" (is always pregnant with the divine will) (I.iv.14) suggests that her daughters do have a paternity of sorts.[20] Bernard also occasionally refers to God using the epithet "Father" (three times in "Megacosmos" iv). For the most part, however, the highest aspect of God, the First Being or Goodness, is not represented in such a way as to encourage reference to human genders. On the contrary, the reader's perception of any equivalence between the First Being and a specifically masculine potentiating principle is fairly carefully deflected.

The strongest evidence for a masculinity in God above and beyond what we can see is Bernard's continued insistence on the femininity of Noys. Where specific attributes of God cannot be forced from anything Bernard says about God, they may perhaps be teased out of the statements describing the relation of Noys to God and to the other feminine deities who are their daughters.

The Difference Which Is Not One: Noys/God and Their Daughters

Two characteristics of Noys are recurrently marked: first, that Noys is an identity with God, differing from God only in the visibility of her labor, but not in the will which is their mutual being; and second, that the femininity of Noys is a positive quality that descends from Noys through Natura to Silva. The interdependence of the goddesses has been emphasized by Dronke and Jolivet, and the identity of Noys with God has been brought out in a variety of ways by many commentators, yet a more detailed reading of the lines and passages that suggest these relationships is still necessary to show how theological questions are being identified with questions of gender and consequently resolved.

The opening lines of "Megacosmos" provide a case in point. Here Nature begins her petition to Noys for the ordering of Silva, the primordial chaotic state of matter:

Congeries informis adhuc, cum Silva teneret
Sub veteri confusa globo primordia rerum,
Visa deo Natura queri mentemque profundam
Conpellasse Noym: 'Vitae viventis imago,
Prima, Noys—deus—orta Deo, substantia veri,
Consilii tenor aeterni, mihi vera Minerva.' ("Megacosmos" i.1–6)

(When Silva, unformed mass, still held
the swirling origins of things in antic heap,
Nature seemed to complain to God, addressing Noys,
deep mind: "You, image of living life, Noys/God,
from God first risen, substance of the truth,
sense of eternal purpose, my Minerva true.") [21]

In this passage we find first the equivalence "Noym, mentem profundam" and then the string of nouns by which Nature both addresses and identifies Noys (I leave out some of the modifying phrases): imago/Noys/Deus/orta/substantia/tenor/Minerva. No English translation can adequately suggest the abruptness with which grammatically opposite genders are thrust together here in Latin, especially in the line "prima Noys deus orta deo substantia veri." However this line is parsed, the masculine "deus" makes emphatic contrast with the grammatical femininity that surrounds it.

As I have rendered the line, feminine "Noys" and masculine "Deus" are bound together by the bracketing modifiers "prima . . . orta," insisting on the indivisibility of Noys and God, something to which Bernard forces our attention from the outset. Yet despite the identity claimed for Noys as God, or perhaps because of it, the grammatical gender contrasts cannot pass unnoticed. Mundanely speaking, the difference between Noys and God is, simply, a difference of gender. But because God and Noys are also, divinely speaking, an identity, one might say that this is a difference that is not one—a difference (to play on Irigaray's sense) both nonexistent and manifold.

The difference may be called manifold because of the manner in which Noys shares her substance with the other goddesses, Natura and Silva. Dronke has noted that all Bernard's feminine theophanies are related and interdependent: Noys is Natura's "source of inspiration—her 'true Minerva'—but also her mother. As Noys . . . is God's firstborn . . . and herself divine, so Natura is 'the blessed fecundity of the womb of Noys,' . . . and Silva is 'Natura's most ancient aspect, the tireless womb of generation.'" [22] The passages Dronke points to here all will be given more detailed analysis, but one thing may be singled out for emphasis right from the start: the key point of contiguity between the three goddesses (Noys, Natura, and Silva) is an anatomical one: it is the womb. As Noys is herself divine, but also always and slightly differently "pregnant with the divine will," so the other two goddesses share in the divinity of Noys specifically through the mark of the feminine, the womb.

Noys opens her response to Nature's plea with an address that links the two of them both divinely and anatomically:

Et tu Natura, uteri mei beata fecunditas, nec degeneras nec desciscis origine qua, filia providentiae, mundo et rebus non desinis providere. ("Megacosmos" ii.1)

(And you, Nature, blessed fruitfulness of my womb, you do not degenerate nor withdraw from the origin on whose account, daughter of Providence, you cease not to be provident with respect to the world and its things.)

The phrase "uteri mei fecunditas" might be taken simply as a circumlocution for "daughter," but the abstract noun ("fecunditas") implies more than this. Nature is not merely the fruit of the womb of Noys, but its very fruitfulness—in fact, the womb itself. Nature's desire is in precisely this sense original and originary; it is the desire of the first Form or Idea of the Womb in Noys for the begetting of the Cosmos. Noys further emphasizes the reflection of herself in Nature in the paronomastic articulation "filia providentiae. . . non desinis providere." Within this phrase, Nature can be seen to enact in the verb "providere" the Providence of which Noys is the nominal form. In one aspect, Noys is simply the ontologically prior Divine Idea of Nature. Yet Noys is bigger than Nature, and Noys's larger function is elaborated in the passage immediately following:

Porro Nois ego, dei ratio profundius exquisita, quam utique de se, alteram se, Usia prima genuit—non in tempore sed ex eo quo consistit aeterno—Noys ego, scientia et arbitraria divine voluntatis ad dispositionem rerum, quemadmodum de consensu eius accipio, sic mee administrationis officia circumduco. ("Megacosmos" ii.1)

(I, Noys, the deeply sought-after reason of God, a second self whom the First Being begot from self, not in time, but from that which is eternal; I, Noys, the divine will's knowledge and judgment for the disposition of things, just as I gather from his agreement [consensu] (with me) [or: from our unanimity, co-meaning], so do I carry out the office of my administration.)

Having at first identified herself so intimately with Nature, Noys now reminds us again of her consensus with God: she is coeternal with God, an "other self," not a creature but, rather, as in Plotinus, an overflowing of the primal divinity from the oneness of being into the alterity of thought.

The desire some scholars have shown to identify Noys/Deus with Christ/Logos is easily understood; such an identification would fall within the traditions on which Bernard's work draws.[23] Yet it must be pointed out how carefully Bernard himself avoids the temptation to make such a connection explicit. Among the many epithets attached to Noys (Mens, Intellectus, Scientia, Sapientia, to name a few) we do not find anywhere the one that would link her indisputably with Christ: Verbum. Had he wished to do so, Bernard could have made the connection patent, but he does not. Indeed, in a narrative of this length, written by a Christian rhetor and dealing with the subject of the creation of the world, one might think that Word is conspicuous by its absence.

But the difficulty of identifying Noys with Logos in the framework of Bernard's poem goes beyond this. It is not simply that the word "verbum" is absent, not simply that the persons of the Trinity are elsewhere represented,[24] not simply that Bernard's Noys is feminine and the Logos masculine—for this situation would pose no intrinsic problem if Noys's femininity had not already come to mean something beyond itself. Noys is not the First Being, but more specifically the Other Self of the First Being; like Christ she is begotten of God's Self, but she differs from Christ in this: although she IS God, she is not ALL of God that there is. Her specific function (the administration of God's Idea) cannot be other than God (for thinking and doing are not distinguishable in God); and yet this function also cannot be God itself, for Noys is manifestly in motion, while the Prima Usia rests in the eternal stillness preceding number, motion, and quality. Noys's femininity here *does* imply a distinction from the persons of the Trinity. In one aspect, the womb she shares with Natura and Silva marks the lack by which she falls short of being the entirety of God. More positively put, it marks that twinning of the primal unity which allows the world and its creatures to come into being.

As one descends the chain of being, the primal unity becomes increasingly diversified, though it continues to reflect the whole in each of its aspects. Thus, in the terms offered by the *Cosmographia*, we see the functions of Noys gradually split apart. Yet each feminine figure can be seen to cast back reflections of goddesses higher up the chain. Just as Noys is God, but not all of God that there is, so Nature is Noys, but not all of Noys that there is; and, finally, Silva is Nature, but not all of Nature that there is. "Erat Yle," writes Bernard,

Nature vultus antiquissimus, generationis uterus indefessus, formarum prima subiectio, materia corporum, substantie fundamentum. ("Megacosmos" ii.4)

(Hyle was the most ancient face of Nature, tireless womb of generation, first understratum of forms, matter of bodies, foundation of substance.)

Hyle, "the most ancient face of Nature," is, as it were, an earlier version of that goddess, a chaotic and indistinct rendering of her, identical in their shared uterine function but temporally prior to the ordered fecundity that Nature both instances and seeks. The identity of Nature and Silva helps to explain why Nature speaks so confidently and intimately of Silva's desire for order and form: Nature pleads her own case; Silva's desire is hers or, more properly perhaps, is her. Silva herself lacks the discrimination that would motivate the articulation of a preference for one form over another, for beauty over chaos.

This lack of discrimination in Silva is associated with the power and copiousness of her fertility, but simultaneously with a certain malign tendency. Of all the goddesses, Silva is the only one in whom can be detected any trace of a character that comes close to being not-God:

Quemadmodum quidem ad conceptus rerum publicos parturitionesque pregnabilis est et fecunda, non secus et ad malum indifferens est natura. Inest enim seminario quedam malignitatis antiquior nota, que prima cause sue fundamina facile non relinquat.("Megacosmos" ii.6)

(Indeed to the extent that [Silva] is commonly pregnable and fecund for the conception and birth of all kinds of creatures, so also is her nature without special regard for evil. For there is in her seed-bed a certain quite ancient character of malignity, which does not easily relinquish the first basis of its cause.)

Silva does not contain evil in any positive sense but is rather simply indifferent to it. The indefatigable fertility of her womb is itself a kind of perversity: she holds nothing back. She is an extreme expression of the plurality and motion that has its beginning in Noys, but unlike Noys, so charged is Silva with her own force that she literally cannot contain herself. The malign mark in her, the character of perversity, comes about not through her association with the nature of matter, but rather through her association with the nature of plurality. The power to proliferate, represented by womb, is visible in Silva at its ungoverned extreme, unlimited and wanton. But it is the same plurality, represented by the same womb, by which Noys differs—insofar as she differs—from her God-self.

In "Megacosmos" iv we learn that Noys is emitted as a ray of the inaccessible light itself, and yet her light is different from its source in that it does not blind. She is

imago nescio dicam an vultus, patris imagine consignatus; hec est dei sapientia, vivis eternitatis formitibus vel nutrita vel genita. De sapientia consilium, voluntas consilio nascitur, de divina mundi molitio voluntate.

Porro dei voluntas omnis bona est. (I.iv.5)

(some kind of image, let me say rather a face stamped with the image of the Father;[25] she is the Wisdom of God, nourished or born from the living tinder of eternity. From Wisdom is born purpose, from purpose will, from the divine will the setting in motion of the world.

Moreover the will of God is entirely good.)

If Noys differs from the inaccessible light by being more visible, this visibility is also the sine qua non of movement in the world, a capacity indistinguishable from the motherhood of Noys. The femininity of these theophanies does not gesture simply at something of a nurturing character, though at certain points it is made to do that, too; nor does it refer to a dichotomy of matter and form, since form resides in Noys and matter in Silva. What womb marks chiefly is plurality and motion, or the potential for plurality and motion, as distinguished from the immobile unity of Being.

There are three phases in the setting in motion of the world: (1) the ordering of Silva by which her son, Mundus, is begotten; (2) the production of Endelichia, the World-Soul; and (3) the marriage of Endelechia to Mundus. The second step, the creation of Endelechia, is preceded by another passage describing Noys. This description of Noys is really a kind of prelude to Endelechia, an introduction to the aspect of Noys from which she is formed:

Erat fons luminis, seminarium vite, bonum bonitatis, divine plenitudo scientiae que mens altissimi nominatur. Ea igitur Noys summi et exsuperantissimi est dei intellectus, et ex eius divinitate nata est Natura, in qua vite viventis ymagines, notiones eterne, mundus intelligibilis, rerum cognitio prefinita. . . . Illic in genere, in specie, in individuali singularitate conscripta, quicquid Yle, quicquid mundus, quicquid parturiunt elementa. . . . Quod igitur tale est, illud eternitati contiguum, idem natura cum deo nec substantia est disparatum. Huiuscemodi igitur sive vite sive lucis origine, vita iubarque rerum, Endelichia, quadam velud emanatione defluxit. ("Megacosmos" ii.13)

(This was the fount of light, seed-bed life, good of goodness, plenitude of divine knowledge which is named the mind of the most high. Thus she, Noys, is the intellect of the high and preeminent God, and Nature was born from her divinity.[26] In [Noys] [were] the images of living life, the eternal notions, the intelligible world, predefined cognition of things. . . . There was written out in kind or species, in individual singularity, whatever Hyle, World, or the elements give birth to. . . . What exists in this way is congruent to eternity, of an identical nature with God, and not disparate in substance. And thus, from the origin of this sort of life or light, there flowed forth the life and splendor of things, Endelichia, as by a kind of emanation.)

Endelichia, the World-Soul, is identified with and mirrors Noys's loftiest qualities. Like Noys, she is feminine, but since Endelichia is emanated (rather than born) from Noys, she is not conjoined to Noys by the uterine function that binds and identifies Noys, Silva, and Nature. Endelichia is "propinquis et contiguis ad Noym natalibus oriunda" (risen from lineage near and contiguous to Noys—"Megacosmos" ii.15)—drawn forth from God itself, or from Noys in her God aspect. Yet we see how near to, and indeed indivisible from, the God aspect is what I have called the womb aspect: the distinction is a matter of emphasizing the eternal stability or immobility of the forms pre-born in Noys, rather than her administrative or motive capacity. Whether as the stable container of forms or the motile administrator of ordered progress, Noys remains the mirror of kind and species and "whatever Hyle, World, or the elements gave birth to." Notions of plurality in the *Cosmographia* always bear something of a feminine stamp, however closely they are joined to the Godhead.

In the passage above, the problematic phrase "et ex eius divinitate nata Natura" gains some of its ambiguity from the fact that it is drawn from the dual-gendered God passage of the Hermetic *Asclepius*—a work whose influence on the *Cosmographia* it is now time to consider in slightly more detail.

"Do you mean that God is of both sexes, O Trismegistus?": The *Cosmographia* and the *Asclepius*

Dronke has noted that the *Asclepius* was, of all Bernard's sources, probably the most important to him. It is chiefly on account of its references to the *Asclepius* that Curtius formed the impression that the *Cosmographia* was "bathed in the atmosphere of a fertility cult"; yet the *Asclepius*, while clearly esoteric and clearly non-Christian, does not really present us with a fertility-cult theology any more than Bernard does. This Hermetic treatise, which was circulated in Latin translation among the works of Apuleius, takes the form of a dialogue between Hermes Trismegistus and Asclepius (though really it is more of a monologue on the part of Hermes, with Asclepius asking occasional questions). The passage in which Trismegistus asserts that God is of two genders clearly had some importance for Bernard because he quotes a number of its phrases verbatim. I quote here certain relevant segments of the dual-gendered God passage:

Hic [Deus] ergo, solus ut omnia, utraque sexus fecunditate plenissimus, semper voluntatis praegnans suae parit semper, quicquid voluerit procreare. Voluntas eius est bonitas omnis. Haec eadem bonitas omnium rerum est ex divinitate eius nata natura, uti sint omnia, sicuti sunt et fuerunt, et futuris omnibus dehinc naturam ex se nascendi sufficiat.[27]

(Therefore God alone, most full like all things with the fecundity of both sexes, always pregnant with his own will, always procreates whatever he wills. His will is all goodness. This goodness of all things is the nature born from his divinity; so

that all things may [continue to] be as they are and were, he furnishes from himself
the nature of being born to all things in futurity.)

In this passage alone we may note three phrases used by Bernard at divergent locations in the *Cosmographia*. In all cases, Bernard uses these
phrases in ways that modify, grossly or slightly, their sense. I have already
noted how Bernard alters the phrase "always pregnant with his own will"
to render a distinction between Noys (who is always pregnant) and God
(whose will she gestates).

In the description of Noys that precedes the account of the emanation of Endelichia, Bernard uses the phrase "ex divinitate eius nata natura."
Here also we observe a modification of sense on Bernard's part. In the *Asclepius* there is no personification of Nature, though the word "natura" is
invariably used to point to the specific qualities of gender and engendering
that Bernard's personified Natura embodies. Thus, here in the *Asclepius*,
the goodness of God's will is linked indissolubly, if abstractly, both with
the "nature born from his divinity" and with the "nature of being born."
In the *Cosmographia*, the context of the phrase "et ex eius divinitate nata
est Natura" (the capital letter is Dronke's) does not make it at all clear
whether "eius" refers to God or Noys. The following "in qua" clearly refers
to Noys and yet seems to link Noys to the precedent "Natura"—thus the
more obvious rendering (which Dronke seems to prefer), "Nature was
born from her (i.e., Noys's) divinity," is rendered problematic by the relative pronoun that follows.

The rendering "[Noys] was the nature born from his divinity" seems
on balance more likely. Because of the quotation's original context in the
Asclepius, however, there is an indissoluble link forged between this particular nature—which is the goodness of God (Noys)—and the function of
engendering specific to Noys, but more specific still to Natura. Though the
pronoun "eius" remains ambiguous, there is really not much doubt that
Bernard intended the word "natura" to invoke both goddesses and to effect
a fusion of their functions. Thus, even while the passage specifically dissoci-
ates Endelichia from the womb function of Noys, it emphasizes the importance of that function by its momentary conflation of Noys and Natura.

While other of Bernard's sources reflect the notion that time mirrors
eternity in the ceaseless engendering capacity of Nature, it is chiefly from
the *Asclepius* that Bernard derives the philosophical correlative that there
must be eternal gender corresponding to worldly gender. Bernard shares
with the Asclepian author, too, some of that reverence for the procreative

act that renders it not merely necessary, but holy, a divine *mysterium*. In the *Asclepius* we read,

Impossibile est enim aliquid eorum, quae sunt, infecundum esse: fecunditate enim dempta ex omnibus, quae sunt, inpossibile erit semper esse quae sunt. . . . procreatione enim uterque plenus est sexus et eius utriusque conexio aut, quod est verius, unitas inconprehensibilis est, quem siue Cupidinem siue Venerem siue utrumque recte poteris nuncupare.

Hoc ergo omni uero uerius manifestiusque mente percipito, quod ex domino illo totius naturae deo hoc sit cunctis in aeternum procreandi inuentum tributumque mysterium, cui summa caritas, laetitia, hilaritas, cupiditas amorque diuinus innatus est.[28]

(For it is impossible for any of the things that exist to be infertile; for if fertility is withdrawn from all things which exist, it will be impossible for the things which exist always to exist. . . . For each sex is full of procreation, and it is the connection of both of them, or more properly speaking, their incomprehensible unity, which you may rightly call Cupid or Venus or both.

This therefore should be grasped in mind more truly and manifestly than any truth: that from God, the Lord of all Nature, is discovered and bestowed on all things this mystery of eternal procreation, in which the sum of charity, happiness, delight, Eros and divine love is innate.)

But if Bernard shares in Hermes's appreciation of voluptuous heterosexual union as described here, still it may be remarked that Bernard carries the notion of divine gender a good deal further, from a philosophical standpoint, than the Asclepian author. The dual-gendered God passage in the *Asclepius* is relatively short and, in terms of the prior subject matter of the work, it even seems a bit startling. The gendering of God appears in some respects almost as an afterthought, a product of Hermes's reflection on the necessity of point-for-point congruence between the eternal realm and the perpetuation of divine forms in time. The influence of this particular passage on Bernard is out of proportion, in fact, to its importance in the *Asclepius* itself. While the Asclepian author emphasizes the inaccessibility and incomprehensibility of the godhead in properly Platonic fashion, he nevertheless refers to God throughout (and even within the dual-gendered God passage) in masculine terms: God is pater, dominus, administrator, effector, gubernator—and is masculine in all pronouns. The masculinity of divine referents and pronouns is characteristic also of the *Timaeus*, which provides the chief precedent for the topos of God's inaccessibility.

Bernard, by contrast, is much more careful of gender than the Asclepian author. His references—whether to feminine Noys, inaccessible

Tugaton, or high Father—are usually clear and deliberate, and where there is conflation or ambiguity of gender referent, this appears also to be deliberate rather than, as in the case of the *Asclepius*, the result of unstated assumptions about divine gender (or simple thoughtlessness). Bernard's use of gender as a means of codifying certain properties of the divine, though it remains largely implicit, is more coherent and philosophically consistent than the explicit assertion of gendered divinity found in the *Asclepius*.

Concluding Observations, or, An Impudent Glance at God's Hidden Pudenda

To the extent that plurality and motion are identified with the feminine in the *Cosmographia*, unity and immobility—as superior and more perfect qualities—become identified with the masculine. This identification may be read consistently through Bernard's narrative, though he never gives it explicit articulation. The identity of the First Being with the masculine is supported both by occasional references to the paternity of God and by a generalized association of masculinity with fire and bright light. As in the *Asclepius*, the duality of masculine and feminine functions in the eternal realm of the *Cosmographia* parallels the earthly duality; from the *Asclepius* Bernard derives the notion that the gendered work of God is a perfect mirror of the divine because the Godhead itself is gendered. But Bernard's mythos differs from the Asclepian author's in rendering as feminine the forces that are responsible for setting the world in motion. In this sense, the femininity of Noys is not merely required as a corollary of earthly genders, but also required by the very hiddenness and immobility that makes the First Being most perfect.

The principles that Bernard invents and elaborates fall within the broad outlines of the tradition of feminine inferiority, and yet there is a novel aspect to this secondariness in the codependence of the genders, of unity on diversity, stillness on motion. If the secondary being, Noys, is less perfect, is different—even by the time of a breath—from the First Being, this imperfection is not merely a falling away from unity but also a doubling into power: without Noys there could be no setting in motion of the world. God, in a certain sense, cannot make a move without Noys, which is no reflection on him, of course, since God IS Noys. Noys, then, may be seen as that which allows the First Being to remain immobile and to move—to remain one and yet to be and engender plurality.

Bernard was one of a group of twelfth-century French writers to engage newly and actively with Plato, particularly with the *Timaeus* and the various commentaries that surrounded, elaborated, and Christianized Plato's cosmogonic myth.[29] Bernard was certainly not alone in his philosophical concern with the problem of the emergence of plurality from unity, intelligibility from Being (which arose in large part from this new concern with the *Timaeus*), nor was he alone in recognizing gender as part of the framework of knowledge, or playing with a parthenogenetic model of divine creation.[30] However, his scientific myth is singular in its use of gender to facilitate, rather than merely complicate, the elucidation of the theological and philosophical problems with which he and other twelfth-century thinkers were engaged.

Judith Butler suggests, among other things, that the "corporeal" ground of sex should not be seen as independent of the gendered "inscription"—the knowledge by which sexual politics operates. Sex and gender, the ontological ground and its epistemic performance, are in humans so entirely codependent that a notional separation between them can have no other function than the political. One of the interesting things about Bernard's allegory is that in his macrocosm, too, the ground of being and its active performance, the Prima Usia and Noys, seem to be codependent in a similar way. It is not that Bernard asserts this: in fact, considerable rhetorical power is spent in asserting the opposite, asserting that Being is primary, that it needs no Other. But it is an inescapable fact of his cosmos that without Noys, the Prima Usia would be unintelligible even to itself.

But the allegory has another level. If Womb is a necessity, it is a necessity chiefly because without it the divine would also be unintelligible to us. Or rather, it would be even more unintelligible than it is. Knowledge, diversity, Endelechia, womb, sex, flesh—all aspects of Noys or her emanations—are thus our necessities, not divine ones at all, and Bernard's poetry recognizes this, too. Gender must be projected into the macrocosmic realm because it is crucial to the microcosmic, or human, realms; the reflection of the one in the other is not allowed to be incomplete. Neither, however, is it allowed to be perfect, literal, point for point. As sex is necessary to reproduction of species in the mundane world, so divine gender must be necessary for the reproduction of divine Ideas. But since our earthly knowledge is insufficient to compass the limits of divine knowledge, this reflection in Bernard's allegory is broken up, differentiated, mobile. If Noys's womb is a mark of secondariness, it is not, as it might be in human terms, a mark of powerlessness, but the reverse; indeed, this representation of the power of womb in the divine realm has the paradoxical effect of inverting certain normal aspects of human quasi-biological gender. The womb, normally interior and invisible, is here what we see, while the penis, normally exterior, does not reveal itself. The receptive womb is what acts, while the active penis is immobile.

I would prefer not to rest in the literality of this reversal, however; it is appropriate that something more nearly approximating Bernard's viewpoint should be heard in my conclusion. And so I will point out once again that if World needs no members, it cannot be assumed that Noys's womb is in even the vaguest sense a literal attribute. Its recurrent marking is not really a logical extension of microcosm into macrocosm, but rather a paradoxical one. Noys's womb is double Nature's single name, a kind of floating anchor that allows Bernard to recognize a distinction in the divine realm that is functional only from the human perspective: a distinction of flesh. In Platonic terms, this does not mean the distinction is not real. It is the flesh, rather, that is phantasmatic. The index of what is real in gender is necessarily the womb, the secondary, which is to say, the distinction rather than its embodiment: that by which we understand.

Bernard was occupied with a common twelfth-century problem in his concern with the derivation of plurality from unity, and his rendering of Noys as God's second self falls within the broad tradition of feminine secondariness. Yet Bernard's allegory is in certain ways unique. This is not merely a comment on its artistry, but also on the peculiarity of his gender ontology and on the theological motivations behind it. Because Bernard's notion of divine gender is removed from, other than, the necessities of flesh that mirror it, the secondary gains in meaning and power precisely what it loses in "naturalness." It is interesting to speculate on how much the opening lines of Alain de Lille's *De planctu nature*, with their violent diatribe against the unnatural grammar of homosexuality, may be a reaction not merely to the innocence of Bernard's cosmos, but also to the potentially dangerous implications of Bernard's playful cosmogony, with its floating womb, its feminine mask of God, and its divine gender liberated from sexual necessity.

If gender is praxis, if it is constituted in performance, then the writing of an allegory that compasses, among other things, divine gender, must be seen as part of this praxis. For allegory, too, is praxis, and Bernard's cosmogonic narrative—in playing with the marks and masks of gender, in shifting this binary construction of knowledge to gods and divine Ideas (whatever else it also does)—must serve the reader as a concrete reminder that it is not merely in our flesh we live, but in our knowledge of it.

Notes

I would like to thank the Social Sciences and Humanities Research Council of Canada for financial support while this paper was being written, and David Townsend for support in general.

   1. Militat adversus Lachesim sollersque renodat
      Mentula Parcarum fila resecta manu.
   Defluit ad renes, cerebri regione remissus,
      Sanguis, et albentis spermatis instar habet.
   Format et effingit sollers Natura liquorem,
      Ut simili genesis ore reducat avos. . . .
   Membra quibus mundus non indiget, illa necesse est
      Physis in humana conditione daret:
   Excubias capitis oculos, modulaminis aures,
      Ductoresque pedes omnificasque manus.

"Microcosmos," 165–82. All quotations drawn from Bernard Silvestris, *Cosmographia*, ed. Peter Dronke. All translations are my own unless otherwise noted.

   2. Judith Butler, *Gender Trouble*, 146.

   3. Butler's discussion of recent writings on genetic sex determination emphasizes the way gender informs the scientific questions asked and answered about sex: "The conclusion here is not that valid and demonstrable claims cannot be made about sex-determination, but rather that cultural assumptions regarding the relative status of men and women and the binary relation of gender itself frame and focus the research into sex-determination. The task of distinguishing sex from gender becomes all the more difficult once we understand that gendered meanings frame the hypothesis and the reasoning of those biomedical inquiries that seek to establish 'sex' for us as it is prior to the cultural meanings that it acquires" (*Gender Trouble*, 109).

   4. Linda Lomperis, "From God's Book to the Play of the Text in *Cosmographia*," 70, n.44. This footnote responds to an article by Jean Jolivet, on which I comment later.

   5. Ernst Robert Curtius, *European Literature and the Latin Middle Ages*, 108–13.

   6. Ibid., 112.

   7. Brian Stock points out that he repeats a mistake made previously by von Bezold: *Myth and Science in the Twelfth Century*, 87; Friedrich von Bezold, *Das Fortleben der antiken Götter im mittelalterlichen Humanismus*, 79.

   8. Etienne Gilson, "La cosmogonie de Bernardus Silvestris," 5–24.

   9. See esp. Marie-Thérèse d'Alverny, "Alain de Lille et la *Theologia*," 121–22 for remarks on Bernard; and more recently Jean Jolivet, "Les principes féminins dans la *Cosmographia* de Bernard Silvestre," 296–305.

   10. Theodore Silverstein, "The Fabulous Cosmogony of Bernard Silvestris," 110.

   11. Stock, *Myth and Science*, 88.

   12. It may be noted here that in terms of the Sapiential tradition, the gender

of Divine Wisdom itself is far from stable. Instances abound of identification between Wisdom and Christ/Logos as well as between Wisdom and the Holy Spirit. On Wisdom see d'Alverny, "Alain de Lille et la *Theologia*" (noted above) and "Le symbolisme de la sagesse et le Christ de Saint Dunstan." Additionally, it was not unusual in the twelfth century to find Christ represented with a variety of feminine attributes quite independently of his links with divine Wisdom. Caroline Walker Bynum's essay "Jesus as Mother and Abbot as Mother" provides key references. In such an atmosphere, complete gender consistency would hardly be expected of Bernard, and it is perhaps unsurprising that consistency was not looked for when so much else seemed to be at stake. Nevertheless, what we find in Bernard's work is, in fact, consistency: a consistency that makes it possible to read the polyvalent Noys with more care than Sapiential figures necessarily invite.

13. See the introduction and notes to Wetherbee, trans., *The "Cosmographia" of Bernardus Silvestris*.

14. See the introduction and notes to his edition, cited above in n. 1.

15. In *L'homme et son univers*, ed. Wenin, 296–305.

16. Jolivet, "Les principes féminins," 301–4.

17. Ibid., 300: "Dans tous les récits où elle est impliquée, dans tous les discours qui lui sont adressés, sa féminité est plus ou moins expressément présente, et inversement rien n'indique en elle le moindre caractère masculin."

18. Ibid.: "Bernard nous présente donc un Premier absolu qui dépasse toute distinction de sexes, et une série de figures originelles exclusivement féminines"; and 301: ". . . ces divers modes de production ne supposent aucun élément masculin."

19. The question of whether God is essentially masculine or "surpasses sex distinction entirely" is problematic from very early on in the Hebrew tradition, as Howard Eilberg-Schwartz points out in *God's Phallus and Other Problems for Men and Monotheism*. Eilberg-Schwartz argues that the Hebrew prohibition of images of the deity may be read more particularly as a prohibition of images of God's phallus; he suggests that in the context of an extreme monotheism, where the one God is understood to be masculine but has no feminine counterpart or consort, the problems surrounding revelation of God's body are implicated as much in homo-eroticism as in spirituality.

20. It may be noted that the line from the *Asclepius* to which this refers makes no distinction of persons; Asclepius's God (referred to here with a masculine pronoun, "hic") is always pregnant with *his own* will (*Asclepius* VI.20, in A. D. Nock and A.-J. Festugière, eds., *Corpus Hermeticum*, vol. 2. All references are to this edition.

21. Dronke suggests a variety of options for punctuating and construing these lines: "prima" could be taken with "imago," and Noys separated by commas from "prima" and "Deus," giving "You, first image of living life, Noys, God risen from God" (thus Wetherbee's translation is construed, if not worded). I have here translated the construction that Dronke prefers, taking "prima. . . orta" to bracket "Noys/Deus."

22. Dronke, introduction to *Cosmographia*, 31.

23. As d'Alverny has shown; see articles cited above, n. 12.

24. A point made by Silverstein, "Fabulous Cosmogony," 108.

25. Wetherbee sees this phrase as evidence of a deliberate distinguishing of Noys from the true Logos (*Cosmographia*, 153, n. 124).

26. Thus Dronke. The line is somewhat ambiguous and might also be rendered "and she is a nature born from his divinity" (as Wetherbee construes it); however, a suggestion of the goddess Natura clearly seems intended. See the discussion below.

27. *Asclepius*, 321.

28. Ibid., 321–22.

29. See Stock, *Myth and Science*, 237–73, for a comparison of Bernard's philosophical concerns with those of his contemporaries, Thierry of Chartres, William of Conches, and Daniel of Morley. Stock's analysis emphasizes differences between the three writers in style and habit of thought. A more recent analysis of Thierry of Chartres by Peter Dronke brings Thierry's neoplatonizing tendencies more sharply into focus. Though Dronke does not mention Bernard Silvestris except in passing, his chapter illuminates the kinds of philosophical problems Thierry felt himself to be confronting in a way that shows Thierry's concerns to be somewhat more similar to Bernard's than Stock allows; Dronke, "Thierry of Chartres," 358–85.

30. Dronke, in the article cited above, quotes Thierry of Chartres: "The divine persons are designated in the masculine gender, though they could be designated by these names: mother, daughter, and gift (*donatio*), like the things they intimate—namely, omnipotence, wisdom, and benignity." It is interesting that this point enters into Thierry's discussion by way of a comment on how names for God are metaphors transferred from human experience: ". . . the names 'Father,' 'Son,' 'Holy Spirit' were first given to created things," says Thierry, and "transferred to God by way of a likeness." The issue of God's gender rises to bridge the gap between the Neoplatonic necessity of divine inscrutability and the human necessity of intelligibility, as I have suggested is also, if differently, the case with Bernard. Dronke notes that Thierry's openness to the use of feminine names for God seems to represent a modification of an earlier view. See Dronke, "Thierry of Chartres," 365 and footnote 28. Quotations are from Thierry's *Glosa* v.22; Dronke refers to the edition by Nikolaus Häring, *Commentaries on Boethius by Thierry of Chartres and His School*, 297.

Scribe quae vides et audis

Hildegard, Her Language, and Her Secretaries

Joan Ferrante

Hildegard of Bingen was the widely respected abbess (technically *magistra*) of a Benedictine convent she had founded and built. But she was also a visionary and prophet whose advice was sought by the mighty and the humble, by kings and emperors, queens and countesses, popes and archbishops, abbesses and abbots, nuns and priests, lay women and lay men. Some she advised in person, others she responded to by letter, in Latin. They turned to her because they had read or heard of her visions, also composed in Latin, or they had heard her speak at a convent or church on one of her several preaching tours. She wrote and spoke not only about personal matters such as morality and responsibility, but also about major public issues, including corruption in secular and religious government, and theological questions about the Trinity and the Eucharist. Hildegard may have hesitated, at first, to write and to preach, but once God made his will clear, she accepted the assignments and carried them out with vigor and skill. She did not hesitate, however, to use Latin. Her Latin may have been more oral than learned (though she was certainly literate), but it was fluent.

For Hildegard, Latin is not the language of the patriarchy, of the Fathers and the Church hierarchy; Latin is the language Hildegard of Bingen shares with God. God speaks to her in Latin, and she transmits the messages to the world in Latin. Paul may have said that women should be silent in church, but God told her to preach, so Hildegard preached to the hierarchy of Paul's church and they listened. Bernard of Clairvaux and Pope Eugene III accepted her written words as God's; bishops and archbishops heard God in her spoken words on her preaching tours. There were some who doubted her—a philosopher who came to scoff but stayed to admire and be buried in her convent (*Vita* 2.12),[1] the churchmen who scorned her because of Eve's transgression—but God chose her to move them.[2] God's word in Hildegard's mouth prevailed, and that word was Latin.

Hildegard admits to a lack of polish in her Latin, but that is no obstacle to her mission nor to her importance—Moses and Jeremiah had similar defects in speech. She is not diffident about using Latin. It is not in any way alien to her since she has used it from childhood to speak and sing to God in psalms, and she is comfortable enough in it to understand God and to transmit his message. It is the message that matters and that is not to be tampered with. Indeed, like John, she threatens any who would change a word of her recorded visions with eternal damnation.[3]

Hildegard expected her scribes and secretaries to take down and copy the words as she spoke them (or as she noted them herself on wax tablets), changing the grammar or spelling where necessary but not the sense. Only her last secretary, Guibert of Gembloux (whose own style was rather ornate) dared to press for stylistic changes, and only in the last two years of her long life, after her major works were written and published. At a time when she was conserving her strength for larger battles, she allowed Guibert to polish her style but not to tamper with the visions. Guibert, like her other secretaries and colleagues (Volmar, Ludwig of St. Eucharius, Godfrey of Disibodenberg), was a great admirer of Hildegard and her visionary gifts. Even when he pressed her about her style, he used the analogy of the Bible—the word of God in a simple style that Jerome had made more elegant in his translation so that it could persuade more effectively.[4]

Since Hildegard's relations with her secretaries are key to understanding her relation to Latin, most of this chapter is devoted to their exchanges and to her reports of their collaboration. Herwegen, Dronke, Schrader, and Führkötter all take Hildegard at her word when she says she allowed no corrections other than grammatical ones to her texts; Derolez, interpreting the implications of manuscript hands and illuminations, doubts her.[5] I suggest that we can take her at her word, if we understand her relationship to her helpers as one of author to copyeditor. The latter may raise a question or make a suggestion about particular words in order to clarify the author's point, and the author may accept the suggestion, seeing it as strengthening his/her text, not as changing the meaning or the style. Certainly we do not think of copyeditors as participating in the composition of our texts, however much we may rely on their careful readings. In this way, I think, Hildegard may have accepted occasional suggestions without in any way surrendering control of her text. On grammatical points, her readers had full sway; on any others, she (or God) had the final word.

The analogy of the author and copyeditor only holds, of course, for those authors who have confidence in what they are saying and how they want to say it. Hildegard saw herself, or at least the import of her messages, as comparable to those God sent through Moses, Jeremiah, John the Evangelist, and Mary. Though she was quite hesitant about her powers when she began, once she had acquired Bernard of Clairvaux's approval and the pope's encouragement, she played her part as God's vessel—calling her a "chosen vessel," Guibert makes an explicit analogy with Paul ("vas es electionis," Gb. 22.12)—with strength and assurance, not hesitating to set the leaders of the secular and religious worlds straight, nor to fight them when she thought she was right.[6] There are, in fact, times when it is virtually impossible to distinguish God's voice from Hildegard's. She did believe that God had chosen her as he chose Mary to carry his word, even before Bernard acknowledged the divine source of her visions. She said in the letter to Bernard that she rose from her sick bed and ran to him, praying him "by the Word that God sent into the Virgin's womb, from which he sucked flesh like honey around the comb," suggestive of the way he seems to be sucking life from Hildegard to give "flesh" to his word. The analogy is even stronger in the *Scivias* when Hildegard says God "sought for a Virgin's candor, and willed that His Word should take His body in her. For the Virgin's mind was by His mystery illumined" (3.13.1). Much later (1175), writing to Guibert, she implicitly compares herself to Paul and John, contrasting herself and the saints with wise men who succumb to vainglory when secrets are opened to them, instead of holding themselves as nothing (VA 103r.44–52). When Guibert wanted to change her style, she reminded him that Moses spoke intimately with God though he felt himself ineloquent and slow of speech, and that Jeremiah demurred that he did not know how to speak (Pitra 29.27).

As she published her visions, Hildegard became more and more assured, listing her other works in the preface to the *Liber vite meritorum*, including natural science, music, poetry, the language she invented, and biblical commentaries.[7] In the preface to the third book, the *Liber divinorum operum*, God tells her, now an old woman but "imbued with the depth of God's mysteries," to "commend what you see with the interior eyes and hear with the interior ears of the soul to stable writing (*stabili scripturae*) for the use of mankind, so they can understand their creator through them, and not refuse to worship him with worthy honor" (PL 197, cols. 741–

42), a monumental assignment. In the last chapter of the same book (cols. 1037–38), the audience is warned that it comes from the book of life, the "scripture" of the Word of God, though through a simple and unlearned female form, and that no man may be so bold as to add to or delete anything from it without sinning against the Holy Spirit, which will not be forgiven here nor in the next world:

Sed liber vitae, qui scriptura Verbi Dei est, per quod omnis creatura apparuit, et quod omnium vitam secundum voluntatem aeterni Patris velut in se praeordinaverat, exspiravit, hanc scripturam per nullam doctrinam humanae scientiae, sed per simplicem et indoctam femineam formam ut sibi placuit mirabiliter edidit. Unde nullus hominum tam audax sit, ut verbis hujus scripturae aliquid augendo apponat, vel minuendo auferat, ne de libro vitae, et de omni beatitudine quae sub sole est deleatur, nisi propter excribrationem litterarum, aut dictionum, quae per inspirationem Spiritus sancti simpliciter prolata sunt, fiat. Qui autem aliter praesumpserit, in Spiritum sanctum peccat. Unde nec hic nec in futuro saeculo illi remittetur. (PL 197, col. 1038B–C).

(But the book of life, which is the writing ("scripture") of the Word of God, through which all creation appeared and which breathed forth the life of all according to the will of the eternal father as he preordained it, brought forth this writing through no doctrine of human learning, but wondrously through a simple and untaught female being as it pleased him. Whence let no man be so bold as to add anything to the words of this writing or take anything away, lest he be deleted from the book of life and from every blessedness that is beneath the sun, except for the correction of letters or words, which were put forth simply through the inspiration of the holy spirit. Whoever presumes otherwise sins against the holy spirit. Which sin will not be remitted neither here nor in the next world.)

The echoes of John at the end of Revelations, even to the book of life, are striking (22: 18–19).[8]

Education

Even while Hildegard speaks with the authority of the Old Testament and the New, she still describes herself as "indoctam." In what sense is she unlearned? There is no question about her knowledge of Latin or her ability to write,[9] and her writings reveal sophistication in thought (on theological as well as medical and psychological matters) and in expression which, unless we credit them all to God or to her collaborators, suggest a rather high degree of learning.[10] At the same time, she must have been conscious of the need to be a tool of God in order to get around Paul's injunction; therefore, all her knowledge, like her prophetic words, must come from God. She apparently had no formal or technical training, such as one might get in the schools, in logic or rhetoric, philosophy or theology,[11] though she must have learned a lot from people she met. Given the number of visits and letters she received in Rupertsberg, and her encounters with learned people on her preaching tours, she must have taken in something in her conversations, but she presumably does not think of that as formal education either. One might say that what she had absorbed and thought about took shape in the visions and could, reasonably enough, be attributed to God.

From the first extant letter to Bernard of Clairvaux, Hildegard makes it clear that she can read Latin, although she does not know Teutonic letters ("litteras in Teutonica lingua, quas nescio," VA 1.21), but she has not learned to analyze a text ("scio in simplicitate legere, non in abscisione textus," VA 1.22). She may be unlearned in external matters, but she is learned in her soul ("indocta de ulla magistratione cum exteriori materia, sed intus in anima mea sum docta," VA 1.24–25), and the visions have taught her to expound the deepest meanings of scriptural texts ("Scio enim in textu interiorem intelligentiam expositionis Psalterii et Evangelii et aliorum voluminum, que monstrantur mihi de hac visione, que tangit pectus meum et animam sicut flamma comburens, docens me hec profunda expositionis," VA 1.17–20). Finally, she does not know how to express what she has learned without the help of the Holy Spirit ("lingua mea non potest proferre, nisi quod me docuit Spiritus Dei," VA 1.10–11), but the visions belabor her to speak, so she asks Bernard what to do.

Despite Hildegard's humble posture, she must have known that acceptance by a major figure, a visionary himself and a friend of popes and kings, would virtually assure her a public voice. Bernard did, indeed, recognize the higher power that worked through her: "What can we teach or admonish where there is interior erudition and anointment teaching about all things?" ("Ubi interior eruditio est et unctio docens de omnibus, quid nos aut docere possumus aut monere?" VA 1r.12–13).

From what Hildegard herself says, and what others say about her early education, it seems that her first teacher, Jutta, though literate and able to teach her the basics of the psalm texts and music, was not formally trained in literature. Hildegard says she did not know how to interpret words or divide syllables (*Scivias*, cited in *Vita* 1.1); that her Latin was not polished ("latinis verbis non limatis," VA 103r.90); and that she "had scarcely any knowledge of literature, as the woman who taught me was not educated," *Vita* 2.2). A prior of Disibodenberg, Adalbert, reminds her that her early education in their monastery was devoted mostly to woman's work ("non alio quam muliebri operi institistis"), and that she was imbued with no other texts than the simple psalter ("non aliis codicibus quam simplici Psalterio imbuta estis," VA 78.10–13). Guibert says something similar in his *Vita* when he tells of her initial fear that if she wrote what she did not know, it would lead to ridicule, because she was "uneducated as to learning in the grammatical art . . . having a knowledge of the psalter in the manner of women, reading scripture simply, without the sharpening of wit of their senses" ("Indocta quippe quantum ad eruditionem artis grammatice erat . . . instar mulierum psalterium solummodo discentium simpliciter scripturas in usu habens legere, non sensus earum acumine ingenii," Gb. 38.375–79): that is, able to read the texts but without training in their interpretation.

Nevertheless, the visions come in unpolished Latin; God, too, speaks in a simple, or oral, rather than literate and literary Latin, and she dictates them in Latin: "I utter them in unpolished Latin just as I hear them through the vision," she tells Guibert.[12] The visions teach her precisely what her simple education had not: "I understood the writings of the prophets, of the Gospels, and of certain other holy philosophers without any human learning, and I did expositions of some of them" ("In eadem visione scripta prophetarum, evangeliorum, et aliorum sanctorum quorundam phylosoforum, sine ulla humana doctrina intellexi, ac quedam ex illis exposui," *Vita* 2.2). (The fact that she understood the writings in the visions suggests that she already knew them.)

Hildegard also claims to have learned music from the visions: "I also brought forth and chanted song and melody in praise of God and saints, without human learning, since I had never studied neums or chant" ("Sed et cantum cum melodia in laudem Dei et sanctorum absque doctrina ullius hominis protuli et cantavi, cum nunquam vel neumam vel cantum aliquem didicissem," *Vita* 2.2). Music is actually for Hildegard a higher former of expression than human language. Whatever Hildegard may say of her deficiencies in Latin, what matters to her is that she delivers God's message in God's words, and her Latin is sufficient for that; it is a medium of communication, not a source of pride or aesthetic satisfaction. She wants it correct, not elegant. But music is a different matter. Though she is able, because of her claimed or real lack of formal training, to ignore the rules of musical composition, she does not see music as a simple means of communication. Instead it is a way for the soul, which is "symphonic," to come closer to the heavenly harmony man lost in the Fall: that is what human music strives for.

In her letter to the prelates of Mainz—who had laid an interdiction on her convent preventing, among other things, the singing of the divine office—Hildegard explains what music does. It helps us "transform and shape the performance of our inner being towards praises of the Creator . . . [and] recall that divine sweetness and praise by which, with the angels, Adam was made jubilant in God before he fell. . . . [I]n Adam's voice before he fell there was the sound of every harmony and the sweetness of the whole art of music"; music has the power to so transform man that he remembers the sweetness of the songs in the heavenly land (VA 23).[13] Hildegard's model for this kind of music is David, who combines words of praise with music as Hildegard does in the *Symphonia*, where her powers of speech and of music, neither constrained by normal human conventions, are extraordinary.[14]

Editorial Assistance

In the words of poetry that accompany her music, as in her medical works, Hildegard speaks in her own words and from her own authority, and she speaks in Latin. She does not acknowledge or seem to feel the need for editorial help. It is only in the visions, in which she is conveying God's message to the Church, that she asks for help, whether because she wants God's words to be correct, or because she knows that the message will be more convincing to much of her audience if they are. Perhaps simply because God has told her to:

[I]lle qui sine defectione magnus est, modo paruum habitaculum tetigit, ut illud miracula videret et ignotas litteras formaret, ac ignotam linguam sonaret. Et dictum est illi: Hoc quod in lingua desuper tibi ostensa non secundum formam humane consuetudinis protuleris, quoniam consuetudo hec tibi data non est, ille qui limam habet, ad aptum sonum hominum expolire non negligat. (VA 8.79–85, to Pope Anastasius, dated 1153–54)

(He who is great without defect touched a small dwelling that it might see miracles and form unknown letters and sound an unknown tongue. And he said to it [her]: what is shown in the language from above you must proffer not according to the form of human custom, since this is not given to you; let him who has the file not fail to polish it to an appropriate sound of men.)

Guibert, in his *Vita*, claims that Volmar "clothed her naked and unpolished words with more attractive / fitting style" ("verba eius, quamlibet nuda et impolita, decentiori sermonis cultu vestire," Gb. 38.404–5), but he may be extrapolating from what he pressed her to do much later. He does qualify his remark with "showing caution of her censorship" ("censoris eius cautelam exhibens). Theodoric cites the letter to the pope (though he names Hadrian) as referring to grammatical corrections alone: "she wrote down in her own hand or from her mouth dictated the contents in their disarrayed state to a certain faithful male attendant. He then rendered their cases, tenses, and conjugations according to the exactness of the grammatical art which she did not have, but he presumed to add nothing at all to them, nor tried to interpret their sense or meaning" (*Vita* 2.1).[15]

At the beginning of the *Scivias* God explains that he made Hildegard fearful about the visions to keep her from being arrogant, causing her to seek out a trustworthy helper, Volmar. At the beginning of the last work, the *Liber divinorum operum*, God makes it clear that neither Hildegard *nor any other person* should intentionally invent anything in it: "Itaque scribe ista non secundum cor tuum, sed secundum testimonium meum, qui sine initio et fine vita sum, nec per te inventa, nec per alium hominem praemeditata, sed per me ante principium mundi praeordinata" (PL 197, cols. 741B–42A). At the end, God asserts that the vision is not the product of human knowledge except in writing (correcting) letters and words, and he delivers the stirring injunction (cited above) against tampering with his work (PL 197, cols. 1038C).[16] I find it hard to believe that Hildegard would have allowed men to do what God forbade.

What Hildegard herself says about those who helped her is repeated formulaically in her visionary works: an acknowledgement of their moral support and unspecified but apparently scribal aid. She makes no distinction between "the man" and "the woman" who helped her[17]—indeed in the first instance the woman is mentioned first—except that she had had to seek out the man. The description implies no more than the most rudimentary kind of secretarial help:

[I]ta quod tandem multis infirmitatibus compulsa, testimonio cuiusdam nobilis et bonorum morum puellae et hominis illius, quem occulte, ut praefatum est, quaesieram et inveneram, manus ad scribendum apposui. (*Scivias*, preface, 83–86)

(Then compelled at last by many illnesses, and by the witness of a certain noble maiden of good conduct, and of that man whom I had secretly sought and found, as mentioned above, I set my hand to the writing.)

Et ego testimonio hominis illius quem, ut in prioribus visionibus prefata sum, occulte quesieram et inveneram, et testimonio cuiusdam puelle mihi assistentis, manus ad scribendum posui. (LVM 1.26–29)

(And I, with the witness of that man whom, as I said in earlier visions, I sought secretly and found, and the witness of a certain girl helping me, I put my hand to writing.)[18]

Ego igitur paupercula et imbecillis forma, testificante homine illo, quem velut
in prioribus visionibus meis praefata sum, occulte quaesieram, et inveneram, testificante etiam eadem puella, cuius in superioribus visionibus mentionem feci,
quamplurimis infirmitatibus contrita, manus tandem ad scribendum tremebunda
converti. (LDO, PL 197, col. 742A–B)

(I, therefore, a small and weak form, with that man testifying whom, as I said in my
earlier visions, I had secretly sought and found, and that girl whom I mentioned in
the above visions also testifying, distressed by many infirmities, I trembling nonetheless turned my hand to writing.)

In the epilogue to the *Liber divinorum operum* in the Wiesbaden manuscript that Herwegen published (308–9), Hildegard speaks at some length
about her various helpers, and she specifies that Volmar corrected the text.
It is likely that the successors she mentions did so as well, though she says
only that they helped:

In tempore illo cum in vera visione cum scriptura huius libri, religioso viro et
observatione regule sancti Benedicti timorato mihi assistente, laborabam, tristicia
animam et corpus meum perforavit, quoniam ab eodem felici viro per conditionem
mortis in hoc mundo orbata separabar. Ipse enim in ministerium dei omnia verba
visionis huius in magno studio sine cessatione laboris audivit et corrigendo dis-
seruit, meque semper monebat, ne propter ullam infirmitatem corporis mei omit-
terem, quin die et nocte in his que mihi in eadem visione ostenderentur, scribendo
laborarem. Sic namque usque in finem suum faciens, in verbis visionum istarum
nunquam saturari potuit; unde ipso defuncto lacrimabili voce ad deum sic dicendo
clamavi; o deus meus, qui cum famulo tuo, quem mihi ad istas visiones diutorem
dedisti, ut tibi placuit fecisti, nunc, ut te decet, me adiuva. Tunc vero reverentissi-
mus et sapientissimus vir coram Deo et hominibus Ludewicus abbas sancti Eucharii
in Treveri, magna misericordia super dolore meo motus est, ita quod per se ipsum
et per alios sapientes stabili instantia auxilium mihi fiducialiter prebuit, et quia ipse
predictum felicem hominem et me ac visiones meas prius bene cognovit, in lacrimabili suspirio de illo, quasi eum a deo suscepissem, gaudebam. Quidam et homo,
qui de nobili gente erat, Wezellinus prepositus scilicet sancti Andree in Colonia,
qui in magna stabilitate honorificos mores coram deo et hominibus habuit et qui
in sanctis desideriis bona opera perficere studebat, cum diligenti studio in amore
spiritus sancti omnia verba visionum istarum audivit et notavit. Idem quoque bea-
tus homo in omni dolore et desolatione mea per se ipsum et per alios sapientes me
consolando adiuvabat et omnia verba visionum istarum sine tedio fideliter audivit et amavit, quum illa super mel et favum ei dulcia erant, sicque per gratiam dei
cum adiutorio predictorum venerabilium virorum scriptura huius libri completa
est. Ego autem de vivente luce, que me visiones istas docuit, vocem sic dicentem
audivi: Istos qui simplicem hominem visiones meas scribentem adiuuabant et con-
solabantur participes mercedis laborum illius faciam. Et ego paupercula in eadem
visione docta dicebam: Domine mi, omnibus qui me in istis visionibus quas ab in-

fantia mea infixisti, magno timore laborantem consolando adiuuabant, mercedem eterne claritatis in celesti Jerusalem dones ita quod per te sine fine in te gaudeant.[19]

(At the time when I was laboring in true vision with the writing of this book, with the help of a devout man, a religious in the observance of the rule of St. Benedict, sorrow pierced my soul and body, since I was separated, bereft of that happy man by death in this world. For he in God's ministry heard all the words of this vision in great zeal with ceaseless labor, and examined them, correcting them; he always admonished me not to omit anything because of bodily weakness, but to labor at writing day and night those things that were shown to me in this vision. So until the end, he could never be sated by the words of these visions; whence I lamented him dead with tearful voice saying to God, "Oh, my God, who did as pleased you with your servant, whom you gave me as helper in these visions, now, as suits you, help me." Then indeed the most revered and most wise man before God and men, Ludwig, abbot of St. Eucharius of Trier, was moved with great mercy for my grief, so that through himself and other wise men he faithfully offered me help with unfailing constancy, and since he knew the aforesaid happy man [Volmar] and me and the earlier visions well, I rejoiced in tearful sighs about him as if I had received him from God. And a certain [other] man, who was of noble stock, provost Wescelin of St. Andrew in Cologne [Hildegard's nephew], who had in great stability honorable behavior towards God and men, and who was zealous to do good works in holy desires, heard and noted all the words of these visions with diligent zeal in love of the Holy Spirit. That blessed man also helped me in all my grief and desolation, consoling me himself and through other wise men, and heard and loved all the words of these visions faithfully without fatigue [tedio], since they were sweet to him beyond honey and honeycombs, so by the grace of God with the help of the foresaid venerable men, the writing of this book was finished. I, however, from the living light, which taught me these visions, heard a voice speaking thus: "I shall make those who helped and consoled a simple man [Hildegard] writing my visions participants in the mercy of the labors." And I, a poor little thing educated in that vision said, "My lord, to all who helped me, consoling me laboring with great fear in these visions which from infancy you thrust into me, may you give the mercy of eternal brilliance in the heavenly Jerusalem so that they may rejoice through you, in you, without end.")

When, in her later years, Hildegard granted her last secretary, Guibert of Gembloux, permission to modify her style in this and other recent writings (see below), she made it clear that this was a departure for her—and not one she relished:

Nam in caeteris sive anterioribus scriptis meis, istud nec puellis quae ex ore meo excipiunt, nec ipsi unice dilecto piae memoriae filio meo Vulmaro, qui ante te in his corrigendis sedulus mihi astitit, unquam concessi, quia nec ille hoc exegit, et simplicitate qua inspirata vel ostensa mihi proferre poteram contentus, non poliendis verborum ornatu, sed tantum secundum regulas grammaticae emendandis quae protulissem, studium apposui[t]. (Pitra 29.27)

(For in my other earlier writings, I never conceded this, not to the girls who took them from my mouth, nor to my uniquely beloved son of pious memory, Volmar, who sedulously helped me before you[20] in correcting them, since he did not demand it, and content with the simplicity with which I could proffer what was inspired and shown to me, put his zeal not to polishing with embellishment of words but only emending what I gave out according to the rules of grammar.)

Whatever Guibert's role at the end, it seems reasonable to believe that Hildegard accepted from her collaborators only corrections of errors in grammar, spelling, or syntax, and perhaps small suggestions about a word here or there that did not modify her simple style.

It is not surprising, given the awe in which her secretaries or "collaborators" seem to have held her, that they did not press more radical changes on her. They recognized her divine election and were happy to serve it in whatever way she chose. It might perhaps be mentioned that all people of position in the Middle Ages—whether religious or secular figures, male or female—employed secretaries. Not just rulers of church and state, but busy religious figures from Jerome to Bernard of Clairvaux, had people taking their dictation, making fair copy from their notes, or putting their thoughts into more elegant or diplomatic or legal form. It was not unusual for a busy abbess to have someone to help her with her correspondence, particularly when she was also publishing so many other works. What was unusual was that most of her works purported to be divine revelations, were accepted by her secretaries as such, and were therefore not to be tampered with by man or woman.

Hildegard and Her Secretaries/Editors: Volmar

We do not have many letters between Hildegard and the various people who we know helped her in her work, except for the last, Guibert, who carefully collected his own as well as her correspondence. It is perhaps an indication of their lesser importance in their own and others' minds that more of the letters from her secretaries were not kept. (This was not, I think, because they were too close to correspond; not all of them were at Rupertsberg and even those who were occasionally wrote). There is only one letter extant from Volmar, provost of Rupertsberg, who was Hildegard's first helper. Volmar occupied a special place because he worked on all of her major visions, and because he apparently had faith in them even before they were officially recognized.[21] We have nothing from Hildegard to him, but we have her remarks about him after he died (in the LDO epilogue) and in God's words in the preface to the Scivias:

[U]nde in amore meo scrutatus est [Hildegard as *homo*] in animo suo, ubi illum inveniret, qui viam salutis curreret. Et quendam invenit et eum amavit, agnoscens quod fidelis homo esset et similis sibi in aliqua parte laboris illius qui ad me tendit. Tenensque eum simul cum illo in omnibus his per supernum studium contendit, ut absconsa miracula mea revelarentur. Et idem homo super semetipsum se non posuit, sed ad illum in ascensione humilitatis et in intentione bonae voluntatis, quem invenit, se in multis suspiriis inclinavit.

(And she searched in her mind as to where she could find someone who would run in the path of salvation. And she found such a one and loved him, knowing that he was a faithful man, working like herself on another part of the work that leads to me. And, holding fast to him, she worked with him in great zeal so that my hidden miracles might be revealed. And she did not seek to exalt herself above herself but with many sighs bowed to him whom she found in the ascent of humility and the intention of good will.)

God speaks of both Volmar and Hildegard as *homo*, reinforcing the sense of their equality as laborers in his work, and applauds her seeking him and accepting his help.

Volmar's single extant letter to Hildegard was probably occasioned by a bout of illness that seemed to threaten her life, inspiring in her friend a moving litany of impending loss for himself and her flock:

Hildigardi, domine reverende, matri dulcissime, magistre sanctissime et symmiste Dei. . . . V[olmarius], filius eius, licet indignus, omnisque concors grex puellarum ipsius. . . . Quamvis, o mater dulcissima, cotidie carneis oculis te videamus, carneis auribus te audiamus, tibi quoque cotidie, ut est iustum, devote adhereamus et Spiritum Sanctum per te loqui nobis intelligamus, absentiam tuam—quod sine lacrimis proferre non possumus—aliquando tamen prout Deo placuerit nobis incumbere non dubitamus, cum te iam amodo carnalibus oculis non videbimus. . . . Tunc enim maior erit meror et miseria nostra quam nunc sit letitia. Ubi tunc responsum de universis casibus suis querentium? Ubi tunc nova interpretatio Scripturarum? Ubi tunc vox inaudite melodie et vox inaudite lingue? Ubi tunc novi et inauditi sermones in festis sanctorum? Ubi tunc ostensio de animabus defunctorum? Ubi tunc manifestatio preteritorum, presentium et futurorum? Ubi tunc expositio naturarum diversarum creaturarum, divina dante gratia cum suavissimis et cum humillimis moribus, et cum materna affectione circa omnes affluentibus visceribus quam in te novimus? . . . Unde et hic manifestissime videtur impletum esse quod Deus stulta et infirma mundi, ut sapientes et fortia confundat, dicitur elegisse. . . .

Plura enim virtutum insignia, plura miraculorum Dei et Sancti Spiritus in te apparent opera quam nos dicere possumus aut dicere velimus. Nam et aliorum est te laudare et predicare, nostrum autem te mirari, venerari et diligere. (VA 195, dated ca. 1170).

(To Hildegard, reverend lady, sweetest mother, most holy master, and truest and
most worthy colleague of God, Volmar, her son, though unworthy, and the whole
harmonious flock of her girls. . . .

Although, sweetest mother, we see you daily with eyes of the flesh, hear you
with ears of the flesh, and devoutly adhere to you daily as is just and perceive the
Holy Spirit to speak through you to us, we do not doubt that sometime as it
pleases God your absence—which we cannot mention without tears—will fall on
us, when we will not see you as now with eyes of the flesh. . . .

For then there will be greater sorrow and misery than there is happiness now.
Where then will be the answer to those asking about all events? Where the new interpretation of Scriptures? Where then the voice of unheard melody and of unheard
language? Where the new and unheard sermons on feast days? Where the revelation about souls of the dead, of past, present, future? Where then the exposition
of the natures of different creatures, with divine grace, with sweetest and humblest
customs, and maternal affection to all from the flowing viscera as we have known
in you?)

Volmar also contrasts the little others can learn who travel, dispute, wake,
and sweat, but have put out the spark of the Holy Spirit in themselves,
while the spirit of prophecy and vision is reborn in a fragile instrument.
"Whence it seems clearly fulfilled that God is said to have chosen the foolish and weak things of the world to confound wise men and strong things."
He insists they speak thus not to denigrate her gift from envy nor to glory
in it, but to show how little is attained by the labor of scholars if they lack
the inspiration of the Spirit within, and to point up the "many remarkable
works of virtues, of miracles of God and the Holy Spirit, more than we can
or wish to say. It is for others to praise and proclaim you, ours to wonder,
venerate, and love."

Ludwig of St. Eucharius

But, of course, it was Volmar, not Hildegard, who died first, leaving her
bereft like an orphan ("velut orphana sola"), laboring alone in God's work,
as she says to another friend, Ludwig, abbot of St. Eucharius of Trier (VA
215r). While Hildegard made appeals even to the pope to get herself a new
provost[22] (since the abbot of Disibodenberg was not honoring his obligation to provide one), Ludwig was a good enough friend to take on the
correction of her last visionary book, the LDO. Described by Hildegard
as "the most revered and most wise man before God and men," Ludwig
was so moved by Hildegard's grief that he also offered others' (perhaps
some of his monks) help with unfailing constancy (see the LDO epilogue
cited above).

Hildegard had corresponded with Ludwig as a loving but stern spiritual adviser, giving him advice about his life and his abbatial duties. She noted his earlier mistakes and his present responsibilities with a parable of a man she had seen "in a true vision." This man had been cultivating his garden zealously until a cloud came over it and he gave it up. Another time, he planted roses and lilies, but they were destroyed by a storm. Then he decided to plant wheat and barley. "This," she says, "was your beginning, somewhat cloudy through various vicissitudes, then by the admonition of the Holy Spirit made better, until fatigue overcame you as a storm does flowers. Now God has pleased to make you a farmer who with great solicitude wherever you look you put the plow rightly in the earth." She tells him to love the good and to correct the vain and delinquent. He should also tolerate with patience those who are "hard stones," not falling on them in anger like an eagle, but doing all things with moderation, lest he disperse the flock of Christ. She suggests that he imbue his sense with the waters of scripture and conversation of the saints, and prevent his body from sowing the devil's wealth. Instead, he should ascend the mountain of virtues, be humble and produce flowers in his brothers as from trees, be a sun through doctrine, a moon through difference, wind through strenuous mastery, air through kindness, fire through beautiful speech/sermon of doctrine. "Begin these in the beautiful dawn and carry them through in bright light, that you may live eternally" (VA 214).

That Ludwig also considered Hildegard his spiritual superior and held her in awe is clear from the one letter extant from him to her, which is filled with hyperbolic but enchantingly conceived praise:

Sancte et Deo dicate virgini H, matri sue dilecte, L, solo nomine abbas de sancto Euchario, salutem et tante devotionis affectionem quod, si quis preter me sciret, vel nihil vel ea que non sunt scibilia sciret.

Satis ridiculosum videretur, si aquilas papiliones, si cervos pulices, si leones lumbrici missis litteris salutarent. Sic, immo plus quam sic mirandum vel ut verius dicam ridendo, quod peccator in divinis vel humanis artibus parum vel nihil valens illi scribere presumit, quam Deus cum mirabili castitatis prerogativa tam alta et tam insigni mirificavit ingenii excellentia ut non solum philosophorum et dialecticorum, verum etiam antiquorum prophetarum exsuperes acumina.

Temerarie tamen presumptioni, mater piissima, solita benignitate non denegabis veniam, cum rescribendi causa fuerit familiaritatis audacia. At tibi scribendum et ad te sepe veniendum non me vie absterrebit difficultas, dum sermonum tuorum me invitet utilitas tanto gratior quanto maiori fuerit studio comparata. Gratius enim possidemus que cum labore acquirimus.

Unde, domina, nostra te non moveat improbitas, quoniam vires quas tibi corporis denegat infirmitas, compatiens administrabit caritas. Litteras a te promissas cum magno desiderio exspecto, quas per presentium latorem mittere non differas. Sed et etiam quod tibi visum fuerit de negotio tibi commisso rescribas." (VA 215)

(Greetings and affection of such devotion that if anyone knew it besides me, he would either know nothing or know things which are not knowable, to the holy virgin Hildegard dedicated to God, his beloved mother, Ludwig, in name only abbot of St. Eucharius. It seems ridiculous enough if butterflies saluted eagles, if fleas saluted stags, if stomachworms saluted lions with their letters, so more than wondrous or truly I should say laughable that a sinner worth little or nothing in divine or human arts should presume to write to one whom God with the marvelous election of chastity magnified so high and with such great excellence of wit that you excede the heights not only of philosophers and dialecticians but also of ancient prophets.

Do not deny favor to such bold presumption, most pious mother, with your accustomed kindness, since the cause of writing back was the boldness of familiarity. But the difficulty of writing to you and coming often to you will not frighten me, while the usefulness of your speech/sermons invites me, so much more pleasing with the greater effort expended. What we acquire with labor we possess more gratefully.

Whence, lady, let our wickedness not move you, since the strengths which infirmity of body denies you, compassionate charity will administer. I await the letters promised by you with great desire, which do not put off sending by the bearer of [this letter]. But also, write back what you think of the business committed to you.)

Ludwig is apparently agreeing to go over the manuscript and asking her to send it back with the messenger, while at the same time asking her advice on something he prefers not to commit to writing.

The fact that Ludwig has accepted the burden of copyediting the manuscript in no way changes the nature of their relationship. Hildegard continues to send him advice, looking to her "true vision." She tells him not to accept a new position or honor ("compel yourself, lest for grace of an honorific name you be moved from the stability of good intention through worldly ways"), even as she acknowledges her need for his help in her humble formula:

Deo etiam et tibi, mitis pater, gratias ago quod infirmitati et dolori meo, que paupercula forma sum, condolere dignatus es, que modo velut orphana sola in opere Dei laboro, quoniam adiutor meus, ut Deo placuit, mihi ablatus est. Librum quo que per gratiam Spiritus Sancti in vera visione cum illo scripsi et, qui nondum finitus est, mox tibi ad corrigendum representabo, cum perfectus et scriptus fuerit. (VA 215r).

(To God and you, gentle father, I give thanks that you deigned to grieve for my infirmity and sorrow, I, a poor little form, who labor now like an orphan alone in the work of God, since my helper, as God pleased, was taken from me. The book which, by the grace of the Holy Spirit in true vision, I wrote with him and is not yet finished, I shall send you to correct as soon as it is finished and written out.)

The same kinds of admonitions and encouragements run through the other extant letters from Hildegard to Ludwig (VA 216, 217), even when she sends the manuscript.

Dronke translates the letter accompanying the manuscript and discusses it as an example of the power Hildegard had acquired for elaborate thought and language (*Women Writers*, 193–94), from which I cite only the part that refers to their collaboration:

Tu autem, o pater, . . . considera qualiter incepisti et quomodo vivendo processisti, quia in pueritia tua stultus eras et in iuventute tua cum temetipso letam securitatem habebas.

Interim tamen quandam causam unicornis, tibi tunc ignotam, quesisti, que scilicet scriptura nostra fuit que plurimum resonat de carnali indumento Filii Dei, qui virginalem naturam diligendo in ipsa velut unicornis in sinu Virginis quiescens, dulcissimo sono pulcherrime fidei omnem Ecclesiam ad se collegit.

Memor esto quoque, o fidelis pater, quid de paupercula mollis forme de eodem predicto indumento Filii Dei sepe audiebas. Et quia per summum iudicem adiutor meus ablatus est, ideo scripturam nostram tibi modo committo, suppliciter rogando quod eam caute serves ac diligenter corrigendo prospicias, ut etiam nomen tuum in libro vite scribatur, in hoc imitando beatum Gregorium qui propter onus Romani presulatus a cithareno sono infusionis Spiritus Sancti numquam dictando cessavit.

Tu etiam ut probus miles celestia arma indue, opera stultitie iuventutis abluendo, ac in angelico vestimento monachilis habitus strenue labora in meridie, priusquam dies inclinetur, quatenus in celestibus tabernaculis in societatem angelorum cum gaudio suscipiaris. (VA 217)

(But you, father, . . . reflect on how you began, how you proceeded in life; for in your childhood you were foolish, and in youth filled with joyous assurance. Meanwhile, you have embarked on an adventure of the unicorn, unknown to you in your youth—and this indeed was my writing, which often carries echoes of the mortal dress of the son of God who, loving a maidenly nature, resting in it like the unicorn in the maiden's lap, gathered the whole Church to himself with the sweetest sound of fairest believing.

Remember too, loyal father, what you often used to hear from a poor little womanly creature soft in form, about that dress of the son of God; and, because my helper has been taken away by the highest judge, I now am entrusting what I have written to you, asking imploringly that you preserve it carefully, and look over it, correcting it lovingly, that your name too may be written in the book of life, imitating the blessed Gregory in this, who, despite the burden of his Roman episcopate, never ceased composing, impelled by the lutelike sound of the infusion of the Holy Spirit.

Put on celestial armour like a noble knight, washing away the deeds of foolish-
ness of your youth, and toil strenuously in the noonday in the angelic robe of your
monk's habit, before the day declines, so that you may be welcomed joyously in
the heavenly tents into the angels' company.) (in Dronke, *Women Writers*, 193–94)

Wescelin

Until a permanent provost was assigned to Rupertsberg, Hildegard also
had help from her nephew Wescelin, as she acknowledges in the LDO
epilogue: "And a certain man, who was of noble stock, provost Wescelin
of St. Andrew in Cologne, who had in great stability honorable behavior
towards God and men, and who was zealous to do good works in holy
desires, heard and noted all the words of these visions with diligent zeal
in love of the Holy Spirit." Wescelin had been asked by Pope Alexander
to make sure Hildegard got the care she had requested for the salvation
of her sisters' souls, and until Rupertsberg agreed to send Godfrey to her,
Wescelin apparently filled in where needed, which included giving secretarial help to Hildegard.

We have no letters from Wescelin to Hildegard, but letters by others
mention him and give vague hints about his role. Wescelin's brother Arnold, archbishop of Trier (SF 177), wrote to his aunt when he became
archbishop to ask her, or God through her, whether his new position was
God's will. He insists he had never sought it, obviously looking for her reassurance and perhaps even congratulations.[23] In the letter, sent through
their mutual friend Ludwig of St. Eucharius, Arnold betrays resentment
of her intimacy with Wescelin,[24] perhaps out of jealousy of his relationship
with their famous aunt or suspicion of his motives:

Amicitia cognatione celestis est, quia senium ei non obest, sed confert, et ubi vera
est, stare nescit, sed in aliquo crescit et proficit cotidie. Cum autem ab ineunte
etate ulnis veri amoris nos amplexati sumus, miramur cur vos adulatorem plus vero
amico diligatis . . . Fratrem nostrum, prepositum sancti Andree, hic adulatorem
vestrum reputamus, nos autem verum amicum intelligi volumus. (VA 27)

(Friendship with kinship is heavenly, since age does not impede but intensifies it,
and where it is true, it does not stand still but grows and advances daily. Since we
have embraced from an early age with the arms of true love, we wonder why you
love a flatterer more than a true friend. . . . We consider our brother, the provost
of St. Andrew, to be a flatterer; we, however, wish to be known as a true friend.)

Guibert mentions that Wescelin, "her nephew and very close intimate
[*familiarissmius*]" returned to Cologne with a roll containing Hildegard's

solutions to questions Guibert and the monks of Villers had sent to her, which he intended to study. When he died, no one knew what had become of them (Gb. 26.828ff). Whether he meant to prepare them for publication, since they were much sought after, or to make some other use of them is not known. Schrader and Führkötter (178) think Wescelin was back in Rupertsberg after Hildegard's death, from 1182 until his own death in 1185, working on the letters. His position, experience with Hildegard, work on the LDO, and cleverness in dealing with people would have made him a logical choice, and Schrader and Führkötter attribute the conception of the Riesenkodex collection to him (though it was produced after his death).

Godfrey of Disibodenberg

Godfrey of Disibodenberg was the provost finally assigned to Rupertsberg as Volmar's successor, according to a letter from Abbot Godfrey of Echternach and St. Eucharius to Guibert of Gembloux (Gb. 41), though Guibert leaves him out of his own accounting.[25] Provost Godfrey began a life of Hildegard at the request of Abbot Godfrey and Hildegard's friend Abbot Ludwig, which Abbot Godfrey sent to Guibert when he was working on his own life. That is the only writing of his to or about her we have.

Godfrey speaks of Hildegard with praise but without extravagant exaggeration. He says she was as distinguished for her birth as for her holiness, precocious in the nature of her visions but shy of revealing them until constrained (1.1). He says of her physical sufferings that she grew stronger in her inner self as severe illnesses wasted her outer self (1.2). He tells of the pope reading aloud from her visions to archbishops and cardinals, and encouraging her to write them down (1.4). He gives examples of people who doubted but were convinced by signs from God of the divine power working through her (1.5). He describes her maternal affection for her nuns, even as she instilled in them the disciplined life, as well as her practical abilities: securing the land for the new monastery by a combination of purchase and exchange; keeping it independent of lay or secular authority and answerable only to the archiepiscopal see; and establishing her claim to the land and money left to her, which she removed from the control of the monks (1.7). Regarding her visions, Godfrey likens Hildegard to the eagle in Ezekiel (a symbol of John the evangelist), who kept moving back and forth from the active to the contemplative life (1.9). Godfrey is thought to have died in 1175 or 1176, leaving Hildegard once again without a secretary. (The account of Hildegard's life was completed by Theodoric of Echternach.)

Hugo of Tholey

Hildegard's brother Hugo of Tholey, canon of Mainz, served as interim provost for some time. Guibert mentions finding a brother of Hildegard's there as provost (Gb. 26.306–7), but there is no mention of his helping her with her writings.

There is one brief letter of severe admonition from Hildegard to Hugh in the collection: "The church tells wondrous things. Sometimes they rush in derision over truth. Whence I admonish you lest you accuse your brother R[oricum] in your heart unjustly and entangle your mind in the error of evil words over him, since God knows that you do not do rightly in this. Beware lest your lord fault you in this your wrath and other similar things. May God spare you in all your sins" (VA 208).

Richardis of Stade and Other Nuns

While Hildegard was going through various crises with her secretaries—the deaths of Volmar and Godfrey and the refusal of Abbot Helenger of Disibodenberg to assign a new provost—she had the continuing help of her sisters. She does not name any of the women who worked with her, though she does acknowledge their assistance. They were the first line of clerical help, taking dictation when necessary, compiling her notes and writings, perhaps even making the copies from which the copyeditors worked. It seems unlikely that they corrected the texts, since they had presumably been trained, as was Hildegard, without sufficient knowledge of grammar. Nevertheless according to Guibert the nuns copied books, so some of them must have been trained in formal hands to do fair copies. The girl who is the first mentioned of all Hildegard's helpers, even before Volmar in the preface to *Scivias* ("by the witness of a certain noble maiden of good conduct and of that man whom I had secretly sought and found") is assumed to be Richardis of Stade.

Richardis's mother had been a major force in helping Hildegard get the support she needed to move the convent to her chosen site of Rupertsberg, and within the convent Richardis was perhaps the sister Hildegard most depended on. The story of Hildegard's attempts to keep Richardis from leaving when she was named head of another convent is well known and need not be rehearsed here.[26] After all her attempts failed, Hildegard wrote Richardis a moving letter of grief and disillusionment in which her strong feelings for Richardis are palpable, but she attempts to cast them as a lesson about all excessive human love. "I transgressed because of the love of a noble man. . . . I tell myself again: 'Woe to me, mother, woe to me, daughter, why did you leave me like an orphan?' I loved the nobility of your customs, the wisdom and chastity, and your soul and all your life so that many said: 'What are you doing?' Let all weep with me who have a sorrow like my sorrow, who had in the love of God such love in their heart and mind for man as I had for you, who in a moment is snatched from them, as you were taken from me" (VA 64). Though the feelings expressed are far stronger than any Hildegard reveals for others, the sense of helpless abandonment in the question "Why did you leave me like an orphan?" recalls her emotional state over twenty years later when Volmar died. This suggests that at least to some small extent her feelings for Richardis were connected with, or had grown out of, their working together on her texts.

In the *Vita*, decades after the events, Hildegard speaks of her affection for Richardis in connection with the *Scivias* (even as she reveals her continuing sense of betrayal and vindication by divine justice):

[C]um librum *Scivias* scriberem, quandam nobilem puellam, supradicte marchionisse filiam, in plena karitate habebam, sicut Paulus Tymotheum, que in diligenti amicitia in omnibus se mihi coniunxerat, et in passionibus mei michi condoluit, donec ipsum librum complevi. Sed post hec propter elegantiam generis sui, ad dignitatem maioris nominis se inclinavit, ut mater cuiusdam sublimis ecclesie nominaretur quod tamen non secundum Deum sed secundum honorem seculi huius quesivit. Hec in alia quadam regione a nobis remota, postquam a me recessit, vitam presentem cum nomine dignitatis cito perdidit. (*Vita* 2.5)

(When I was writing the book *Scivias*, I held in full love as Paul did Timothy a certain noble girl, daughter of the marchioness, who joined herself to me in earnest friendship in all things and grieved with me in my sufferings until I completed that book. But afterwards, because of the position of her family, she inclined toward the honor of a higher name, to be named mother/abbess of a lofty church, which she sought not for God, but for worldly honor. After she left me, she swiftly lost the present life with the honorable name in a remote region far from us.)[27]

We have no letters from Richardis herself, though there is one from her niece Adelheid, who also left Rupertsberg to become an abbess (of Gandersheim). There is, however, no indication that the younger Adelheid

was involved with Hildegard's writing. Herwegen has suggested that a
third cousin of Richardis, Hiltrude, was one of Hildegard's helpers, citing
a reference in Trithemius's *Chronicle of Spanheim* for the year 1148:

S. Hildegardis . . . ad montem S. Ruperti . . . cum XVIII sacris monialibus tran-
sivit, interquas una erat Hiltrudis, filia comitis Megendhardi, virgo sanctissimae
conversationis, et beatae Hildegardi multum familiaris, ob cuius intuitum Comes
pater multa eidem loco beneficia impendit. (cited by Herwegen, 305)

(Saint Hildegard went to Rupertsberg with eighteen dedicated nuns, among them,
Hiltrud, daughter of Count Megenhard, a virgin of very holy behavior, and very
close to blessed Hildegard, on account of which the count, her father, gave great
benefices to that place.)

Hildegard also mentioned the girls who took dictation from her ("puellis
quae ex ore meo excipiunt") to Guibert of Gembloux (Pitra 29.27), so we
know she had secretarial help from various nuns, but we know nothing
more about them.

Guibert of Gembloux

Guibert was Hildegard's last secretary.[28] After writing admiring letters and
posing theological questions for her to answer for himself and the monks
of Villers, Guibert made a visit to her that only increased his enthusiasm.
He then suggested to her or encouraged her to ask him to come as her secretary—he must have let her know the invitation would be welcome, since
his monastery was under no obligation to staff hers—and arranged to get
permission to serve in that capacity, where he remained for two years until
she died (Gb. vii).

   Once Guibert got to Rupertsberg, he pressed Hildegard to allow him
to do more than correct grammar. Having a more ornate style himself,
he tried to convince her that she could reach an audience that would be
put off by her simple style only in more elegant language.[29] Hildegard,
although stating firmly that her former secretaries had never asked or been
granted such permission (Pitra 29.27), gave it, either because she was old
and weak, with more important battles still to wage (cf. VA), or because
the documents involved were the life of St. Martin (a saint Guibert was
especially devoted to) and her letter collection (to be revised according to a
scheme Volmar had probably had worked out, with her agreement, before
he died). Perhaps as she came to the end of her life, already a legend and an

important voice, Hildegard was also thinking of the effects of her message on future audiences (though she did not allow him to tamper with her earlier writings). Newman thinks Guibert reworked the letter in which she granted him permission, overstating his victory, but she also recognizes Guibert's style in Hildegard's life of St. Martin (*Sister of Wisdom*, 24).

Guibert first made contact with Hildegard, as many people did, by letters, his filled with lavish praise for her special gifts and defense of her special position. His reverence for her is perhaps best understood by his reaction to the arrival of her first response. When he heard it had come, Guibert rushed to pick it up and then was so overcome—both by fear that it might threaten his destruction, and by excitement that "it contained something venerable and magnificent" ("aliquid venerabile et magnificum in eo contineri," Gb. 18.39–40)—that he put it on the altar unread and spent the night prostrate in prayer before he opened it. He prayed for the Holy Spirit to make him worthy of the reading and acute in understanding it, and when he finally read it two or three times in silence, he was "transformed and almost come into ecstasy for the wonder of the words, for what they said was beyond my strength and seemed more the voice of the spirit of an angelic tongue than of man. I blessed the father of lights who . . . filled your soul with such splendors" (18.30–56).

In his first letter, Guibert expresses his awe of Hildegard and her writings, saying he and his fellows were hindered by their sins from understanding them directly, and begging her to help them:

Excellentis et meriti et nominis cum reverentia michi nominande Christi famule Hildegardi. . . . Insolita et omnibus pene seculis hactenus inaudita Spiritus Sancti munera tibi, o mater venerabilis, prerogata nos, ad quoscumque scripta tua perveniunt. . . etsi illa peccatis nostris obstantibus immediate percipere non meremur, per te tamen . . . dum his redundas et distillas, frequenter hauriamus. (Gb. 16.1–11)

(To the servant of Christ, Hildegard, excellent in merit and name, to be named by me with reverence. . . . To whomever they come, your requested writings, gifts to you from the holy spirit, unusual and almost unheard of through all time until now, o venerable mother, though we do not deserve to perceive them directly because of our sins, yet we frequently drink them in just as you pour them out and distill them.)

Guibert often addresses Hildegard as another Mary: "Ave, ergo, post Mariam gratia plena, Dominus tecum, benedicta tu in mulieribus, et benedictus sermo oris tui" ("Hail, full of grace after Mary, the Lord is with you, blessed are you among women, and blessed the speech of your mouth,"

Gb. 22.18–20; cf. Gb. 16.23–26). Here Guibert not only uses the words of the prayer to Mary, but by substituting "the speech of your mouth" for "the fruit of your womb," he suggests that Mary and Hildegard have a similar role, both giving human expression to the word of God. He also connects Hildegard with Mary as a counter Eve:

[O] mirandam indesinenter et predicandam circa genus humanum benigni pietatem Redemptoris, qui per eum quo mors intraverat sexum in matre ipsius vita restituitur, et de qua manu pestifer potus perditionis illatus nobis fuerat, de hac eadem manu in te salutaribus doctrinis antidotus recuperationis nobis refunditur. (Gb. 16.40–45; cf. 18.63–69)

(O wondrous piety of the benign Redeemer to be preached to human kind, who through that sex by which death entered, life was restored in his mother; from whose hand the pestiferous drink of perdition was offered to us, from that hand the antidote of recovery was poured out for us in you with salutary doctrine.)

Guibert emphasizes Hildegard's sex and the unusual aspect of God's choice, making a particularly telling point when he calls her a chosen vessel ("vas electionis") like Paul, putting her on the same level with the man whose word prevented women teaching:

Tu per gratiam Dei vas es electionis effecta, Deo carissima, angelis grata, hominibus necessaria et dilecta ad dirigendos pedes eorum in viam vite, ad cognoscendam magnificentiam potestatis eterne. Agnoscunt enim in sacris excellentie tue meritis sexum femineum divinitus honorari, videntes gloriam tuam, gloriam quasi regenerate a Patre, plena gratie et veritatis. (Gb. 22.12–17).

(You by the grace of God are made a chosen vessel, most dear to God, pleasing to angels, beloved of men and necessary to guiding their feet on the road of life to know the magnificence of eternal power. For they recognize in the sacred merits of your excellence that the female sex is divinely honored, seeing your glory, a glory that is as of one brought forth from the Father, full of grace and truth.)

Indeed, in the midst of an effusive description of the public reception of her letter (which he translated into French for an admiring audience), he reports that someone (Derolez suggests it was he, [Gb. 225]) specifically defended her public teaching:

Mulierem in ecclesia docere non permittit apostolus; sed hec, per assumptionem spiritus ab hac conditione soluta . . . et si imperita sermone, sed non scientia, in doctrina sua sana, qua multos instruit, lac consolationis rudibus et vinum correptionis fortioribus quasi duobus affluenter fundit uberibus. Se quamvis eam interius unctio magistra doceat de omnibus iubeatque, sicut in scriptis eius invenitur, ut ea, que ei suggerit in occulto, fiducialiter ad instruendos auditores proferat in aperto, memor tamen et sexus et conditionis proprie, et maxime predicte interdicitonis, paret spiritui neque quem spiritus mittit obviat apostolo, libris et sermonibus, fidei catholice per omnia consonis, erudiens ecclesiam, nec tamen more eorum, qui declamatorie loqui solent ad populum, disserens in ecclesia. (Gb. 18.240–55)

(The apostle does not permit a woman to teach in church; but she, through her reception of the spirit is released from this condition . . . and if she is unskilled in speech, she is not in learning, but healthy in her doctrine by which she instructs many, and pours the milk of consolation for the untaught and the wine of correction for the strong as from two breasts. If magisterial anointing teaches her within and orders her about all things, as is found in her writings, so that those things which it suggests in secret she faithfully conveys to instruct her hearers openly, mindful of her sex and condition, and especially of that interdiction, she obeys the spirit and does not oppose the apostle whom the spirit sends, instructing the Church with books and sermons consonant in all things with the Catholic faith, not in the manner of those who are accustomed to declaim to the people, [but] discoursing in church.)

Hildegard is said to be exempt from the veil by which married women must be covered. She "trancends womanly oppression with great height; comparable in eminence not just to whomever, but to the highest men, looking on the glory of the Lord revealed directly, she is transformed in that image from clarity [light] to clarity, as by the Lord's spirit" (". . . muliebrem depressionem altitudine multa transcendit; et non quorumlibet, sed summorum eminentie comparata virorum, revelata facie gloriam Domini speculans, in eandem transformatur imaginem, a claritate in claritatem, tamquam a Domini spiritu" 18.256–63). This seems to be a defense of her preaching both by the authority of God and under the aegis of ecclesiastical authority (in contrast to the preaching of rabble-rousers). Hildegard is to be thought of not as a lay or married woman, but as the equivalent of special men. Indeed, as the speaker says, on the testimony of her familiars, God compels her to preach; if she hesitates to obey, not from sluggishness or obstinacy but from feminine fear or virginal modesty, she suddenly gets quite rigid, "her body seems not like human flesh but inflexible wood, and this rigor is not relaxed until she fulfills the orders" (18.294–305).

It is not only Guibert who is overwhelmed by Hildegard's letter, but also a learned abbot who compares her favorably to the most respected theologians of France, who are much farther from divine truth:

[V]ir magni nominis et multe scientie, domnus Rubertus, Vallis Regie quondam abbas, cum ei ipsa legeretur epistola, tacitus sedens, diligenter et crebro agitans caput, sic affectus est, ut vix expectato fine erumperet, cum gravitate tamen, et

contestaretur non cuiusquam esse nisi Spiritus Sancti verba que audisset. 'Nec opi-
nor, inquit, vim et altitudinem quorundam verborum, in hac epistola positorum,
summos huius temporis Francie magistros, quantovis polleant acumine ingenii, ex
integro posse consequi, nisi eo spiritu quo dicta sunt revelante. Illi quidem arenti
corde et crepantibus buccis perstrepunt, languentes circa questiones et pugnas, de
quibus oriuntur rixe, non intelligentes de quibus loquuntur vel de quibus affir-
mant; et laciniosis contentionum funibus et se et alios inexplicabiliter irretiunt.
Hec autem beata, disciplinari assidue, ut audio, infirmitatis verbere purgata et in
sui custodiam cohibita, mitis et humilis corde unum illud, quod solum est nec-
essarium, id est beate gloriam Trinitatis, in simplicitate purissime mentis contem-
plans, de plenitudine illa intus haurit, quod ad sitientum relevandam sitim foras
fundit. (Gb. 18.139–57)

(Robert, once abbot of Val-Roi, a man of great name and much learning, sat silent
while the letter was read, shaking his head, so affected that he scarcely waited for
the end to declare that her words were nothing if not of the Holy Spirit, "Nor do
I think that the highest masters of this time in France, however sharp their wit,
could completely attain the power and depth of certain words in this letter, except if dictated by that spirit. Indeed, not understanding what they are saying or
affirming, they make great noises with burning hearts and rattling babblings, get-
ting ill over questions . . . which give rise to battles; and they snare themselves and
others with entangled ropes of contentions. She, however, blessed, assiduously
disciplined, purged as I hear with the scourge of illness . . . humble and gentle of
heart, contemplating what alone is necessary, the glory of the blessed Trinity, in
the simplicity of purest mind, pours out from the plenitude she drinks within to
relieve those thirsting.")

Guibert was not without some reservations, at least at first. He sent a
series of questions about her visions: whether she forgot them once they
were written down, whether she dictated in Latin or in German (which
someone else translated), and whether she was literate and knew holy
scriptures (Gb. 16.92–102).[30] Clearly he wondered whether it was she or
others who were in control of the reports of the visions, and the letter that
answered the questions and put those doubts to rest is the one that elicited
such enthusiasm from Guibert and Robert of Val-Roi (VA 103r). In the
letter, Hildegard says she does not perceive the visions with her five physical senses, but in her soul, though always with her eyes open, never losing
consciousness, day or night. She sees, hears, and knows simultaneously,
and remembers it long afterwards, and she speaks what she hears in unpolished Latin, just as she hears them in the vision, "for I am not taught
to write as philosophers write." In other words, God speaks to her in the
simple Latin of the New Testament, not in the complicated language of
philosophers and rhetoricians. The "shadow of the living brightness" is

always with her, giving her answers to the questions people ask. Though she answered his questions graciously, Hildegard also sent a personal message for Guibert, perhaps in response to his admonitions against pride.[31]

Guibert finally made a brief visit himself to Hildegard, and when he returned to Gembloux, he stopped at the abbey of Villers. His reports of what she had told him, as well as his frequent recitals of the previous letter (which he apparently carried with him), enflamed the monks to compose a series of theological questions that Guibert, in his new capacity as her "familiar," sent on to her (Gb. 19). He adds deferentially that if she has already answered some of the questions in her works, she should let them know where they can find the solutions or should send them the passages. He and the monks pressed her again and again for the answers (Gb. 20, 21, 23, 24, 25), their insistence a testimony to the importance they attributed to her as an authoritative source of theological doctrine and divine truth.[32] When Guibert heard a false rumor of Hildegard's death, he wrote to the nuns of Rupertsberg, asking them to send him whatever she had finished, or if she was still alive, as he hoped, to urge her to finish and send them (Gb. 23).[33] When he discovered she was alive, he was pleased but immediately asked for the answers (Gb. 24). After Guibert became her secretary, and the monks of Villers sent thirty-four more questions (Gb. 25), Guibert wrote back that she was too busy, too weak, and too old to answer any more (Gb. 26). He also wrote that though there were answers to some questions, they were not clear enough—"sometimes the author of obscurity and ambiguity, she wrote briefly what did not satisfy to their necessary elucidation" (Gb. 26.822ff.)—a remark that might describe many of her earlier answers and which suggests here that Guibert was trying to control their publication.[34]

In the letter that accompanied the first set of questions, Guibert offers condolences on the death of Hildegard's secretary, Volmar, but since Volmar had died in 1173, and the letter was apparently written in 1176, the death he had heard of must have been Godfrey's. Since Guibert reworked his own letters, it is unlikely that this was a simple error, because he could have corrected it. Guibert knew that Godfrey of Disibodenberg was Volmar's successor from Godfrey of St. Eucharius's letter to him (Gb. 41.26–27). It thus seems more plausible that Guibert intentionally suppresses the fact that Godfrey was her secretary. He does the same thing when he narrates his own history with Hildegard. After the death of Volmar, Guibert says that he was summoned at the counsel of friends to console her in Volmar's place (Gb. 26). This is revisionist history, as in Guibert's statement that Volmar had "taken her simple unpolished visions and illumined them with a cultivated style" ("visionum eius seriem simplici et impolito sermone ab ea prolatam excipiens, stili quo poterat cultu illustrabat," Gb. 26.291–93). I think Guibert wanted to be remembered as Volmar's successor—as the other man who helped to form Hildegard's opus—and consciously suppressed the existence of an obvious rival, the more recent secretary and fellow biographer, giving himself more authority for his stylistic revisions.

It is clear from everything Hildegard herself says that the role Guibert attributed to Volmar was not one she allowed him, though as I suggested earlier, tactful copyediting might well have been accepted. What Guibert pressed on Hildegard, however, was more serious revision. As Newman describes it, the life of St. Martin corrected by Guibert's eloquence "can scarcely be recognized as Hildegard's. Purists can at least rejoice that their collaboration began only after the seer's major works were completed" (*Sister of Wisdom*, 24). In the comments Hildegard sent Guibert with the vision of the life of St. Martin he was to correct, she asks him, in this as in the other works he would help her with, to add or subtract nothing and to change only "where the order or the rules of correct Latin are violated" (quoted in *Sister of Wisdom*, 23). But she concedes that if he prefers, she will allow something she has not otherwise permitted: that is, to "clothe the whole sequence of the vision in a more becoming garment of speech," always preserving the truth of the meanings. She accepts what was apparently Guibert's argument (cf. Pitra 29.26, "veluti ex tuo . . . ingenio soles dicere") that just as condiments may be necesssary to make useful foods appetizing, so rhetorical touches may be needed for ears "accustomed to an urbane style":

In quorum correctione sic et caeterorum in quibus emendandis tua defectui meo diligenter suffragatur dilectio, id observare debes, ut nihil addens vel detrahens, sive mutans, tantum ubi a tramite vel regulis justae latinitatis excessum est, solertiam reformationis adhibeas, aut si malueris, quod et in hac epistola praeter morem concessi, totam visionis seriem, observata omnibus sensuum veritate, decentiori sermonis cultu vestire non negligas, quoniam sicut quilibet cibi quatenus ex se utiles, nisi aliunde conditi, non appetuntur, sic et quaevis scripta, salutaribus licet referta monitis, si non aliquo eloquii colore commendantur, auribus urbani styli assuefactis fastidiuntur.(Pitra 29.25)

(When you correct [the *Life of St. Martin*] and the other works, in the emending of which your love kindly supports my deficiency, you should keep to this rule: that adding, subtracting, and changing nothing, you apply your skill only to make corrections where the order or the rules of correct Latin are violated. Or if you prefer—and this is something I have conceded in this letter beyond my normal practice—you need not hesitate to clothe the whole sequence of the vision in a more becoming garment of speech, preserving the true sense in every part. For even as foods nourishing in themselves do not appeal to the appetite unless they are seasoned somehow, so writings, although full of salutary advice, displease ears accustomed to an urbane style if they are not recommended by some color of eloquence.) (*Sister of Wisdom*, 23)

Guibert had argued that as harmony allured the hearer while dissonance offended (appealing to her musical sense), so honorable speech provokes and attracts and inspires readers, while inept sayings annoy and repel them. She includes in the material he may rework only what she has so far written *to him* and what she may yet write ("caetera, quae vel hactenus ad te scripsi seu deinceps scriptura sum . . . quae, sicut dixi, specialiter ad te vel jam direxi, vel forte post haec mihi dirigenda videbuntur" Pitra 29.26). Although Hildegard insists on the integrity of the content of her visions, she grants what Guibert said about the writings of the prophets and apostles, whose simple, uncultivated style in Hebrew or Greek zealous interpreters transposed to Latin, polishing and shining the text, so that it would not irritate those who loved God but impress itself more easily on their hearts and adhere there more tenaciously. Jerome, in particular, translated not word for word, but sense for sense ("non verbum a verbo, sed sensus reddatur ex sensu"). Thus Hildegard says she will not compel Guibert to follow step for step, as long as he does not move away from the footprints of her journey.

Even though she yields this much to Guibert (possibly knowing or strongly believing she will write no more major works), Hildegard clearly prefers her earlier mode, in which she permitted no changes beyond simple corrections, and no one, not even her beloved Volmar, asked to do more. Volmar was "content with the simplicity in which I expressed what was shown to me," and so, she implies, Guibert should be. "The defects of my Latin eloquence should not scandalize you or any readers" ("Nec vero te, seu quempiam mea legentium, iste latini eloquii quem patior defectus, scandalizet," Pitra 29.27), when Moses, who conversed intimately with God, acknowledged himself to be ineloquent and slow of speech, and accepted as an interpreter from God his brother Aaron to explain what he could not on his own. Jeremiah also testified that he did not know how to speak, but inexperienced in speech though not in learning, he showed himself an outstanding preacher, not only by voice, but also in dictating (Pitra 29.27). Hildegard, too, accepts what she lacks with humility and glorifies God for what she received: the revelations (Pitra 29.28).

It is impossible to know how far Hildegard bent to accommodate Guibert's arguments. It is certainly possible that, not expecting to write much more, she granted what he asked to keep him happy or, more important, to keep him with her while she conserved her energy. It is hard to imagine her changing her view drastically, since she had always thought of herself as God's vessel, relaying his message, and these were God's words she wrote down and dictated. One might argue, not altogether facetiously, that if God had thought elegance of speech was important, he would have supplied her with a knowledge of rhetoric as he did of theology and biblical exegesis. Instead, the language Hildegard heard from God in her visions was an oral Latin, with the endings probably not very clear, but it was good enough to get God's message to her and through her to the Church hierarchy and the public. It was the message that mattered, not the medium.

Notes

1. The *Vita sanctae Hildegardis* by Godfrey of Disibodenberg and Theodoric of Echternach was edited by Monika Klaes, CCCM 126 (Turnholt: Brepols, 1993); a translation of the PL 197 edition was done by Anna Silvas in "Saint Hildegard of Bingen and the *Vita sanctae Hildegardis*," *Tjurunga* 29 (1985): 4–25; 30 (1986): 32–41; 32 (1987): 46–59. References to the *Vita* in this chapter refer to this life, not to the life by Guibert of Gembloux, which can be found in *Guiberti Gemblacensis epistolae*, ed. Albert Derolez. The *Epistolae* are cited as Gb.; the life cited as Gb. 38.

2. The references to Eve occur in the prefaces to books 1 and 2 of the *Scivias*, edited by Adelgundis Führkötter and Angela Carlevaris; it was translated by Columba Hart and Jane Bishop.

3. God makes this threat in the last chapter of the *Liber divinorum operum simplicis hominis*, PL 197, col. 1038, cited hereafter as LDO.

4. So Hildegard reports in the piece she sent him for his correction, which can be found in *Analecta sancte Hildegardis opera spicilegio solesmensi parata*, vol. 8 of *Analecta sacra*, ed. J. B. Pitra, hereafter cited as Pitra; the present letter (on pp. 415–34) cited as Pitra 29.

5. Hildephonse Herwegen, "Les collaborateurs de Sainte Hildegarde"; Peter Dronke, *Women Writers of the Middle Ages*; Marianna Schrader and Adelgundis Führkötter, *Die Echtheit des Schrifttums der heiligen Hildegard von Bingen*; Albert Derolez, "The Genesis of Hildegard of Bingen's 'Liber divinorum operum'" and "Deux notes concernant Hildegarde de Bingen." Dronke (307 n.11) thinks Derolez's conclusions go beyond the codicological evidence, and I agree.

6. The unusual circumstance of Hildegard's preaching tours, in which she preached to clergy and bishops, is justified by an admirer who says she is exempt from the condition imposed by Paul that does not permit women to teach in church because she is instructed by the spirit (Gb. 18.240ff). She speaks of her-

self in a letter as a timid, poor little thing, who exhausted herself speaking before masters and doctors and other wise men in whatever major places they lived ("ego autem timida et paupercula per duos annos valde fatigata sum, ut coram magistris et doctoribus ac caeteris sapientibus in quibusdam majoribus locis ubi mansio illorum est, vivente voce ista proferrem" [*Hildegardis Bingensis Epistolarium*, ed. Lieven Van Acker—hereafter cited as VA—15r to bishops of the church]), but note the prestige of that audience. For the first two volumes of her letters, see VA. The other letters must still be consulted in PL 197, Pitra, or Adelgundis Führkötter's German translation of Hildegard von Bingen, *Briefwechsel*.

7. The text has now been edited by Angela Carlevaris, *Hildegardis liber vite meritorum*, hereafter cited as LVM. A translation based on the text in Pitra was done by Bruce W. Hozeski, *The Book of the Rewards of Life*.

8. If direct echoes of John are missing in the earlier works, the dangers of changing her/God's words are nonetheless clear. God says at the end of the *Scivias*: "sed si quis haec verba digiti Dei temere absconderit et ea per rabiem suam minuerit aut in alienum locum alicuius humani sensus causa abduxerit et ita deriserit, ille reprobatus sit. Et digitus Dei conteret illum" (whoever rashly conceals these words written by the finger of God, madly abridging them, or for any human reason taking them to a strange place and scoffing at them, let him be reprobate; and the finger of God shall crush him). God has just said that he would conquer the strong who scorn him with the small and weak as he did Goliath with a boy and Holofernes with Judith (*Visio* 13.16, 640–45). Compare this to the end of LVM: "Et hec vera sunt; et qui verus est ea sic manifestari veraciter voluit. Quapropter si quis per supereminentem mentem Scripturarum et proprietatis sue aliquid eis in contrarietate addiderit, penis hic descriptis subiacere dignus est; aut si quis aliquid ab eis per contrarietatem abstulerit, dignus est ut a gaudiis hic ostensis deleatur" (LVM 6.45, ll.897–902).

9. Hildegard's physical writing is mentioned in the *Vita* by both Godfrey ("mox ut illa scribendi opus, quod non didicerat, adtemptavit," 1.3) and Theodoric ("manu propria scripsit," 2.1). She herself says in the prologues: "manus ad scribendum apposui" ("I put my hand to writing," *Scivias*) and "manus tandem ad scribendum tremebunda converti" ("trembling I turned my hand to writing," LDO, col. 742A). That she could write as well as read suggests that she had more than the most rudimentary education, though she probably was not taught a formal hand. Still, the nuns did copy books in her convent at Rupertsberg, so some of them must have been taught such a hand (Gb. 38.59).

10. Dronke describes her command of Latin style as "forceful and colourful, and at times as subtle and brilliant, as any in the twelfth century" (*Women Writers*, 200, cf. 194), though he is aware of its occasional awkwardnesses. He also notes apropos her learning that people are still trying to track down her sources (ibid., 200). Elsewhere he suggests as sources for the *Scivias* Donatus and various Stoic writers, as well as Lucan and possibly Seneca and Cicero ("Problemata Hildegardiana," 108).

11. She says in a letter to Pope Eugene that she has not been taught by philosophers ("indocta de philosophis," VA 2), and to Guibert that the visions do not teach her to write as philosophers write ("sicut philosophi scribunt scribere in visione hac non doceor," VA 103r.91–92).

12. "Latinisque verbis non limatis ea profero, quemadmodum illa in visione audio" (VA 103r.88–92). For a partial translation of this letter, see Dronke, *Women Writers*, 168–69.

13. For a partial translation of the letter, see Dronke, *Women Writers*, 197–98. For more on Hildegard and music, see Marianne Richert Pfau, "Music and Text in Hildegard's Antiphons," and Bruce Holsinger, "The Flesh of the Voice: Embodiment and the Homoerotics of Devotion in the Music of Hildegard of Bingen (1098–1179)."

14. "Quis vero non miretur, quod cantum dulcissime melodie mirabili protulit symphonia, et litteras prius non visas" ("Who would not marvel at the chant she brought forth of sweetest melody with wondrous harmony, and the letters never seen before," *Vita*, 2.1).

15. Klaes attributes the discrepancy to Theodoric's negligence, *Vita*, 129. For more on the confusion, see Schrader and Führkötter, *Die Echtheit*, 119–20.

16. Hildegard wrote to Guibert at the end of her life that she had permitted no one, not the girls who took dictation, nor her beloved Volmar, to change her writings (Pitra 29.27). See p. 111.

17. It cannot be coincidental that God is often presented through feminine attributes, Hildegard herself as sexually neutral or androgynous (*homo* used with masculine adjectives), and her co-workers as a sexually balanced team. Whether consciously or not, Hildegard sets up a pattern of authority that is not, or not exclusively, patriarchal.

18. Since Richardis of Stade, the nun who was her particular helper and friend, left her in 1151, long before the composition of the last two books of visions, Hildegard is either recalling the experience of the first book as the crucial moment for her writing or alluding to other supportive companions. This seems less likely, even though she certainly had them, because her description of the pair—"the man I secretly sought and found" and the young girl—is virtually formulaic, and in the LDO she implies that it is the same pair.

19. The text is from Herwegen, with corrections by Dronke (*Women Writers*, n. 93), who cited the section on Ludwig. I quote it in full because it is not easily obtainable. There is some question whether *stabili instantia* means that Ludwig came for a long stay to work on the book (a possibility raised by Schrader and Führkötter, *Die Echtheit*, 146 n. 91) or that he worked with "unfailing constancy," as Dronke thinks.

20. Either this is an instance of Guibert suppressing (by deleting reference to) the existence of other secretaries (see below), as though he were Volmar's only successor; or else Hildegard is using Volmar as the model: if Volmar did not do it, certainly others would not have dared? Barbara Newman thinks Guibert has reworked the letter to exaggerate his victory in the battle over style (*Sister of Wisdom: St. Hildegard's Theology of the Feminine*, 24). Hildegard was in fact dead by then ("novi vos eam vehementer dilexisse," Guibert says to Philip of Cologne when he sends it to him, Pitra 28).

21. Of Volmar, who died in 1173, Godfrey's life says Hildegard was content with one faithful colleague for the grammar she did not know—the cases, tenses, and genders—one who did not presume to add to or delete what affected the sense:

"uno solo fideli viro symmista [the same word he uses of her, VA 195] contenta, qui ad evidentiam grammatice artis, quam ipsa nesciebat, casus, tempora et genera quidem disponere, sed ad sensum vel intellectum eorum nichil omnino addere presumebat vel demere" (*Vita* 2.1). Volmar worked on the three major visions with her and probably collected her letters, doing some reordering among and within them with her consent (MS Wr); the later revisions and amplifications (MS R) were probably done by Guibert (see also John Coakley's review of the Van Acker edition, *Speculum* 68 (1993): 1132–33).

22. A letter from Hildegard to Pope Alexander after Volmar's death says, "I and my sisters bend our knees before your paternal piety, praying that you deign to look on the poverty of a poor, little form, for we are now in great tribulation, since the abbot of St. Disibodenberg and his brothers deny the privileges and choice we have always had. About which there must always be great caution providing for us . . . since if they do not concede what we ask, devout and religious men, spiritual religion will be completely destroyed among us" (VA 10.24–32). In response, the pope wrote to Wescelin, provost of St. Andrew's in Cologne and Hildegard's nephew, asking him to look into the matter and settle it, and if they cannot get the provost from Disibodenberg to make sure that they have a competent one from elsewhere (VA 10r). Wescelin himself apparently filled in until Godfrey was assigned.

23. Instead of giving Arnold the desired reassurance, Hildegard warns him that all power is from God and that he should avoid whatever is without God, lest he fall in pride with the first angel, Satan. She reminds him that God loves the poor, not the rich, and commends justice and truth to him. She says she looked to the true light as he asked, but could hardly see the beginning of good works (VA 27r).

24. Van Acker dates this letter 1169, well before the death of Volmar, so Wescelin was not yet filling in for him at Rupertsberg. He may, however, have spent time with his aunt before he was asked by the pope to look into her problem.

25. Schrader and Führkötter suggest that Godfrey of Echternach and St. Eucharius, before he became abbot, may have been called in by Ludwig to help Hildegard, one of the "alios sapientes" she says he found to help her (SF 181).

26. See Sabina Flanagan, "Spiritualis Amicitia in a Twelfth-Century Convent? Hildegard of Bingen and Richardis of Stade," and Dronke, *Women Writers*, 154–59, which includes a translation of Hildegard's letter to Richardis.

27. In his report to Hildegard of his sister's death, Richardis's brother Hartwig, archbishop of Bremen, suggested that Richardis returned her affection—either because it was true, or because he wished to restore good will with Hildegard, who had accused him of simony in the transactions: "I ask you, if I am worthy, as I can, love her as she loved you; and if she seemed deficient in any way, it was not from her but from me; at least consider the tears which she shed when she left that convent, which many witnessed. And if death had not impeded her, she would have come to you" (VA 13).

28. Fortunately, Guibert collected the letters in which he recorded his relations with Hildegard and her convent, an unusual source of information about her and the community, as well as about one of the close companions of her last years. There are three letters to Guibert from Hildegard (VA 103r, 106r, and 109r

to Guibert and the monks of Villers), and eight to Hildegard from Guibert, some of them with or for the monks of Villers. Guibert also corresponded with Hildegard's convent before and after her death, and he continued to correspond with one of the nuns, Gertrude, who seems to have become a particular friend. He also wrote to fellow monks about her life and her convent.

29. The editor of Guibert's letters, Albert Derolez, cites Cartellieri on Guibert's heavy style ("entsetzlich schwülstig und weitschweifig") and comments himself: "c'est surtout en écrivant aux grands de ce monde, les évêques et les abbés, que ses lettres deviennent interminables et perdent parfois tout intérêt" (Gb. ix). Herwegen says that Guibert's style "manque absolument de simplicité et de naturel," and that he was "un homme possédé de la manie de corriger et de changer" ("Collaborateurs," 392).

30. When he got no answer, but the promise of one in the future, he sent more questions about the visions: whether she had them awake or asleep, what the title *Scivias* meant, and whether there were other works. He also asked about the customs of her convent, why her nuns wore crowns, and what diversity there was among them—questions that had also been raised by Tengswind of Andernach (VA 52).

31. "But you, son of God, who seek him in faith, and who seek from him that he save you, attend to the eagle flying to the cloud with both wings, who if he is harmed in one remains on earth and cannot raise himself, though he would willingly rise to fly. So also man flies with two [wings] of rationality—knowledge of good and evil: the right wing is good knowledge, the left bad, and bad ministers to good, and good is sharpened by bad and ruled, and the wise [man] is completed in all things by it. Now however, o dear son of God, God raises the wings of your knowledge to the right roads so that although you lick sin from a taste for it, since you are born so that you cannot be without sin, yet you do not eat it. In this way, o upright soldier, act in this battle so that you can be in heavenly harmony, so that God can say to you: 'You are from the sons of Israel who by the zeal of heavenly desire look through the grating onto the highest mountain'" (VA 103.139–57).

At the end of his letter requesting answers to his and the monks' questions, Guibert made a more specific comment about pride. Begging her to pray until God gives her the answers, he reminded her of what Gregory testified about holy prophets, that they sometimes said things from their own spirit that they believed came from the spirit of prophecy, and thus she, too, should beware lest she impute to the Holy Spirit what came from her spirit. This seems a tactless remark to make and unnecessarily sanctimonious, unless he suspected or had heard suspicions that some of her pronouncements represented her own views rather than God's.

32. In her answers to Guibert's letters 20 and 24, Hildegard excuses her failure to send the answers to the questions, saying that she has "looked to the true light" for answers to their questions and is working on them—though bereft of her consolation and busy with the affairs of the monastery (VA 106r); and that she has worked on them but is busy with other writings and held back by sickness, so has only completed fourteen answers (VA 109r).

33. The thirty-five questions are in epistola 19 of Guibert's letters. The questions with Hildegard's thirty-eight answers (she handled multiple-part questions

separately) are also in PL 197, cols. 1037–52. Ralph of Villers later sent thirty-four new questions to Hildegard through Guibert (epistola 25), but those answers are not extant. For a discussion of some of Hildegard's answers in relation to the contemporary monastic versus scholastic approaches to theology, see Anne C. Bartlett, "Commentary, Polemic, and Prophecy in Hildegard of Bingen's *Solutiones triginta octo quaestionum*."

34. Guibert also told of a misfortune that later befell the solutions that did exist (Gb. 26.828 ff.). After her nephew Wescelin, who had collected all the solutions in a roll and taken them with him to Cologne to study them, died, the roll disappeared. Guibert suspected the answers were stolen. With no hope of recovering them, he suggested that the monks of Villers investigate the questions in learned books or send them to some of the more experienced masters of France in Cîteaux, a *pis aller*, but all they can do now that she is dead.

Sex and the Single Amazon in Twelfth-Century Latin Epic

David Townsend

"I even made poor Louis take me on Crusade. How's that for blasphemy? I dressed my maids as Amazons and rode bare-breasted halfway to Damascus. Louis had a seizure and I damn near died of windburn, but the troops were dazzled." This is Eleanor of Aquitaine speaking, not perhaps as she was, but as she is imagined in *The Lion in Winter*.[1] As a teenager going to summer stock in southern Indiana, I was shocked and delighted by Eleanor's reminiscences of the Second Crusade, as by the other Plantagenet perversities acted out that muggy July night. When I was sixteen, this became the twelfth century for me, soon to be reinforced by the film version of the play and supplemented by Kenneth Clark's *Civilisation* episode on the age of the cathedrals.[2] But Clark, alas, offered neither Amazons nor a homosexual heir to the throne of Henry II.

When I was a child, I read as a child, but having become a medievalist, I put away childish interpretations. In the intervening twenty-five years, I have learned with a vengeance to distrust such popularizations. I now know that in regard to the image of Eleanor trotting through a bitterly contested Middle East done up as an Amazon, "our caution . . . cannot be too extreme." Eleanor indeed went East with female companions, and a Greek chronicler toward the end of the twelfth century likened her to a second Penthesilea, suggesting that her fellows "behaved in an even more masculine way than the Amazons." But not until we reach the Victorian account by a disapproving Agnes Strickland do we actually find the queen and her ladies themselves donning Amazon garb.[3] So much for windburn and bedazzled troops. Perhaps (I still cannot help thinking during occasional lapses) the twelfth century was poorer for the loss.

On the other hand, Eleanor surely knew an Amazon when she saw one. Benoit de Sainte-Maure would dedicate the massive *Roman de Troie* to her about ten years after the Crusade. There Penthesilea and her army appear with much pomp and in considerable detail.[4] Maybe Eleanor, beholding her anachronistic representation, might approve: *si non è vero, è ben trovato*. I long for the imagined Eleanor's subversion of the rules others made for her. I remember the space her nostalgic recollection opened for me, as I churned through the void between my own anomalous desires and the brutally enforced norms of a respectable small town. Professionally, however, I have to settle for Amazons where I can find them.

Penthesilea, thee I invoke.

* * *

Walter of Châtillon's long Latin epic, the *Alexandreis*, dates from the last quarter of the twelfth century.[5] At the beginning of Book 8, after his conquest of Darius and before the Indian campaigns that lead swiftly to his hubris-ridden downfall, Alexander the Great receives a visit from Talestris, Queen of the Amazons:

Lamenting Memnon's death with endless grief,
three times the Dawn had strewn her radiant beams
through all the earth, when earth's sole conqueror,
valiant and swiftly lunging toward all peril,
approached Hyrcania's boundaries with his host.   5
He'd scarcely gained the victory, or heard
the supplications of the lisping Bagoas
to grant bloodstained Narbazanes his life,
when Queen Talestris of the Amazons,
aflame with her desire to see the king,
approached the camp with virgin retinue.   10
All peoples dwelling from the Caucasus
to rushing Phasis' wide-encircling stream
received this woman's laws. When once an audience
was granted to her with the king, she swiftly
descended from her horse, with quiver slung
from her left arm, two spear-shafts in her right.   15
(The dress of Amazons does not obscure
their bodies wholly. On the left, their chests
are bared; their garments settle on the rest,
and hide what must be hidden, though the soft
raiment doesn't fall below the knee-joint.
The left teat is preserved until adulthood
to nurse their infants of the female sex;

the other one receives an early searing
to ease their wielding of the pliant bow,
and leave them unencumbered for the javelin.)   23
    Perusing, then, the king with wary eye,
Talestris marveled that his meagre body
ill fit his fame, and silently she pondered
where the great virtue of the unvanquished prince
might lie concealed: the simple savage mind
respects and judges all according to
their bodies' beauty and their splendid raiment,
and thinks none capable of mighty deeds,
save those whom nature has seen fit to bless
with shapely body and a charming form.
But sometimes mightier courage dwells inside
a middling body, and illustrious power
transgresses all the body's limbs to rule
somewhere within obscure and darkened members.   35
    And so the queen, asked once for what she'd come,
whether she sought some great boon of the king,
responded that she'd come to fill her womb
and leave again to bear an offspring shared
with such a prince: she judged herself as worthy
that from her he might sire a kingdom's heirs.
If from that birth a noble woman issued,
the daughter would attain her mother's realms;
if there came forth a male, he'd be returned
for nourishment under his father's tutelage.
The king inquired whether Talestris cared
to take up arms beneath him, but she pleaded
her realm now lacked a guardian. Finally
she took the gift of thirteen nights, and gained
what she was seeking. Then she turned her steps
back to her realm's throne and ancestral cities.[6]

    Some modern readers still know Walter better for his lyrical and
satirical poems in the accentual meters that appealed to post-romantic conceptions of medieval literature: these works are conducive to the wide appreciation of the "Goliardic" Latin verse long associated with Helen Waddell's "Wandering Scholars."[7] Walter also wrote an extended prose treatise
against the Jews.[8] But Walter's hexameter epic was his *magnum opus*, at-
tested by some two hundred surviving manuscripts, many of them heavily
and systematically glossed.[9] Nor was the popularity of the poem restricted
to the thirteenth century's burgeoning academic culture. Vernacular adaptations testify to the breadth of its appeal.[10] The work's currency in circles

of high political power was already presupposed by its dedication: Walter's patron William of the White Hands, bishop of Sens from 1169 to 1176 and archbishop of Reims from 1176 to 1202, was also the uncle of Philip Augustus.[11]

The poem draws on a Latin prose text of the early imperial period, the *Historiae Alexandri Magni Macedonis* of Quintus Curtius Rufus, as its principal source.[12] Walter sometimes follows Curtius very closely indeed, but at others he amply demonstrates his willingness to handle that text more freely: he modifies or omits episodes, adds digressions (often to provide epic coloration), and conflates the text with other sources.[13]

Twentieth-century criticism of the *Alexandreis* has in large part organized itself around several central topoi of traditional philological criticism. Treatments often focus on the epic's classicizing tendencies, so that Walter comes to be judged by his success or failure at reproducing the aesthetic, and to some extent the ethos, of the Gold and Silver Latin epic.[14] Much attention is paid to Walter's use of Curtius and to his synthesis of this with other materials from the Alexander legend and from the Latin poetic tradition.[15] And extensive argument obtains over the engagement or withdrawal of the text from the pressing political issues of its day.[16]

Insofar as the poem resonates against the controversies surrounding the French prosecution of the Crusades, we can read it as one of medieval high culture's principal monuments to the long history of Orientalism.[17] Its literary constructions of the newly accessible East must necessarily evoke as intertexts other, more fantastic materials in the Alexander tradition, like the *Letter of Alexander to Aristotle* imbedded in another vastly popular Latin text, the *Historia de preliis*.[18] Less foregrounded in the poem, and thus understandably bypassed in recent criticism, is the representation of gender: Walter generally presents Alexander as a sexless being in a homosocial environment, and indeed, Walter's practice of omitting many of the episodes in Curtius that cast a pall over Alexander's character covers the traces of gender and sexuality issues.[19] But the appearance of the Amazon queen affords a remarkably easy entrée into such concerns. A close reading of the passage reveals a deeply imbedded problematic of gender, a problematic that intersects the incipient Orientalism of this underread masterpiece of the twelfth century.

Memnonis eterno deplorans funera luctu,
Tercia luciferos terras Aurora per omnes
Spargebat radios cum fortis et impiger ille

Terrarum domitor, in cuncta pericula preceps,
Hyrcanos subiit armato milite fines.   5

The opening lines of Book 8, with their conventional epic allusion to
Aurora's grief at the tomb of Memnon, betray an immediate debt to Ovid's
Metamorphoses and to the *Aeneid*.[20] But at the caesura of line 3 comes a first
seam in the construction of the passage, as the text moves from mythological description to the representation of martial prowess. We could read
this juxtaposition as entirely commonplace, a derivation from the previous epic tradition. But in the *Alexandreis* it reflects the amalgamation of
two profoundly different kinds of source, namely the epics and the prose
historiographical discourse of Curtius. Much criticism focuses upon the
synthesis of these voices, but it is possible instead to read the poem as exist-
ing at the intersection of their dialogic tensions, as constituted precisely by
the intertextual relays that the reader must negotiate to construe the text.[21]
In the gap that opens up in the middle of the passage's third line, there
arises, overlapping but not coinciding with the dialogue between these
competing discourses, a gendered tension between the passivity of the
female Dawn and the behavior of the Macedonian conqueror. Although
one could read this tension as purely conventional, verbal repetition mili-
tates against such a dismissal: *terras* of line 2 is set off against *terrarum* of
line 4 in almost exactly symmetrical relation to the caesura of line 3: while
Aurora scatters her tears through all lands, the still-unnamed Alexander
appears as those lands' conqueror. Both gender and the militarist expan-
sionism of Alexander's project thus become visible in this space.

Quos ubi perdomuit uitamque cruentus ab ipso
Narbazanes molli Bagoa supplicante recepit,
Haut mora, uisendi succensa cupidine regis,
Gentis Amazoniae uenit regina Talestris
Castraque uirginibus subiit comitata ducentis.   10

Two lines of circumstantial detail now intervene between the opening
of the book and the arrival of Talestris. Here we learn that Alexander spares
the treasonous Persian general Narbazanes at the prompting of "effeminate
Bagoas." With this reference, the text encodes an interpretive lack, depend-
ing as it does for comprehension on a network of references that undermine
the work's self-sufficiency. A late thirteenth-century gloss from Vienna,
National Library 568 reflects the necessity of such supplementation:

Hic dicit quod Narbazanes reconciliatus fuit Alexandro per blanda uerba, sed
auctor subticet ueritatem quoniam Narbazanes duos filios pulcerrimos habuit qui-

bus abutebatur Alexander. Qui ab Alexandro inpetrauerunt pacem patri suo Nar-
bazani, sed quoniam hoc Alexandro fuit dedecus, et ideo tacuit auctor.

(Here he says that Narbazanes was reconciled to Alexander by pretty words, but
the author hushes up the truth that Narbazanes had two very beautiful sons whom
Alexander abused. They begged peace for their father Narbazanes from Alexander; but since this redounds to Alexander's dishonor, so, therefore, the author
keeps quiet.) [22]

This gloss paradoxically serves to clarify that the poem's ideal reader is
well aware of what it praises Walter for omitting. Once it is clear that this
ideal reader is already familiar with such material from Curtius and other
sources, we can recognize these lines as a kind of *praeteritio*, highlighting
precisely what they purport to omit. If Walter is attempting to whitewash
Alexander here, as this and other glosses in the same manuscript rather disingenuously suggest,[23] and as some modern scholars have asserted more
generally of the hero's portrayal in the poem, we must concede that he has
been singularly clumsy about it. Even given the choice of detail with which
Walter contextualizes Talestris's arrival, he could have omitted Bagoas
altogether; and even given Bagoas's presence, Walter surely could have
spared him the epithet "molly." If we choose to ignore the text's signposts
toward Alexander's gender and sexuality, we can only rescue Alexander's
normative virility by casting aspersions on Walter's competence to produce the effects critics have proposed he intended.

Omnibus hec populis, dorso quos Caucasus illinc
Circuit, hinc rapidi circumdat Phasidos amnis,
Iura dabat mulier. cui primo ut copia facta est
Regis, equo rapide descendit, spicula dextra
Bina ferens, leuo pharetram suspensa lacerto.   15

   The text's immediate valorizations of gender and sexuality as interpretive issues allow us, then, no facile dismissal of Talestris's entrance as
though its details were inevitable in the representation of the Amazon
queen, and so unworthy of sustained attention. Walter does indeed follow
Curtius's account very closely for the rest of the episode,[24] but details of
his adaptation depart tellingly from mechanical versification of the source.
The ensuing lines give particular emphasis to Talestris's gender by radically
splitting the nominative subject between the demonstrative *hec* of line 11
and *mulier*, line 13, at the final position in its sentence. The victorious
Alexander has just granted clemency to a parricide at the prompting of
his catamite; now a ruler who governs a wide territory described in some
geographical detail is emphatically asserted, at the last possible moment in

the sytactical unit, to be a woman. She swiftly dismounts and carries two javelins and a quiver with her to her audience with the king.

Vestis Amazonibus non totum corpus obumbrat.
Pectoris a leua nudatur, cetera uestis
Occupat et celat celanda, nichil tamen infra
Iuncturam genuum descendit mollis amictus.
Leua papilla manet et conseruatur adultis,   20
Cuius lacte infans sexus muliebris alatur.
Non intacta manet sed aduritur altera lentos
Prompcius ut tendant arcus et spicula uibrent.

Lines 16–23 present something like an ethnographical description.[25] If the attention to detail given the garb of the Amazons represents a kind of cultural tourism, the searing away of the right breast in childhood can be read as the inscription of their society's organization upon their bodies. In this context, Amazonian dress becomes a kind of gloss both supplementing and partially covering over the body-as-text. In that gloss, the dialectic of concealment and revelation, thematically announced in line 16—"the Amazons' garb does not veil the whole body"—unsettles any perceived naturalism of dress and its relation to the body's social meaning. The left breast—that left intact by Amazon society—is revealed; their garments cover "the rest," and particularly, we are told, "conceal what ought to be concealed."

Perhaps the phrase *celat celanda* merely provides a poetic variation on the preceding *cetera occupat*; Walter has added it to an otherwise close paraphrase of Curtius's corresponding sentence. But the nature of what must be concealed is here manifold. The exposure of the female breast already suggests that *celanda* means something significantly different to the Amazons than to Western society. *Celanda* clearly denotes the sexual organs and substitutes for another gerundive, *pudenda*. The text thus imputes universality to the prohibition against exposing the sexual organs. But the relation of *cetera* to *celanda* remains indeterminate and so leaves open the question of what, in the eyes of the Amazons themselves, must be concealed. At the end of line 19 we pass from the description of Amazon fashion to their practice of nursing children: females only, so that the boys both vanish from our sight and are the focus of our attention by yet another *praeteritio* (of which the missing term is this time not Curtius, but the reader's consciousness of gender as a binary opposition) and so to the cauterization of the right breast. In light of the sartorial gloss that has preceded the reading of the Amazon body, it is not clear whether the missing breast is simply part of the *cetera* which happen to be concealed, or part of the *celanda* that must be rendered invisible. Nor, if the absence of the breast is indeed a *celandum*, is it self-evident in whose eyes it is a site for potential shame: in those of Walter and his readers, or in those of the Amazons themselves.[26]

I read these lines as thus implicated not only in a tension between concealment and revelation, but more deeply in the gendered dialectic of sexual organs as lack or possession of the phallic signifier of cultural power.[27] Under concealment and revelation there lies the more fundamental grid of the male and female genitalia and the divergent meanings of their concealment. If the male sexual organs must be concealed, it is in order to keep the phallus veiled, and so to protect it against challenges to what Kaja Silverman has called the "dominant fiction" that the phallus as transcendent guarantor of power and cultural meaning is equivalent to the penis. Unveiling the phallus risks the beholder's recognition that phallic transcendence is hardly matched by "the" male organ's limitation and mutability.[28] If the female genitalia must be concealed, according to that same dominant fiction it is because the scandal of lack must be covered over. The ideology of patriarchy demands that we must understand sexual difference as what the female body is deprived of.

But the seared breast of the Amazon queen introduces a third term of difference into the obsession with the phallus or its absence as the binary opposition upon which gender is founded. The seared breast represents the construction of social power not upon a naturalized lack, a "castration" that is the always already given of female bodily existence, but rather upon a choice determined by the contingent norms of a given society, a choice by which the excision of the biologically natural effects not the deprivation of power, but an access to it. Talestris's cauterization *produces* the power of her socially determined subjectivity. Patriarchy maps its metaphor of "castration" onto the female body in order to secure the dominant fiction, but the lack it imputes remains figurative. Amazon society, by contrast, demands a literal and physically exacted deprivation, but it offers inclusion in the social body as compensation for that introduction of lack into the subject. I want to suggest that enormous conceptual strain is thus placed on a continued patriarchal reading of Talestris's body: by juxtaposing the patriarchal imposition of a figurative lack onto the subject with the Amazons' imposition of a literal one, the text problematizes the very notion of "castration" upon which the dominant fiction depends.

Talestris's cauterization is not simply a reverse "castration" by which the female aspires to hardness and is thus masculinized: Talestris remains very much a woman, coming to Alexander with the possibility of conception in mind, and capable of nurturing a child with the breast that her dress reveals. The concealment of the female *celanda* is refigured. No longer does that concealment mask an ontological "lack." It veils, rather, a socially determined lack that carries with it the consequence of socially constructed power. The bow and javelins wielded by the Amazons, those same weapons with which Talestris has already made her appearance before the Macedonian king, are the visible tokens of that power. Such weapons, in Alexander's eyes, might well stand for the phallus, but to Talestris, they are rather the tokens of her status as a woman inducted into Amazon society, and it is to her perspective that we will be more compellingly guided in the lines that follow.

> Perlustrans igitur attento lumine regem,
> Mirata est fame non respondere Talestris   25
> Exiguum corpus, taciturnaque uersat apud se
> Principis indomiti uirtus ubi tanta lateret.
> Barbara simplicitas a maiestate uenusti
> Corporis atque habitu ueneratur et estimat omnes,
> Magnorumque operum nullos putat esse capaces   30
> Preter eos, conferre quibus natura decorum
> Dignata est corpus specieque beare uenusta.
> Sed modico prestat interdum corpore maior
> Magnipotens animus, transgressaque corporis artus
> Regnat in obscuris preclara potentia membris.   35

The text now stands poised between a dominant fiction of male plenitude and a realization of Amazon "castration" as a positive term effecting the possibility of being-in-society. It is at the same time poised between the dominant fiction (that phallus and penis are one) and a space in which Talestris's own subjective vision of her self becomes articulable. If the text has regarded Talestris, up to this point, as the object of its gaze, Talestris now gazes back. In line 24, she "wanders over" the king with a careful eye and finds his scanty body lacking. In her silence she speculates—as she does not, explicitly, in Curtius's version—as to where the *virtus* of this man lies. In the Latin, even more than in the English of our own readings, the line between virtue and virility begins to blur as we ponder etymology, to say nothing of raw sound. Alexander's virtue, and with it his power and his manliness, hides somewhere Talestris cannot lay eyes on it. Talestris's silent contemplation focuses our attention on the fact that the emperor is indeed clothed—and for good reason. Her unspoken speculations as to what he may, or may not, have under the hood throws the notion of the phallus's veiled power back on itself. Her aporia ridicules the phallus precisely in its concealment. If Alexander's hidden parts aren't more impressive than what he shows off, she's clearly decided, then he's hardly the eighth wonder of the world she came to inspect.

A medieval audience was, if anything, more likely than a modern one to have grasped the comic incongruities of Alexander's position. Thomas Laqueur has traced in much detail the dominance of a so-called "one-sex" model of sexual difference in Western culture up until the late eighteenth century.[29] In a world where sexual difference, according to such a paradigm, signified greater or lesser perfection on a continuum, and where women were seen as beings possessing analogous sexual equipment to men's (but turned outside in as a sign of their inferior status), the signification of power by the phallus must have been even further valorized than it is for twentieth-century readers, who have simultaneous access to other conceptions of difference that have come to the fore since the Enlightenment—"two-sex" conceptions that, for better or worse, imagine sexual difference not as degrees of perfection ranking individuals along a single scale, but as a more fundamental dimorphism of somatic and psychological reality.

If the text allows such a rupture as I have delineated in the dominant fiction of phallic signification and power, if it opens such a space for the expression of Talestris's female subjectivity, it nevertheless moves immediately to contain the threat that this heterodox perspective represents. I am struck by the fact, however, that it circumscribes Talestris's alternatively gendered gaze as partial and inauthentic not in terms of sex, but, rather, generalizes upon the barbarian simplicity that fails to recognize the distinction of inward power from external appearance. Walter has introduced the dangerous possibility that Talestris's female subjectivity signifies a construction of gender in society alternative to Alexander's normative *virtus*. Now Walter negates that possibility by appealing not to gender, much less to sex, but to an ethnically marked distinction between hermeneutic sophistication and naive observation. Talestris fails to read Alexander's *virtus* appreciatively not because she is a woman, but because she is a barbarian. By thus reinforcing gender polemic with projections of cultural alterity, the text escalates its defense of Alexander. But, as is often the case, pulling out the big guns is perhaps here something of a sign of desperation; nor is the recognition of that desperation merely a reading of the text against its own monologic grain. Other passages in the *Alexandreis* also suggest a commingling of voices that undermines the privileging of any one among them. The indeterminacy of the poem's dialogic relations leaves the reader adrift to order their hierarchy, or not to do so, in the freedom of his or her own reception.[30] But, more specifically, the baldness of this representation of the ethnic Other, reflective of the text's position in the history of xenophobia in the West, creates for itself in nine lines perhaps as many difficulties as it lays to rest—difficulties I try to sketch out in the paragraphs that follow.

These lines assimilate the evaluation of the relation between body and inner virtue to the typological interpretation of the text: inside the bodily *integumentum* resides the mighty spirit, a kernel of meaning that the barbarian cannot grasp, but in which lies the body's true significance.[31] Yet in order to accumulate its assertions of the invisibility of inner virtue, the passage focuses precisely on that body which it chides Talestris for regarding without reference to what lies hidden within it. In nine lines the body appears four times (*corporis*, line 29; *corpus*, line 32; *corpore*, line 33; *corpore*, line 34), returning repeatedly even as the text urges the reader's understanding to transcend it, lest he or she, too, turn out to be a barbarian. Nor has this body yet escaped from the literal-minded gaze of Talestris against which Walter protests so profusely: the body is still represented as Talestris chooses to evaluate it, and the text merely reacts against this vision by negating it. Alexander's outward appearance lacks the "maiestas uenusti corporis" (the majesty of a lovely body); the positive term of this discourse remains the status of those "upon whom nature has seen fit to bestow a seemly body of charming appearance."

Notably absent here is any assertion, in contradiction of Talestris's gaze, that Alexander's male body is to be judged by a male standard of appearance. The language the text uses to suggest that prettiness isn't everything represents Alexander's physical presence in language more generally used of women: *venustas* is by both etymology and classical usage the property of Venus, not of Mars.[32] Talestris doesn't merely find the king lacking; she finds him lacking according to a standard by which women are judged, but here itself employed by a woman. Perhaps she would be more favorably impressed by her fellow Amazons. The defense of Alexander's inner majesty only serves to intensify the predicament in which Talestris's silent appraisal has left him.

According to categories aligned with post-Lacanian feminism, the defense attempts to shield the phallus from Talestris's single-mindedly physical, and so literal, gaze. If it succeeds in vindicating Alexander's possession

of the phallus as the transcendent signifier of power, it does so by deny-
ing the unproblematic equivalence of the phallus with the penis, of power
with the specificity of the male body. If Alexander's virtue is vindicated
at the expense of that virtue's straightforward connection with his physical stature, a crack has opened in the dominant fiction. "Mighty spirit"
must "transgress" the body's limbs in order to sustain its rule; "illustrious power" has retreated to a habitation *in obscuris membris*. Thus the text
leaves Alexander stuck on the horns of its dilemma.

It remains unclear, however, whether even here the phallus can rest
safe from Talestris's scrutiny. Her evaluation, at once cool and salacious,
may well continue to speculate as to just which obscure members have become the place of retreat. A hermeneutically informed understanding, of
course, would recognize that these members are figurative, and that the
body's types and shadows have their ending in the transcendent dwelling
place of virtue. But for a moment, learned reader, give Talestris her way:
like the queen she is, she will probably have it in any case. What if these
obscure members are themselves still physical? *Obscurus* is, in fact, in this
context a rather strange choice of words on Walter's part; and the entire
sentence is his free elaboration of his source. Its usual meanings run along
the lines of "gloomy, dark, obscure."[33] In Virgil, a grove is *obscurus*; the
night is *obscura*; of language, the word can mean obscure or incomprehensible. The *obscurum* is imperfectly known, uncertain, concealed from
knowledge. The word suggests only with some contortion the higher intelligibility of inward understanding. If these out-of-sight members are
physical, they are indeed covered over, and so darkened. We are back to
the organs, then, that earlier were described as universally *celanda*, requiring concealment. These may well be Alexander's private parts, the declared
goal of Talestris's sojourn: after all, she has come, as she will soon tell us,
specifically to be inseminated by the universal conqueror.

Even so, these organs are more than concealed; potentially, they are
unintelligible or indistinct, and as such they plausibly evoke Luce Irigaray's exploration of the indeterminacy of the female body.[34] Perhaps, if
these *membra* are physical, they belong to Alexander and still point ahead
to Talestris's imminent acquisition of what she's come for; but perhaps
they represent an alternative somatic correlative of power altogether. Perhaps they are the organs of Talestris's own fecundity—not only obscure in
their concealment, but *unheimlich* in the castration fear they engender in a
patriarchal subjectivity constituted in terror of the potential loss of phallic
power.[35] (Perhaps, indeed, this is an eruption of "two-sex" thinking against

the dominant ideology of the age.) These possibilities converge, at both interpretive and literal-narrative levels, in the climax of Talestris's appearance.

> Ergo rogata semel ad quid regina ueniret,
> Anne aliquid uellet a principe poscere magnum,
> Se uenisse refert ut pleno uentre regressa
> Communem pariat cum tanto principe prolem,
> Dignam se reputans de qua rex gignere regni   40
> Debeat heredes. fuerit si femina partu
> Prodita, maternis pocietur filia regnis.
> Si mas extiterit, patri reddetur alendus.
> Querit Alexander sub eone uacare Talestris
> Miliciae uelit. illa suum custode carere   45
> Causatur regnum. tandem pro munere noctem
> Ter deciesque tulit, et quod querebat adepta
> Ad solium regni patriasque reuertitur urbes.

Alexander wants to know whether Talestris has come to ask for something big. She replies straightforwardly enough. She wants to go back
home pregnant with a child sired by so great a prince. She judges *herself*
worthy to mother the offspring of Alexander. Her proposal is thoroughly
contractual: if the issue of this union is a woman (and a woman of rank,
femina, at that), she'll inherit the "maternal realms." A male child will
be returned to sender. The language is overwhelmingly loaded. Talestris's
daughter will emerge into the world a gendered being, born into a matrix
of social relations in which her standing is guaranteed by her mother and
her society.[36] Talestris's potential male offspring is scarcely even represented as her son: *mas* can apply to humans, animals, and even plants. This
child awaits an identity that, if it is imparted at all, will be received at the
hands of its father, to whom it will be restored "for sustenance."[37]

The fate of such a child is indeed precarious. Perhaps one can read the
gerundive *alendus* straightforwardly as "to be nourished." But it emphasizes just as plausibly that the child is in a state of requiring nourishment,
"needing to be nourished." How Alexander will accomplish this in the absence of the child's mother is unclear. Of course, he will provide the boy
with a wetnurse, but in the framework of the entire episode's continuous
focus on the physical, I cannot but attend to the fact that here Talestris's
own source of power, entirely outside the discourse of the phallus, comes
to the margin of awareness. Talestris's left breast is capable of nurturing
her daughter, as her right arm displays the prowess that will guarantee that
daughter's position in Amazon society. Alexander must rely, for the nour-

ishment of the male child that may come of this union, upon an unnamed and unacknowledged woman. That child will already have been born from Talestris's own *obscura membra*, whose power depends on no tenuous relay between the body and its concealment of *virtus*: her literal body is itself its own power, in need of no act of tropological alienation.

Talestris thus refuses to look beyond Alexander's physical stature for what she is seeking not out of arbitrarily and willfully bad hermeneutics, but out of knowledge and choice. She knows what she wants from the start, and her search for a somatic *virtus* (a *muliertas*, if you will) will not be diverted, either by the defensive tactics of the (possibly disingenuous) narrator or by Alexander's own initial parry of her request: immediately following her proposal, Alexander changes the subject, in what looks very much like a counter-offer. Would the Amazon not like to make some time for warfare under *him* (*vacare sub eo*, where Curtius had read *cum ipso militare*, to fight *with* him)? Falling back once again on figurative language as a defense of his prowess, Alexander devises a way to make sure he remains on top, at least metaphorically: whether he will be able to maintain that relation in a more physically constituted relationship, like the one Talestris proposes, is perhaps a more open question. But Talestris, in a rather lady-like gesture allowing the gentleman to save face, pleads a previous engagement: her kingdom, without her, would lack a guardian. "At last, as a gift, she carries the night thirteen times, and having gained what she was seeking, returns to her kingdom's throne and to the cities of her ancestors."

Talestris has clearly won this combat for discursive space, which has rather unobtrusively raged for forty-eight lines of an epic generally read in the twentieth century, when read at all, as an inscription of the dominant cultural values of its time. She does not merely receive the gift of thirteen nights; she carries them one by one, each encounter with Alexander an active exercise of her choice. Finally, with supreme irony, she returns to her *patrias urbes*. What can this (yet another detail Walter adds gratuitously to Curtius's version) possibly mean, in a society that is not merely matrilineal, but exclusively female? In both prose and verse, I have rendered *patrias* as "ancestral"; R. Telfryn Pritchard, in his prose translation, gives his reader "native."[38] But how, in idiomatic English, might we capture the jarring incongruity of a term at the center of whose connotation lies fatherhood as conceived by the tribes of Latium?

One answer is straightforward enough, given the context: Talestris has it all. By biological fact, the Amazons all have fathers. That those fathers are rendered invisible and absent in Amazon society suggests that in Talestris's social discourse it is *she* who represents the Lacanian Name-of-the-Father and so wields the phallus that is its signifier. The fiction of any natural correspondence of the phallus to male anatomy is shattered. In its abjection from phallic signification, the penis has become the unspeakable term of human intercourse, as are the female genitalia in the patriarchal world into which she has made her brief counterinsurgence. Behind the catachresis of the notion that the Amazon cities could be "paternal" lies another trope. By synecdoche the paternal function is here absorbed into the maternal, which is thereby universalized. In much the same way, though with reversed polarity, patriarchal discourse has long insisted that the universalizing language of "man" incorporates the experience of women.

Talestris would thus bring forth her subjectivity out of a most unlikely context, but only at the price of fulfilling, on another level, the deepest stereotypical fear of patriarchy, that female power inevitably carries with it the threat of male castration. Another possibility is perhaps in the first instance born of my own desire, but not at the expense, I'd still maintain, of the text's integrity. Talestris has indeed shattered the illusion of any natural correspondence between the Law of being-in-society and the particulars of male anatomy. But the foreclosure she effects appears as castration only from within that illusion of the equivalence of phallus and penis. In contrast to what the text fears that she threatens to take away, and to what Alexander himself seems to fear in his counter-offer to take the queen on as a sidekick in combat, she offers Alexander that same physicality with which she insists on regarding him. Even as she puts the phallus in jeopardy, she holds out to Alexander the reality of his body, and the pleasure of thirteen nights with a real woman whose spear stands propped in the corner, and whose body itself bears the marks of her prestige. The text gives no indication that he can or does recognize such an offer for what it is. He is perhaps too obsessed with *aliquid magnum*, some big thing he should be bestowing out of his own turgid sense of largesse. But Talestris resolutely puts forward what to patriarchy is as much a scandal as the threat of castration. She makes it clear that she has indeed come for what Alexander has below the belt, but on her terms, not his. In so doing, she ultimately unveils not the phallus, but rather the penis, the sign not of transcendent power but of the male body's partiality and contingency. She offers Alexander a freedom that he appears unable to accept.

At the same time, her offer does suggest an alternative explanation for her return to the *patrias urbes*. Perhaps, by insistently calling the body the body, and by resisting the metaphorical identifications that crush somatic reality under the weight of cultural significations, Amazon society offers a space for an alternative male subjectivity, one in which fatherhood signifies not power and disembodiment, but the body's real presence. The *Historia de preliis* describes the carefully controlled circumstances under which the Amazons come together with the men of their race.[39] Nothing in the account suggests the subjugation of the men. Walter, to be sure, chose here to follow Curtius instead; but the *Historia*'s alternative account, as we have already seen, remained accessible to a range of contemporary readers, as surely as did Curtius at those points where Walter departed from him.

Still, in the *Historia de preliis* I cannot find the presence of men, and so my own presence as embodied reader, *within* Amazonia itself. Nor can I find it in later medieval accounts. In the late fourteenth century, in *The Book of the City of Ladies*, Christine de Pizan described the founding of the Amazon state as the reconstitution of a society in which men had previously made great slaughter.[40] Perhaps we should count Christine, one of the most erudite women of her day, among Walter of Châtillon's readers: by her time, the *Alexandreis* had been a standard of the literary curriculum for nearly two centuries. So I have to go still further afield in search of Amazon men.

I have to shift to my own horizons and leap from twelfth-century epic to twentieth-century feminist science fiction. In *The Gate to Women's Country*, Sheri S. Tepper constructs her own cities of women, peopled by the descendants of those who survived a nuclear holocaust. Beyond the town walls lie the garrisons—a militaristic, exclusively male culture where men in touch with the Warrior Within can chant and drum to their hearts' content.[41] In Women's Country only a few "soft" males find a place. Reproduction is assured for both communities by carefully controlled periods of mating between the women's and men's societies, and mothers surrender the male offspring of these unions to their "warrior fathers" at the age of five. At age fifteen, the boys choose whether to become warriors or to return through the Gate to Women's Country. But the zealously guarded secret of Women's Country is that the fathers of the children these unions ostensibly produce are not the testosterone-poisoning cases encountered at the semiannual carnivals. The true fathers are the men harbored within Women's Country itself. Rejects and refugees of the dominant patriarchy that supposes itself the source of life, they are possessed of their own concealed and tenderer strengths.

Tepper's vision poses its own problems. Her women govern their cities by elitist meritocracy, and with very little humor. Her elimination of male aggression by sustained selective breeding explains sexual oppression by appeal to a crudely essentialist biologism. By that same blithe faith in genetics she dismisses diversity of sexual preference as a treatable hormone imbalance. In any case, Talestris's society is, of course, not Women's Country. But it does appear to be a place where everyone knows what women want, and where men who learn the answer to that vexed question perhaps also find the reality of their own embodiment.

Walter of Châtillon was no feminist. The *Alexandreis* is no feminist text. But it *is* a work of remarkable and underappreciated subtlety, and its commingling of voices allows a great deal to slip through the gaps of its construction. If it celebrates Alexander, it does so with continuously ironic qualification. If it purports, however half-heartedly, to defend him from Talestris's momentary gaze, it creates room for her to speak in the gaps between its dialogically juxtaposed languages. How many medieval readers of the poem may have heard her voice? Perhaps no one can answer that question definitively. If the copious surviving glosses on the poem settle the matter, the answer lies in a manuscript I have not seen, and whose annotations are not printed. Clearly, at least some people in the twelfth century *were* capable of appreciating a dirty joke. Some could perceive the margins around normative masculine identity, as the copious eleventh- and twelfth-century literatures against and in favor of homosexual activity attest—margins that the literature of romance was also exploring in a generally heterosexual context.[42] Then, as now, such a reading might well have struggled against an orthodox reception of the text. Finally, the twelfth century I imagine as a modern reader includes, after all, Eleanor of Aquitaine (or at least, as on a palimpsest, the divine Katherine Hepburn in bogus Plantagenet drag) dressing her women as Amazons and riding barebreasted halfway to Damascus. If I write, willfully enough, my own gloss on Walter, I expect that it will be covered over in its turn. Mine, too, is another voice in the margin of his text.

Notes

This essay first appeared in slightly different form in *University of Toronto Quarterly* 64,2 (Spring 1995): 255–73. It is reprinted by permission of the University of Toronto Press.

1. James Goldman, *The Lion in Winter*, 43.
2. Kenneth Clark, *Civilisation: A Personal View*, chap. 2.
3. D. D. R. Owen, *Eleanor of Aquitaine: Queen and Legend*, esp. 148–52.

4. Ibid.; Benoit de Sainte-Maure, *Le Roman de Troie*, line 23,357 and following.

5. H. Christensen (*Das Alexanderlied Walters von Châtillon*, 10) dates the composition of the poem to 1176–1182; A. C. Dionisotti ("Walter of Châtillon and the Greeks," 90–6) argues for substantial completion by 1176.

6. The verse translation is my own: *The Alexandreis of Walter of Châtillon: A Twelfth-Century Epic*. This chapter glosses not my translation, itself an interpretation of the text, but the Latin original of lines 8.1–48 as they appear in *Galteri de Castellione Alexandreis*, ed. Marvin Colker (hereafter cited as Colker, *Alexandreis*), 199–201. My readings will suggest aspects of Walter's text from which the translation may be seen to diverge. The reader of this chapter will have to weigh my rendering dialogically against the exposition provided in the following pages. For easier cross-reference, I have provided line numbers against the verse translation, corresponding to the quoted blocks of the Latin text.

7. Helen Waddell, *The Wandering Scholars*. Walter's rhythmical verses have been available in good editions for generations, thanks to *Moralisch-satirische Gedichte Walters von Châtillon*; the *Alexandreis* subsequently waited fifty years for Colker's services.

8. Walter of Châtillon, *Tractatus contra Judaeos*.

9. For a census of surviving manuscripts, see Colker, *Alexandreis*, xxxiii–xxxviii; for the glossing tradition, see R. DeCesare, *Glosse latine e antico-francese all' "Alexandreis" di Gautier de Châtillon*. For excerpts from the glosses of four manuscripts, see Colker, *Alexandreis*, 277–514.

10. Colker, *Alexandreis*, xviii–xx.

11. John R. Williams, "William of the White Hands and Men of Letters."

12. *Quintus Curtius*, ed. and trans. John C. Rolfe, 2 vols.

13. For Walter's sources, see the summary by R. Telfryn Pritchard in the introduction to his prose translation of the poem, 11–14.

14. E.g., Max Manitius, 3: 924–25; Otto Zwierlein, *Der prägende Einfluss des antiken Epos auf die "Alexandreis" des Walter von Châtillon*, 87 et passim.

15. E.g., Christensen, *Das Alexanderlied*, 102–64.

16. F. J. E. Raby (*A History of Secular Latin Poetry in the Middle Ages*, 2: 79) denies any engagement with current affairs; asserting the resonance against contemporary events are Henriette Harich (*Alexander Epicus: Studien zur Alexandreis Walters von Châtillon*, 2–3) and Maura Keyne Lafferty ("Reading Latin Epic: Walter of Châtillon's *Alexandreis*," 163–89).

17. I use the term "Orientalism" loosely to include the antecedents of a discourse that Edward Said's seminal treatment *Orientalism* represented as achieving full coherence only centuries later. Much textual evidence suggests that this discourse had already attained considerable impetus and efficiency before the age of modern empires or, indeed, before the European onslaught on the Americas. The term's application in the twelfth century is further complicated by the fact that so much of the ideology's force derived from the application of ethnography to peoples on the northern and western peripheries of Europe (see Robert Bartlett, *Gerald of Wales, 1146–1223*, esp. 157–210 on ethnography).

18. R. Telfryn Pritchard, ed. and trans., *The History of Alexander's Battles: His-*

toria de preliis—The J₁ Version; George Cary (*The Medieval Alexander*) provides an account of the rich and varied development of the Alexander tradition in the centuries before and after Walter.

19. Pritchard, *Alexandreis*, 10.

20. Cf. *Metamorphoses* 13.578–79; *Aeneid* 4.584–85 and 9.459–60.

21. David Townsend, "*Mihi barbaries incognita linguae*: Other Voices and Other Visions in Walter of Châtillon's *Alexandreis*."

22. Gloss printed in Colker, *Alexandreis*, 458; the translation is mine.

23. The glossator of the Vienna manuscript, in fact, seems especially eager to point out the possibility of homosexual elements in the legend and then to commend Walter for his omissions. A gloss on 2.437 is even plainer about it: "*conscius archanis* quia simul peragebant uicium sodomiticum. Vel *conscius* aliis rebus archanis et melius secundum propositum auctoris quoniam auctor celat in hoc libro que sunt celanda" (Colker, 384) (*conscious of his secrets* because at the time they were committing the vice of Sodom; or *conscious* of other secret matters, and better thus according to the author's intention, since in this book the author conceals those things which ought to be concealed). On the resonance of the glossator's phrase "celat . . . celanda" with the passage I discuss here, see below.

24. Curtius, 6.v.24–32.

25. On the classical precedents for Walter's inclusion of such detail, see Richard F. Thomas, *Lands and Peoples in Roman Poetry: The Ethnographical Tradition*; on the ideological implications of appeals to ethnography in the late twelfth century, see n. 17 above.

26. At this juncture I want to juxtapose with my reading the current politics of breast cancer and mastectomy. The *New York Times Magazine* for 15 August 1993 ran Susan Ferraro's essay "The Anguished Politics of Breast Cancer" as its lead story, using for its cover illustration one of the poster-sized photographic self-portraits of New York artist Matuschka. Strongly sidelit, head swathed in white fabric blown by an off-camera fan, the subject looks to her left with some introspection and wistfulness but holds her arms at an angle of self-assurance. The conventions are those of fashion photography, but the low-backed white dress is skewed to reveal the scar of a radical mastectomy, with the caption, "You can't look away any more." Matuschka's work has been more recently and extensively featured in Delaynie Rudner, "The Censored Scar."

About the time I wrote this chapter, a friend was struggling to decide on her treatment after a lumpectomy, and I remembered Matuschka's image as one of extraordinary courage, combined with uncompromising self-assertion. Perhaps I also respond to it because its shocking appropriation of a commercialized aesthetic employs the same tactic as the AIDS imagery collective Gran Fury in the late 1980s and early 90s: AIDS (unlike breast cancer) is a health risk in which I have a first-person stake. In any case, the scandal of the image exposes what Alexander, and perhaps Walter, would sooner drape in cloth.

27. Jacques Lacan, "The Signification of the Phallus."

28. Kaja Silverman, *Male Subjectivity at the Margins*, 15–51. See also Charles Bernheimer, "Penile Reference in Phallic Theory."

29. Thomas Laqueur, *Making Sex: Body and Gender from the Greeks to Freud*.

30. Townsend, *"Mihi barbaries,"* 26–28.

31. Carolyn Dinshaw has been among the more recent to trace the conventionally gendered distinction of (carnal/feminine) letter and (spiritual/masculine) typology in the Pauline tradition (*Chaucer's Sexual Poetics*, 21–22).

32. Cicero, *De officiis* 1.130: "cum. . . pulchritudinis duo genera sint. . . uenustatem muliebrem ducere debemus, dignitatem uirilem." (OLD, s.v. *venustas*, def. 2). Walter has heightened the effect of Curtius, who uses the word *corpus* only once in the source passage, and *venustas* not at all.

33. OLD, s.v. *obscurus*.

34. Luce Irigaray, "This Sex Which Is Not One."

35. Sigmund Freud, "The Uncanny."

36. Some readers may join me in remembering the ecstatic shouts of Joannie Caucus's day-care charge Ellie (in *Doonesbury* in the early 70s) on hearing the news of her sister's birth: "It's a woman! It's a baby woman!" (Gary Trudeau, *"And What Do We Have for the Witnesses, Johnnie?"*)

37. This problem of the indeterminate identity of the male child might well provide an entrée into a wider gendered reading of the poem as a whole, since it gathers into the discussion Alexander's own obsessions with parentage, often suppressed by Walter but abundantly present in the intertext against which the poem presses: plagued by the rumors of his own illegitimate status as the child of the sorceror Nectanabus, he compensates by his concern to gain the title "son of Jove"—a title which by the end of the poem constitutes a principal indication of the hubris that will bring him to the unfavorable, and fatal, attention of the goddess Natura.

38. Pritchard, *Alexandreis*, 180.

39. Pritchard, *The History of Alexander's Battles*, 77–79.

40. Christine de Pizan, *The Book of the City of Ladies*, 40–41.

41. Sheri S. Tepper, *The Gate to Women's Country*.

42. John Boswell, *Christianity, Social Tolerance, and Homosexuality: Gay People in Western Europe from the Beginning of the Christian Era to the Fourteenth Century*, 207–302. The romances of Chrétien de Troyes are predicated on the double binds of masculine identity; in *Erec and Enide*, in particular, the social perils of excessive sexual love, however licit its context, dominate the narrative (*The Complete Romances of Chrétien de Troyes*, 31–35).

The Color of Salvation

Desire, Death, and the Second Crusade in Bernard of Clairvaux's *Sermons on the Song of Songs*

Bruce Holsinger

In the introduction to *A History of Anglo-Latin Literature, 1066–1422*, his magisterial survey of Latin literary production in the British Isles from the Norman Conquest to Henry V, A. G. Rigg characterizes the book's project as it relates to one of many daunting tasks still facing medieval Latinists:

> In 1612, after several voyages to what is now Canada, Samuel Champlain drew a map. In light of what we know now, it was not a very good map (in fact, he revised it later); its outlines were vague and its depictions of the hinterland negligible. He could probably have made a better map; if he had consulted all the natives and explored all the inlets and creeks, he would have made a very good map indeed, but he would probably never have lived long enough to complete it. This book is a bit like Champlain's map. It suffers from too sketchy a knowledge of the primary sources and even more from too little reading in secondary works. It is full of hasty generalizations, even prejudices. It is, however, a map of sorts, and, as such, it is something that has not been available before. The absence of explorers in post-Conquest Anglo-Latin literature is largely explained by the lack of any sort of guide, however inadequate. I hope that my rough sketch map—even in four hundred pages it is scarcely more than an outline—will encourage others to enter the territory and to describe it more thoroughly.[1]

Imagining himself as a colonial cartographer, Rigg encourages others to follow in his path by casting Anglo-Latin literature as an unknown land and people to be mapped and known through intellectual labor. As "explorers" in this uncharted literary "territory," medievalists are invited to consult "the natives," the texts themselves, in hopes of filling in the blank spaces that remain in the book's "rough sketch map" of the past.

Rigg clearly intended his extended metaphor as nothing more than a self-effacing admission of his study's potential biases and oversights. Yet it is perhaps no coincidence that he chose to cast his project in colonialist terms, for in its bold recovery of a specific literary tradition—"post-Conquest Anglo-Latin literature"—the book posits a *terminus a quo* that foregrounds the historical status of that very tradition as an ecclesiastically privileged discourse of colonialism. Though Rigg would undoubtedly be the first to eschew the metaphorical innocence he attributes to his subject, in other words, the terms of the metaphor beg the question of how Latin itself served as a colonialist idiom for a variety of medieval individuals and institutions intent upon staking their claims to dominion over foreign lands and populations. Indeed, Robert Bartlett has recently suggested that the historical trajectory of the western Middle Ages more generally represents a *longue durée* of "conquest and colonization" that gradually consolidated the geographical identity of Europe by the late fourteenth century. Building on his earlier study of medieval "colonial aristocracies,"[2] Bartlett argues that the doubling in size of Latin Christendom between 950 and 1350 can be attributed in large part to a continuous process of invasive expansion—the establishment of colonial bishoprics, religious houses, and aristocratic fiefdoms—through numerous western incursions into the eastern Mediterranean.[3] The Crusades, in particular, were characterized by a "supra-national quality" that transcended linguistic differentiation and, when successful, symbolized the global triumph of Latin Christendom—in the words of Matthew Paris, the ascendancy of the "Latin race" (*gens latina*).[4] While the study of the literature of European imperialism and colonialism since the early modern period has focused primarily upon vernacular writings, then, we should recognize that these specifically nationalist discourses stand at the end of a diverse and venerable tradition of Latin textuality that served to support or memorialize *pre*- or *proto*-nationalist colonial regimes. It may be no exaggeration to say that the most enduring "imagined community" in the Middle Ages, in Benedict Anderson's influential phrase, was constituted precisely by Latin, one of "the sacred silent languages . . . through which the great global communities of the past were imagined."[5]

The following pages will suggest that it was just such a global imagination that inspired the Latinate hermeneutical labors of Bernard of Clairvaux at a significant point during the composition, compilation, and publication of his *Sermones super Cantica canticorum*. In the following passage, taken from the twenty-seventh Sermon, Bernard comments on the scriptural image of the *pelles Salomonis* (skins of Solomon, Song of Songs 1:4) in an attempt to consolidate the written authority of his own hermeneutical performance through the *auctoritas* of biblical and patristic citation. Though a typical gesture in the medieval commentary tradition, Bernard casts his intepretative net particularly widely:

> Do you not now see what heavens Ecclesia possesses within her, that she herself, in her universality, is an immense heaven, stretching out "from sea to sea, and from the river to the ends of the earth"? . . . Just like our mother above, this one, though still a pilgrim, has her own heaven: spiritual men outstanding in their lives and reputations, men of genuine faith, unshaken hope, generous love, men raised to the heights of contemplation. . . . They proclaim the glory of God, and stretched out like skins [*pelles*] over all the earth, make known the law of life and knowledge written by God's finger into their own lives, "to give knowledge of salvation to his people." They show forth [*ostendunt*] the gospel of peace, because they are the skins of Solomon.[6]

This vivid image of the Church's global reach resonates with Augustine's well-known description of the *Liber celestis* in *Confessions* 13:

> You know, O Lord, how you clothed men with skins when by sin they became mortal. In the same way you have spread out the heavens like a canopy of skins, and these heavens are your Book, your words in which no note of discord jars, set over us through the ministry of mortal men. Those men are dead, and by their death this solid shield, the authority of your words delivered to us through them, is raised on high to shelter all that lies beneath it.[7]

If Bernard had this passage in mind when fashioning his own model of Christian dominion, he nevertheless recasts its imagery in important ways. For Augustine, the *pelles* stretched over the earth constitute the "solid shield" of God's authority, its timelessness and perdurance. In Bernard's imagination, however, these same skins represent the temporal authority of the Church as embodied in the redemptive actions of its preachers and law givers. The nature of this authority is indicated by Bernard's citation from Psalm 72, which enjoins the "enemies" of God to "lick his dust" (*pulverem lingent*) and "all kings [to] fall down before him, all nations [to] serve him" (Psalm 72:8–10). The result is a hermeneutical crystallization of text, body, and dominion in which God's finger literally inscribes "the law" of Scripture onto the *living* bodies—not, as in Augustine, the dead skins—of "spiritual men," who themselves are both contained within the womb of Ecclesia and stretched like "skins of Solomon" across the surface of the earth. Figuring writing as a discourse of *auctoritas* encompassed within the female body of Ecclesia but transmitted by the skins and lives of men, Bernard imagines a textual community of writing, reading, and dissemination in which his own texts play a defining role. Paradoxically, then, even as Bernard lovingly explicates the Bible within the intimate space of the cloister, he casts the *Sermons on the Song of Songs*—one of the founding texts of affective spirituality and long regarded as a hallmark of the new spirit of interiority characterizing twelfth-century religious practice—as a work of truly global pretensions, a text seeking to provoke in its readers and auditors the desire for Christian dominion "over all the earth."

To say this, however, is not to reduce the *Sermons* to functionalist propagandism, as though they were written with Christian conquest as their sole or even primary aim. The following pages will focus for the most part on Bernard's engagement with a single biblical verse through just six of the eighty-six sermons in the cycle. As we shall see, however, the abbot's extended meditation on this verse's perplexing imagery recruits religious devotion within a monastic community into the service of a universalizing production of gendered desire and racialized violence that ultimately subsumes the more local resonances of his predicatory exegesis. By moving back and forth between Bernard's idiosyncratic explication of the Song of Songs and the politicized context in which the *Sermons* themselves circulated, I hope to account for both the public Bernard sought to interpellate as well as the audience that actually received and read his texts.[8] In both cases, I will suggest, Bernard sought to produce an eroticized longing for conquest, incorporation, and sacrifice at a historical moment in which Latin Christendom, in his eyes, desperately needed to ideologize its everyday practices and rituals toward the reconquest and continued colonization of the Holy Land.

Any inquiry into the political implications of Bernard's devotional works must engage with one of the enduring cruces of Bernardine studies: what John Sommerfeldt has identified as "the inconsistency between Bernard's description of the proper epistemological method and social role of the monk and his own intellectual activity and apostolate."[9] For Sommerfeldt himself, this seeming inconsistency does not impinge on the abbot's devotional and pedagogical writings: "Bernard's activity in the world does not contradict his sociological and epistemological principles which separated the ways of life, spheres of activity, and means to truth of monk, secular cleric, and layman. Bernard's own life is explicable in terms of his theory but did not correspond with the general lines of it."[10]

The particular "means to truth" Sommerfeldt refers to here is, of

course, "monastic theology," a phrase coined by the modern dean of Cistercian studies, Dom Jean Leclercq, as a means of expressing the inward,
ruminative flavor of Cistercian thought and spirituality.[11] For Leclercq,
monastic theology represents an eschewal of the worldly concerns of bishops, schoolmen, and the laity in favor of contemplative deliberation and
an intensive concentration on the soul's journey to God. Leclercq's notion
of monastic theology is only one of many attempts to separate Bernard's
inner devotional life from the vagaries of his political life; as Adriaan Bredero notes, this same tension between the introverted contemplative and
the extroverted polemicist, the loving abbot and the "chimerical" politi-
cian, has for centuries shaped the outlines of the scholarly literature both
on Bernard himself and on Cistercian religiosity more generally.[12]

Nowhere in Bernard's oeuvre does the political appear more estranged
from the devotional than in the *Sermons on the Song of Songs*, which Michael
Casey has recently dubbed "the supreme example of monastic theology," an
understandable appellation given the way in which Bernard himself casts
the mode and purpose of his sermonizing.[13] Bernard returned to Clairvaux from Rome in 1138 after helping to resolve a bitter and long-standing
dispute at the Curia between Innocent II and his rival, Anacletus II (the
"Lion" referred to below). Soon afterward he resumed the sermon cycle,
writing his return from Rome to Clairvaux into the opening rhetoric of
sermon 24:

On this third return from Rome, my brothers, a more merciful eye has looked
down from heaven and a more serene countenance has smiled on us. The Lion's
rage has cooled, wickedness has ceased, the Church has found peace. . . . I have
been granted to your desires. . . . And because you wish me to continue the sermons I began a while back on the Song of Songs, I gladly acquiesce, thinking it
better to resume where I broke off than to commence with something new. (24.1)

Bernard casts the act of sermonizing as a turn away from the public
sphere of papal politics and toward the cloistered intimacy of the monastery, from the affairs of worldly governance he disingenuously describes
as "inconsequential" (24.1) to the mundane affairs of his local community and the "desires" of his immediate auditors. An oft-cited example of
Bernard thinking the world out of his spirituality, this passage initiates the
second redaction of sermon 24, which he revised specifically to reflect his
return from Rome. Coming home thus furnished Bernard with the narrative *materia* for a new beginning that is at the same time a reassuring sign
of his sermons' continuity with the quotidian rhythms of life at Clairvaux.

We should be cautious, however, in allowing Bernard to convince us of the delimited provenance of his sermons. To take the most obvious example, Bernard wrote sermons 65 and 66 in direct response to a request by Everwin, provost of the Steinfeld Premonstratensians, for his help in stemming the rising tide of neo-Catharism in the Rhineland.[14] In sermon 65, commenting on the "little foxes" (*vulpes parvulae*) of the Song of Songs, Bernard makes clear that the implications of his preaching extend far beyond the walls of the cloister:

As far as our domestic vine is concerned—which is what you are—I think that in two sermons I have given you sufficient warning to protect you from the wiles of three kinds of foxes. . . . But it is not so with the vineyard of the Lord—that one, I mean, which encompasses the world, of which we are a part—a vine great beyond measure. . . . And the more I dwell on our domestic matters, the less use I am in matters of general concern. I am greatly troubled for that vine when I see the multitude of those who would spoil it, the number of its defenders, and the difficulty of its defence. (65.1)

While according to Bernard these heretical "foxes" should be defeated *non armis, sed argumentis*, his sermons functioned nevertheless as interventions in a highly politicized dispute that had already resulted in the burning of heretics by an orthodox mob after their unsuccessful bid for clemency in front of the Archbishop of Cologne.[15] Like Ecclesia, the "vine great beyond measure" is a *global* vine, threatened on all sides by its enemies; as such, it must be addressed even when preaching to a limited audience.

As Leclercq himself has argued, moreover (though with quite different results), we should resist privileging the ostensibly oral attributes of the *Sermons*—as though they exist in their present form as they were delivered in chapter—and acknowledge as well the power these works were accorded precisely as material texts, which was truly prodigious.[16] By Leclercq's (perhaps inflated) estimates, Bernard's works survive in some 1,500 manuscripts, many of which date from his own lifetime.[17] The *Sermons on the Song of Songs*, in particular, influenced continental culture across language, genre, and medium, inspiring iconographical creativity in manuscript illumination and the plastic arts and, in a few cases, even influencing the language of charters.[18] In the twelfth century alone, manuscripts of the *Sermons* were received and copied by houses of every major religious order as far east as present-day Poland, and by mid-century they had shown up in the libraries of many cathedral schools as well.[19] Perhaps most remarkably (and a fact to which I will return in concluding this chapter), more than half of the *Sermons* were translated into French at the turn of the century.[20]

Internal and external evidence tells us that the specific sermons considered here initiate a distinct cycle (sermons 24 through 49), that was emended by Bernard and published from Clairvaux no later than 1145.[21] This was a momentous year for Western Christendom.[22] Reports of the fall of Edessa in September of 1144 reached the newly elected Eugenius III in official form the following autumn, and as a former monk of Clairvaux under Bernard, the pope turned immediately to his former abbot for advice. Meanwhile, upon hearing of the threat to the Christian Jerusalem, King Louis VII consulted with Godfrey de la Roche, the bishop of Langres and also a former Cistercian, who blessed the king's decision to embark on crusade. Soon afterward, of course, Bernard himself preached the crusade at Vézelay to great approbation and, it would appear, with much success.[23] That so many current and former Cistercians were involved from the outset—not simply in preaching the Second Crusade, but also in making the very decision to initiate it—suggests that there may be more compatibility between "monastic spirituality" and such political endeavors than scholars have previously allowed.

As Bernard's internal reference to his 1138 return from Rome indicates, sermons 24 through 29 were originally composed prior to 1140, well before the launching of the Second Crusade. Despite many oblique references to contemporary politics throughout the *Sermons*, moreover, Bernard makes no explicit mention of crusading per se, a fact that has not been lost on Cistercian scholars invested in keeping Bernard's spirituality free from the taint of history.[24] As Penny J. Cole has recently pointed out in her study of crusade preaching, this modern tendency follows numerous medieval Cistercian efforts to dissociate Bernard "as far as possible" from the Second Crusade following its failure, a process that was helped along after the abbot's death by the probable destruction of documents attesting to his role in its instigation.[25]

Yet Bernard's thoughts had been directed to the Holy Land and the implications of crusading for at least a decade before these particular sermons began to be circulated outside of Clairvaux. The second half of *De laude novae militiae*, Bernard's treatise on the Knights Templar written between 1128 and 1131,[26] constructs an allegorical and tropological cartography of holy places in the East, culminating in a description of the "events at Jerusalem" that have "shaken the world": "The islands hearken, and the people from afar give ear. They swarm forth from East and West, as a flood stream bringing glory to the nations and a rushing river gladdening the city of God." Just as East meets West in Jerusalem, the Knights Templar themselves are "a multitude coming forth to reinforce the few" in their role as armed protectors of the western pilgrims and colonizers who followed in the wake of the First Crusade.[27]

Cole suggests that the notoriety of the *De laude* may have been partially responsible for Bernard's initial consultation by Eugenius about the advisability of the Second Crusade.[28] Perhaps so, for Bernard was certainly not consulted for his profound knowledge of either Islam itself or the nature of crusading warfare. Unlike his sometime friend Peter the Venerable, who was disgusted by the general ignorance of Islam among western Christians, Bernard seems not to have taken great pains to learn about the enemy he himself helped to invent. If, as James Kritzeck has argued, "Peter's warfare was single-mindedly against false doctrine, not against men,"[29] Bernard's was emphatically against both; as he writes in the *De laude*, "a new kind of knighthood . . . ceaselessly wages a twofold war both against flesh and blood and against a spiritual army of evil in the heavens" (1.1).

Before exploring in more detail the rhetorical and tactical efficacy of the *Sermons* within the cultural environment that produced the Second Crusade, I want to make several more general points about the ideological stakes of Bernard's allegoresis. Although the Song of Songs represents perhaps the ultimate biblical testimonial to heterosexual love and marriage, and though it was of course read throughout the Middle Ages as an allegory of the relationship between the masculine and the feminine—whether Christ and the human *anima* or God and Ecclesia[30]—for Bernard and many other commentators it served primarily as a means of contemplating relations between men. Thus Caroline Walker Bynum argues that the so-called "feminization of language" so characteristic of twelfth-century Cistercian piety functioned primarily to articulate male-male structures of authority and subordination.[31] More recently, Brian McGuire has described "Bernard's loves" as "circumscribed and so male-oriented that they eliminated even interest in what we call courtly love"; for McGuire, "Bernard enjoyed living in an all-male world and found more than sufficient emotional sustenance in his bonds with other men."[32] In the case of Cistercian devotional literature inspired by the Song of Songs, of course, these relationships of love and authority were articulated through the imagery of courtship, desire, and, ultimately, consummation between the Bridegroom and the Bride.

Indeed, nurture and sustenance were not the only supposedly "feminine" attributes Bernard located in the figure of the Bride. When Bernard lingers in the *Sermons* over particularly provocative verses—for example, "inter ubera commorabitur" (between the breasts he shall linger, 1:12); "amore langueo leva eius sub capite meo" (I languish in love, his left arm under my head, 2:5–6)—he of course speaks as the feminine *sponsa* or *anima*. But he also speaks as a man, one who yearns as passionately for union with the body of Christ as does the Bride for the Bridegroom on the literal level of the biblical text. Writing and preaching to other men, Bernard repeatedly encourages them to appropriate the eroticized role of Bride for themselves and fantasize *her* relationship with the Bridegroom as their *own*: to kiss Christ's body from head to toe, to penetrate him with their gaze, to be penetrated in turn and overcome by his love. At numerous moments in the *Sermons*, moreover, Bernard goes out of his way to stress the role of the body in this desirous dynamic: "[Our] souls have need of a body. Without it we cannot attain to that form of knowledge by which alone we are elevated toward the contemplation of truths essential to happiness" (5.1).

In *De diligendo Deo*, his treatise on the nature of human love for God, Bernard conceives of this union, in which body will rejoin the soul in an eternal embrace with Christ, as more perfect and pleasurable than that of the soul alone, almost suggesting, as Bynum has argued, that "body adds greater capacity for ecstasy to the soul"[33]: "The sick, dead, and resurrected body is a help to the soul who loves God; the first for the fruits of penance, the second for repose, and the third for consummation [*ad consummationem*]. Truly the soul does not want to be perfected [*perfici*], without that from whose good services it feels it has benefited."[34] As Bernard makes clear in his *Sermons*, the relationship between Bride and Bridegroom in the Song of Songs mysteriously prefigures the individual's nuptial *consummatio* with Christ. My point here is that we must separate the strictly heteronormative framework of the Song of Songs itself from the various modes of desire the biblical text enabled as it was glossed, allegorized, preached, and consumed in the Middle Ages, not all or even most of which desires were heterosexual. The feminization of religious language beginning in the twelfth century—and surviving in the writings of later poets such as Richard Crashaw and John Donne—was, in no uncertain terms, a *homoerotics* of religious language at the same time.[35]

Crucially, however, male-male relations in Bernard's *Sermons* are figured primarily through female bodies, whether that of Ecclesia, the Bride, or, in some cases, the Virgin. In this sense, they are "homosocial" relations, in Eve Kosofsky Sedgwick's influential term, that express "a desire to consolidate partnership with authoritative males in and through the bodies of females."[36] And in sermons 25 through 29, male homosocial relations are grounded specifically in a *black* female body. The Bride's words, "I am black but beautiful, daughters of Jerusalem, like the tents of Kedar, like the curtains of Solomon" ("Nigra sum sed formosa, filiae Hierusalem, sicut tabernacula Cedar, sicut pelles Salomonis"), provoke Bernard both to explore the somatic and ethical significance of skin color and to instill thereby a militaristic will in his readers to overcome the alterity that the Bride's blackness comes to represent. In this respect, I want to suggest, Bernard's rhetoric anticipates the tendency of later colonialist writings to deploy what Anne McClintock has recently termed a discourse of "porno-tropics," a "metaphysics of gender violence" in which female figures are "planted like fetishes at the ambiguous points of contact, at the borders and orifices of the contest zone."[37] As McClintock and others have shown, western regimes have often eroticized the geographical spaces they seek to colonize as ethnically or racially other female bodies, bodies whose sexual topographies are designed to provoke a collective desire for penetration and domination within the public that encounters them. For Bernard, however, unlike the many later writers, artists, and cartographers adduced by McClintock, it is the western male subject himself whose body paradoxically represents the ultimate object of colonialist desire. Enjoining his male readers to perform the objectified role of the Bride themselves, Bernard positions himself, his auditors, and the militant host his sermons address precisely as the abject victims of ethnic and religious violence, as blackened and feminized Christian subjects who must perform their own ravishment and defeat before they can hope to triumph. The erotics of Christian devotion and the desire for Christian dominion ineluctably converge as Bernard charts his hermeneutical path across an unfamiliar textual terrain.

As sermon 25 begins, Bernard attributes the Bride's subjection to slander in the Song of Songs by the "daughters of Jerusalem" directly to her blackness of skin: "I mentioned in the previous sermon that the bride was compelled to give an answer to her envious assailants, who seemed to be physically part of the group of maidens, but alienated from them in spirit. She said: 'I am black but beautiful, daughters of Jerusalem.' It would appear that they disparage and slander her on account of her blackness" (25.1). Despite the humiliating alterity of the Bride's blackness, however, Bernard immediately asserts that her darkened skin, like her feminine virtue, provides a model of patience, nurture, and humility for leaders: "Perfection of this kind is commendable for all, but is the model for prelates who wish to be worthy. Good and faithful superiors know that they have been chosen,

not for the vain prestige of holding office, but to take care of ailing souls"
(25.2). The simultaneous abjection and exemplarity inherent in blackness
produces a hermeneutical tension between "color" and "form," surface and
depth, a tension that Bernard incorporates into the redemptive frame of
his allegoresis:

> Let us next examine what was meant by saying: "I am black but beautiful." Is this
> a contradiction in terms? Certainly not. These remarks of mine are for simple per-
> sons who have not learned to distinguish between color and form; form refers to
> the shape of a thing, blackness is a color. Not everything therefore that is black is
> on that account ugly. For example blackness in the pupil of the eye is not unbe-
> coming; black gems look glamorous in ornamental settings, and black locks above
> a pale face enhance its beauty and charm. You may easily verify this in any number
> of things, for instances abound in which you will find beautiful shapes with dis-
> agreeable colors on the surface. And so the bride, despite the gracefulness of her
> person, is not without the stigma of blackness, but this is only in the place of her
> pilgrimage. (25.3)

Here Bernard articulates what we might call an epistemology of skin
color, one in which the knowability of corporeal signs is produced through
the categorical contrast between blackness and whiteness. But the two
sides of this coin are by no means equal, for blackness serves precisely to
bring out the essential beauty of whiteness: dark skin is a "stigma," black
hair a "disagreeable color" that nevertheless "enhance[s] the beauty of a
pale face." These colorized contrasts are refracted as well through alliterative and assonant oppositions in the Latin: for example, *decoloria* (discolored) and *decora* (lovely), *pulchritudine* (beauty) and *nigredinis* (blackness). Throughout the sermon Bernard also exploits the standard play on
forma and *formosa*: all black things, he asserts, are not *deforme* (ugly or
without form); they may also be *formosa* (beautiful). Beauty resides—mor-
phologically and empirically—in the form, but only the whiteness of a
"pale face" can serve to beautify this form in the material world.

This spectacular contrast between blackness and whiteness as articulated through corporeal signs proves to have profound moral and eschatological implications. Despite the Bride's blackness in "the place of her
pilgrimage," Bernard writes, "It will be otherwise when the Bridegroom
in his glory will take her to himself 'in splendor, without spot or wrinkle
or any such thing.' But if she were to say now that her color is not black,
she would be deceiving herself and the truth would not be in her" (25.3).
Bernard cites Ephesians 5:27 ("non habentem maculam aut rugam aut aliquid eius modi") to figure the black, wrinkled, and stigmatized body as the
earthly body, and the pure, smooth, and whitened body as the resurrection

body; the resurrection itself promises to erase "the stigma of blackness," the visible mark of the body's corruptibility.

The same verse is deployed in both the *Third Sermon for All Saints* and *On Loving God* to express the desire of the glorified soul for the resurrection body whose "spots" and "wrinkles" will disappear at the end of time.[38] In other places, Bernard figures the resurrection body as the white robe of Revelations, a robe dirtied with dust and discoloration (*maculam*) in its earthly form, but redeemed as pure, white, and immutable at the Resurrection; or as the "tent" (*tabernacula*) of Psalm 90, which "no sickness [shall] come near" after it is redeemed.[39] Bernard's imagery leaves little room for doubt: if the relationship between Bride and Bridegroom in the Song of Songs promises for its readers a consummational union with Christ at the end of time, the bodies that embrace will be *white* bodies, glistening and immutable. In this life, the very sight of blackness constitutes the eschatological promise of salvational incorporation precisely by reminding the Christian that it will be redeemed and, more insidiously, erased in the end.

But if the blackened body of the Bride is the ostensible focus of his exegesis, Bernard turns more frequently in these sermons to the exemplary trials, tribulations, and beauties of men:

Shall I point out to you a person at once both black and beautiful? . . . This was St. Paul. Daughters of Jerusalem, do you measure Paul in terms of his bodily presence, and despise him as blemished and ugly because you see only a runt of a man who has suffered hunger and thirst, cold and nakedness, the hardship of constant labor, countless beatings, often to the verge of death? These are the experiences that denigrate Paul; for this the Doctor of the Nations is reputed abject, dishonorable, black, beneath notice, a scrap of this world's refuse. (25.5)

Paul's exemplary blackness, Bernard suggests, derives from the abjecting trials of his earthly life, the deprivations he suffered while alive. Again Bernard's language is highly performative: Paul was reputed *inglorius, ignobilis, niger, obscurus*, a string of adjectives through which Bernard replicates the percussiveness of the physical and verbal beatings Paul endured at the hands of his tormentors by rhetorically hurling his own invective at the saint, an effect augmented through the anagrammatical beginnings (*ing-*, *ign-*, *nig-*) of the first three terms: just as form implies beauty, abjection and dishonor imply blackness. Paul's blackness, however, must be "merely external," for he was considered worthy to be "rapt into paradise" (25.5) during his earthly life.

Even the cross itself "involves the stigma of blackness," for "it is also in the pattern and the likeness" of Christ's body (25.8). Because this body was "pierced through for our faults [and] crushed for our sins," the humiliating physicality of Christ's Passion constitutes "the reason for his blackness" (25.8). Bernard asks his readers to "look steadily at him in his filth-covered cloak, livid from blows, smeared with spittle, pale as death: surely then you must pronounce him black" (25.9). "Pale as death" (*pallidum morte*), however, Christ's body during his earthly life is not literally black, stigmatized by darkened *pelles*. Solomon's, by contrast, decidedly is:

Solomon; I even embrace [*amplector*] Solomon himself under his black skin. For though Solomon seems black, it is only in the skin [*in pelle*]. Outwardly, in the skin, he is black, but not within. . . . Within is the shining whiteness of divinity [*divinitatis candor*], the graciousness of his virtues, the splendor of grace, the purity of innocence. But covering it all is the abject color of infirmity [*despicabilior infirmitatis color*] . . . I recognize here the form of our sin-blackened nature; I recognize those garments of skin that clothed our sinning first parents. [Christ] even brought this blackness on himself by assuming the condition of slave, and becoming as men are, he was seen as a man. (28.2)

Here again, black skin—whether shrouding Solomon or enveloping all of postlapsarian humanity and thus marking its fall from grace—represents a necessary but temporary aberration that endures only to be redeemed by the cleansing whiteness of salvation. Embracing Solomon in his imagination, Bernard does so only by reaching through and triumphing over his blackened *pelles*, which will ultimately be sloughed for the pure, essential, and enduring whiteness beneath. Throughout these sermons Bernard's rhetoric oscillates between a compassionate empathy for the suffering soul and an alienating objectification of the blackened body, both the Bride's and that of her typological progeny.

How are we to account for Bernard's insistent preoccupation with skin color in these six sermons? What did it mean in the mid-twelfth century to have an essentializing conviction that perfected bodies are white bodies, bodies that must shed their darkened skin in order to reach the whitened and resurrected state desired by the Christian subject? And finally, how might such representations be implicated in the public sphere in which the *Sermons on the Song of Songs* circulated?

First, it seems clear that skin color in twelfth-century Europe was not, in the words of Henry Louis Gates, taken as a sign "of ultimate, irreducible difference between cultures, linguistic groups, or adherents of specific belief systems" that the biologized notion of "race" has come to signify in modern formulations.[40] As Steven Kruger and John Friedman have shown, conversion to Christianity was often imagined in medieval literature as a metamorphosis of bodies from black to white, a transformation that exemplifies the perceived malleability of skin color in the period.[41] Yet as Bernard's rhetoric makes clear in no uncertain terms, it is *white* skin that represents the Christian ideal, an assumption that asks us to scrutinize the *Sermons on the Song of Songs* for what they reveal about, in bell hooks's phrase, "white identity and the way essentialism informs representations of whiteness." For hooks, the general inattention among scholars concerned with race and representation to the essentializing production of whiteness "enables the voice of the non-white Other to be heard by a larger audience even as it denies the specificity of that voice, or as it recoups it for its own use" in a quasi-cannibalistic "eating of the other" through cultural production.[42]

Hooks's particular formulation of this issue, of course, reflects her critical engagement with the culture and society of late capitalism; we should be cautious, to say the least, in seeking to illuminate twelfth-century constructions of "white identity" in theoretical terms that arise from specific contemporary struggles over race, class, and ethnicity. Despite these caveats, however, hooks usefully alerts us to the many senses in which western culture has hypostasized "whiteness"—particularly whiteness of skin—as purity, origin, and ideal through appropriative and abjecting representations of blackness; in so doing, she demonstrates that "white identity" in whatever form is often constructed precisely in opposition to an inessential, aberrational blackness taken on or sloughed at will. In this broader sense, the conjunction of color, voice, and identity in the *Sermons* is emphatically essentialist, part of an ancient strain in Christian theology casting the whiteness of the resurrection body as the very *absence* of color.[43] Starting with "*Nigra sum,*" two simple words spoken by the Bride in the Song of Songs, Bernard produces an elaborate metonymic spectacle in which black bodies are repeatedly and energetically gazed at, beaten, and penetrated, only to shed their darkened skin and reveal the underlying whiteness of the Christian soul and, finally, the resurrection body.

Bernard uses precisely these terms to characterize the temporal conflict between Christianity and Islam in the *De laude novae militiae.* In this earlier treatise, Bernard contends that Islam represents a "discoloration" of the pure whiteness of the earthly Jerusalem, and clashes of color embody the moral and military conflict between the two faiths and worlds. The Islamic hordes are led by "princes of darkness" (*tenebrarum principes*), while the Templars are enjoined to occupy the Temple of Jerusalem, which is "polluted" with the darkness of Islam, and "cleanse it and the other holy places of every un-Christian stain."[44] This imagery is characteristic of a more general moralizing use of color found in a number of mid-twelfth-century Latin religious works. In the popular *Vision of Tondal* (1149), devils appear "nigri sicut carbones" ("black as charcoal") as a mark of their distance from God.[45] In the *Scivias* (1141–51), Hildegard of Bingen recounts a vision of "black children" entering the womb of Ecclesia, moving through her body, and exiting her mouth "stripped [of] the black skin" and "clothed . . . in a pure white garment," "snatched from the Devil and restored to God."[46]

Somatic blackness was also deployed in this period specifically to stigmatize Muslims. As Ruth Mellinkoff has shown, dark skin consistently appears as a sign of the "belittlement and vilification" of Saracens in the medieval visual arts.[47] Bernard's images resonate in particular with a twelfth-century vernacular literary tradition in which the perceived contrast between the blackness of Islam and the whiteness of Christianity served explicitly as anti-Muslim propaganda. Perhaps the most influential examples of this phenomenon appear in the *Chanson de Roland*, one of the most violent and widely diffused pieces of anti-Muslim literature in the years surrounding the First Crusade.[48] Here the religious alterity of the Saracen Abisme, who "fears not God, the Son of Saint Mary," is writ large on his countenance: "Black is that man as molten pitch that seethes."[49] Roland himself gazes upon other such "misbegotten men," who appear "more black than ink is on the pen, / With no part white but their teeth."[50] Samir Marzouki has gone so far as to argue that for the *Roland* author skin color was "un indice moral ainsi qu'un indice social," in which the Saracen, "hâlé par le soleil, était considéré comme laid et par conséquent immoral."[51]

Similar imagery can be found in many other twelfth-century *chansons de geste*, part and parcel of a general paranoia over possible Muslim invasion of Europe. What Norman Daniel has termed the "barbaric Christian nationalism" of the *chansons*, which frequently cast cannibalism and the Christian rape of Saracen women in a favorable light,[52] constructs somatic contrasts between black and white with little regard for the regional and ethnic specificity of either Christian or non-Christian bodies. Thus the daughter of a Persian giant in *Maugis d'Aigremont* appears "plus noire que nuz charbons trieblez."[53] As in Bernard's sermons, many of the *chansons* represent whiteness as the essential or ideal state of the human body, while blackness can be erased or appropriated at will. In *Blancandin*, the hero "make[s] himself a Saracen" ("Sarrazin dist qu'il se fera") by rubbing his *visaige* with *une herbe*, after which he becomes "plus noirs que poiz bollie" ("darker than a boiled pea").[54] As Daniel suggests, the Saracen Balan in *Aspremont* may be represented as more conducive to conversion at the court of Charlemagne because he is already more fair-skinned than his companions.[55] And a Christian girl in male disguise darkens her skin to appear Saracen-like in *Floovant*.[56]

Nor were the *chansons de geste* the only vernacular works that represented religious and ethnic difference in terms of skin color. To take a well-known and particularly vivid example, Wolfram von Eschenbach's early thirteenth-century *Parzival* begins by likening humanity's moral state to "the color of a magpie": "The companion of disloyalty . . . has black for his color and takes on the shade of darkness. A man with steadfast thoughts clings to white."[57] In the same chapter, Gahmuret falls in love with Belakane, a Moorish queen "black of color"; when Belakane eventually gives birth to their son Feirefiz, the infant's skin is "of two colors. God had decided to work a miracle in him: he shone with colors white and black."[58]

As in Wolfram's image of the magpie, the intermingling of black and white, Saracen and Christian, is simultaneously a moralized contrast visible on the surface of the body itself. In several of these examples, moreover, the blackness of Saracens' skin is likened to the color of objects from the material world, such as boiled peas, charcoal, or pitch, in what Paul Bancourt has termed an "expressive comparison" strikingly similar to Bernard's characterization of the Bride's blackness in terms of black locks, gems, and "the pupil of the eye."[59] Equally prevalent are images of skin as black like ink on a page or pen, as in the *Roland* and *Maugis*; near the end of *Parzival*, when Parzival and Feirefiz are finally reconciled, the former likens his half-brother's skin to "a parchment written on, black-and-white here and there."[60] In these examples, the blackness of Saracen skin becomes a somatic simulacrum of the very act of writing, perhaps exposing an anxious awareness among Christian writers of the fictionality of the ethnic and religious essentialisms they themselves were inscribing. As we have seen, in the *Sermons* Bernard similarly exploits the conjunction between the parchment-like *pelles* of Ecclesia's book and the blackened *pelles* of the Bride, Solomon, and Paul.

Like many contemporary vernacular writers, then, Bernard imagines the contrast between blackness and whiteness not simply as a sign of difference between *individual* bodies, but also as a universalizing moral, political, and eschatological canvas on which to portray the global conflict between Christianity and Islam. Within this conflict, to paraphrase Judith

Butler, individual bodies come to "matter"—to materialize both ontologically and politically—precisely through their varying degrees of blackness
and whiteness, a scheme that constitutes the color not only of skin, but also
of clothing and armor as they cover bodies redeemed or bodies doomed.
When Bernard turns in the *De laude* (4.7) to the external appearance of the
Knights Templar (who, while dressed in undyed white like the *moines blancs*
themselves, "seldom wash and never set their hair"), he describes them in
their ideal state as "tousled, defiled with dust, darkened [*fusci*] by the sun
and their armor." Like the Bride, the soldiers are blackened by their earthly
tribulations, but white and gleaming underneath with the promise of salvation. For Bernard, as for the many vernacular poets whose works were
being performed just as the *Sermons* reached their initial audience, Islam
constitutes the temporarily polluting but ultimately redemptive stain on
the essential whiteness of Christianity, Holy Church, the earthly Jerusalem, and the Knights Templar themselves.

The globalized semiotics of color through which Bernard characterizes the relationship between Christianity and Islam in *De laude* resurfaces
in sermons 25 through 29 by means of an etymological connection found
in the literature of the early Church. Citing Jerome's treatise on Hebrew
names,[61] Bernard writes, "It is obvious that 'Kedar,' meaning darkness
[*tenebrae*], corresponds to blackness." *Tenebrae*, as we have just seen, is
the term that connotes the moral blackness of Islam in the *De laude*, and
Bernard reiterates this parallel in an impassioned effort to provoke desires
for militancy, conquest, and sacrifice in his text's public. Thus the opening
section of sermon 26 focuses on the blackened skin of the Bride in an explicit image of embodied warfare:

All must be able to see that tents can suggest the notion of darkness. For what is
meant by tents but our bodies, in which we wander as pilgrims? "For we have not
here a lasting city, but we seek one that is to come." We even wage war in them,
like soldiers in tents, like violent men taking the kingdom by force. In a word, "the
life of man upon earth is a warfare," and as long as we do battle in this body "we
are away from the Lord," away from the light. (26.1)

While the likening of *tabernacula* to *corpus* was a standard medieval
allegory, Bernard reads the temporality of this somatic tent through a chain
of metonymic associations—darkness-blackness, tents-bodies, pilgrimage-
holy war—that constitute a thinly disguised series of allusions to crusading, an act both individual and collective in which Christian soldiers seek
a "promised city," "take it by force," and "do battle in this body" in order

to escape their own bodily darkness for the whiteness of salvation. The crusading body is not a permanent home or native residence, but a peripatetic *tabernaculum*, an ever-present but mobile reminder of humanity's displacement from the true Holy Land above: "Our bodily dwelling-place therefore, is neither a citizen's residence nor one's native home, but rather a soldier's tent or traveller's hut. This body, I repeat, is a tent, a tent of Kedar, that now intervenes to deprive the souls for a while of the vision of the infinite light, permitting that it be seen 'in a mirror dimly,' but not face to face" (26.1). While the blackened body "intervenes"—while life in the body endures, in other words—the soul is prevented from achieving its desired goal of union with the divine.

Indeed, it is only through death itself—as well as the acknowledgment of its inevitability—that Bernard's rhetoric of militarism achieves the desirous intensity it seems to demand. Attempting to instill in his readers the will to "take the kingdom by force" at the opening of sermon 26, Bernard invites them to consider the indispensability of violent self-sacrifice in the most literal of senses. When "blackness appears on the body of the Church," as he puts it, "some souls long to die, that freed from the body, they may fly to the embraces of Christ. . . . A man such as this is aware that one cannot dwell in a tent of Kedar and lead a pure life, free of stain . . . without some degree of blackness [*quantulacumque nigredine*]; so he longs to die and be divested of it" (26.2). For Bernard, the devotional subject must "long to die," be willing to die and fly into the arms of Christ, in order to rid the body—and, more importantly, the "body of the Church"—of the "blackness" of affliction.

The "longing to die" that Bernard seeks to produce proves more than metaphorical, for in emendating his *Sermons* for distribution, Bernard chose to insert his moving elegy for his deceased brother Gerard at precisely this moment (26.3–14). The abruptness of Bernard's transition from exegesis to elegy appears at first glance to be a spontaneous sign of his affection, an involuntary interruption of the sermon's flow in which the abbot expresses the profound sense of loss he feels while "cast[ing] the clay over the body of him I loved, destined soon to be at one with the clay" (26.3): "We were of one heart and one soul; the sword pierced both my soul and his, and cutting them apart, placed one in heaven but abandoned the other in the mire. I am that unhappy portion prostrate in the mud, mutilated by the loss of its nobler part. . . . I feel it; the wound is deep" (26.9). Like Paul, like the Bride herself, Bernard is abject, muddied, and mutilated by the piercing violence of his loss.

Brian McGuire has recently suggested that the inclusion of this elegy within the sermon-cycle shows how Bernard's "tears of human loss could become an expression of faith, hope, and love" for the Christian life of his community.[62] Yet the spontaneity of Bernard's elegiac performance might also be read as a deliberate attempt to instill in his readers and auditors a longing for and acceptance of death, both their own and one another's. For however wrenching the death of a close companion may be, Bernard writes, it is inevitable, and desirable in its very inevitability. As he addresses his brother, "What a harvest of joys, what a profusion of blessings is yours. In place of my insignificant person you have the abiding presence of Christ, and mingling with the angelic choirs you feel our absence no loss" (26.5). After his bodily death and union with Christ, Gerard's whole being is "engulfed in that sea of endless happiness," his human spirit "changed into a movement of divine love" (26.5).

As Bernard imagines it here, death is salvific not simply in terms of the individual redemption it promises, but also for the collective will to action it can inspire. Not only should the departure of Gerard not be begrudged, but his example should teach that the desire to survive must be secondary to the will to sacrifice. Bernard thus deploys the very death of his brother to constitute his community and his readers around the body he mourns and the loss he endures by instilling the collective "desire to die" in the service of Christ that the ideal crusader must possess. As he writes in the *De laude*, "to inflict death or to die for Christ is no sin, but rather, an abundant claim to glory. In the first case one gains for Christ, and in the second one gains Christ himself" (3.3). Like Bernard, Gerard, and the monastic community, moreover, the Templars "live as brothers in joyful and sober company, without wives or children" (4.7).

Throughout this valorization of death and sacrifice, in which Bernard implicitly parallels his own mournful abjection with the abject blackness of the Bride, we can perceive what Louise Fradenburg has recently termed "the construction of the subject through sacrifice," indeed "the production of the subject for death" that characterizes so many medieval discourses of selfhood in their profound dependence upon loss as fundamentally constitutive of Christian subjectivity.[63] After Bernard's death, in fact, Clairvaux would become a popular site for both religious and aristocratic men to come to await their own death and burial.[64] As Fradenburg recognizes, such sacrificial instantiations of the religious subject do not entail an effacement of pleasure: Bernard's mournful elegy to his brother initiates an increasingly eroticized trajectory of loss, rapture, and salvation through the next three sermons, in which the struggle against fleshliness and communal dissidence becomes coextensive with the global struggle for Jerusalem.

Sermon 27 opens with an inquiry into the precise nature of the *pelles Solomonis*, the celestial skins "whose beauty delights the bride because so like her own" (27.1). For the platonizing Bernard, this resemblance constitutes an unmistakable sign of the "heavenly origin" of the Bride, who "retains a natural likeness to it in the land of unlikeness . . . as an exile on earth" (27.6). The Bride's exilic blackness provokes Bernard's most explicit meditation on the typological parallel between the earthly and heavenly Jerusalems that, as scholars such as Bernard McGinn, Hans-Dietrich Kahl, and D. H. Green have demonstrated, was so central to the medieval spiritualization of the crusades:[65]

These gifts reveal a power that is more of heaven than of earth. They clearly indicate that a soul thus endowed is truly from heaven. But Scripture is clearer still: "I saw the holy city, the new Jerusalem, coming down out of heaven from God, prepared as a bride adorned for her husband. And I heard a great voice from the throne saying: 'Behold the dwelling of God is with men. He will dwell among them.'" But why? In order to win a bride for himself from among men. (27.6)

Identifying the Bride herself as the "new Jerusalem" from Revelations 21, Bernard depicts her descent to the *earthly* Jerusalem as its heaven-sent redemption, which nevertheless demands the participation of all the members of the Church's body: "it pleased [Christ] to summon the Church from among men and unite it with the one from heaven, that there might be but the one bride and one Bridegroom. The one from heaven perfects the earthly one; it does not make two." The consummation of "Jesus the Bridegroom and Jerusalem the *bride*" (27.7) is at the same time a gathering "among men" in Jerusalem the *city* as the individual and collective Brides of Christ.

Articulating his own desire to participate in this collective union, Bernard writes, "If only he would anoint my soul with the oil of his mercy, to extend it like a curtain of skin that expands when anointed" (27.9). The soul wishing "to be able to make sufficient room" for the love of Christ must also be one that "grows and advances toward 'mature manhood, to the measure of the stature of the fullness of Christ'" (27.10). Bernard implies that being united with and filled by Christ, whose own heart "is filled with a love that embraces everybody," can occur only in Jerusalem, where the loving soul will "endeavor to take the kingdom of love by force, until this holy warrior [*pius invasor*] helps you succeed in possessing it even to its farthest bounds" (27.11). In sermon 28, this *pius invasor* constitutes a homosocial bond between brothers on earth and between men and Christ:

To be discolored by the sun may also mean to be on fire with fraternal love, to weep with those who weep, to rejoice with those who rejoice, to be weak with those who are weak, to burn with indignation when someone is led into sin. She can also say this: "Christ the Sun of Justice had made me swarthy in color, because I am faint with love of him." This languor drains the color from the countenance, and makes the soul swoon with desire. (28.13)

The origin of such a "fraternal love" between men, writes Bernard, lies in a burning desire to unite with Christ and, like the Bride, to assume the "stigma" of blackness in contrast to his splendor: "Which of us so burns with holy love that in his longing to see Christ he wearies of all the color-fulness of this world's prestige and gaiety and casts it from him. . . . Well may she say: the sun has discolored me by the contrast of its splendor; when I draw near to it I see myself in its light to be dusky, even black, and I despise my filthiness. But otherwise I am truly beautiful" (28.13). While the subject is constructed so as to "despise" its own blackness, humanity's "longing to see Christ" after death nevertheless inspires the will to endure such *denigratio* for the redemptive promise of whiteness.

As the next sermon begins, Bernard turns away from the phrase "Nigra sum" for a moment to explicate verse 1:5, "My mother's sons turned their anger to me." The "mother's sons" whose anger the Bride endured seem to be Judas, Annas, and Caiaphas, the Jews who "hanged Jesus . . . on a tree": "It is about these and others of that same race [*de illa gente*] who are known to have opposed the Christian name, that the bride complains when she says: 'My mother's sons turned their anger on me'" (29.1). Yet Bernard asks the Bride, "Why then do you complain so particularly about your mother's sons, when you are so well aware that men of various nations [*aliis nationibus*] have so often assailed you?" (29.2)—for Jews are not the only "enemies" of the Church. Even as he insists that the Bride's words should be taken to refer specifically to domestic dissension, Bernard invokes once again the global struggles "from every nation under heaven" that afflict the Church:

And so, with all possible care, I study what is set before me in these words of the bride, and for my own instruction and security take note that persecution by members of the household is alone mentioned by name, whereas she passes over in silence numerous and grave trials which she is known to endure all over the world from every nation under heaven, from pagans [*infidelibus*], from heretics and schismatics. Aware as I am of the discernment of the bride, I know it was neither by chance nor through forgetfulness that she omitted these. The truth is that she expresses her grief so openly about what hurts her so acutely, and what she thinks we must use all vigilance to avoid. And what is it that hurts her? It is internal and domestic dissension [*Malum utique intestinum ac domesticum*]. (29.2)

Following Peter the Venerable, Bernard casts Muslims as pagans or infidels (*infideles*) who threaten the Church's well-being just as he excoriates the "abominable and detestable vice" of dissension and anger threatening the placid life of the monastic household (29.3). Fraternal conflict within the walls of the cloister is a microcosmic reflection of the global conflict without, the cloister itself a site from which this conflict can be commented upon and negotiated.

When Bernard further explores the implications of domestic discord near the sermon's conclusion, he represents the violence and hostility of the Church's enemies as a salvific trial for both Ecclesia and its individual members: "The Church, or the soul who loves God, can say that the sun has changed her color by commissioning and equipping some of her mother's sons to make salutary warfare against her, and lead her captive to his faith and love, pierced with those arrows of which Scripture says: 'The warrior's arrows are sharp,' and again: 'Your arrows have pierced deep into me'" (29.7). Even violent warfare against the Church by the discolored brothers of the sun can be "salutary," Bernard writes, as long as it is resisted by "the soul who loves God" and is willing to die for and in *his* son.

In much the same spirit, Bernard addresses the earthly Jerusalem in the *De laude*: "If God has permitted you to be so often beseiged, it has only been to furnish brave men an occasion for valor and immortality" (5.11). Yet Bernard never lets his reader forget the jeopardizing and sacrificial aspects of this warfare: "See then, if the Saint who, for his own good, demands to be attacked and pierced with arrows, is not acting prudently when he says: 'Pierce my flesh with your fear.' How excellent that arrow of fear that pierces and kills the desires of the flesh, that the spirit may be saved" (29.7). Paradoxically, the sanctified body of the Christian soldier must itself be pierced and penetrated repeatedly in order for its fleshly desires to be quenched:

There is another arrow: the living and active word of God that cuts more keenly than any two-edged sword, of which our Savior said: "I have not come to send peace but the sword." "A polished arrow" too is that special love of Christ, which not only pierced Mary's soul but penetrated through and through, so that even the tiniest space in her virginal breast was permeated by love. . . . It transpierced her thus that it might come down even to us, and of that fullness we might all receive. She would become the mother of that love whose father is the God who is love; and when that love was brought to birth he would place his tent in the sun, that the Scripture might be fulfilled: "I will make you the Light of the Nations, so that you may be my salvation to the ends of the earth." (29.8)

Here the gender of God's chosen object of love switches abruptly from female to male, the Virgin's rapturous penetration by the arrow of God prefiguring "ours" by the body of Christ. Like the Templars, moreover, "blackened by the sun and their armor," Christ pitches his own *tabernacula* in the sun in order to bring "salvation to the ends of the earth," a gesture indelibly binding the desire of the soul for Christ to Ecclesia's desire for global conquest and salvation.

Finally, as he so often does, Bernard localizes this struggle within the individuated human subject, moving from first-person plural (*acciperemus*) to first-person singular (*putaverim*), from the "we" who desire the "polished arrow" to the "I" who longs for the sword: "I would reckon myself happy if at rare moments I felt at least the prick of the point of that sword. Even if only bearing love's slightest wound, I could still say: 'I am wounded with love.' How I long not only to be wounded in this manner but to be attacked over and over again until the color and heat of that which wars against the spirit is overcome" (29.8). From the gentle intimacy of the kiss of "the kiss of the mouth" (*osculo oris sui*) that so preoccupies him in the early sermons, Bernard has moved to the "prick of the point of the sword" (*cuspide huius gladii pungi*), the penetrative ravishment of the devotional body promising redemption.

Here, too, Bernard's vocabulary is inescapably violent: *expugnari, militat*. While this exegetical spectacle lends credence to McClintock's suggestion that the Western tradition has often figured colonial conquest as "an erotics of ravishment,"[66] for Bernard this ravishment is specifically homoerotic and, equally important, self-directed. Though Ecclesia herself is "in joy and thanksgiving and a spirit of triumph that she has been found worthy both to be and to be called dark and discolored [*fusca seu decolor*] for the name and love of Christ," Bernard's vision of personal salvation entails the eroticized conquest of blackness, the violently libidinous "erasure of color" (*exterminationem coloris*) from the lives and flesh of men (29.9). Even as an experiential participation in blackness promises Christian salvation for the crusader, blackened skin and darkened bodies must be overcome in order to achieve it.

For Bernard, then, the color of salvation is white. The sermons I have been discussing are devoted in large measure to convincing their public that whiteness represents the truth and finality of redemption and resurrection, a conviction Bernard seeks to instill through a cannibalizing subsumption of ethnic and religious difference within the trajectory of Christian salvation. Even the resisting reader can be lulled by the literary beauty of Bernard's Latin, the erotic intensity of his belief, and the integrity of his spiritual vision into forgetting the lethal formulations of violence upon which these rhetorics are founded. In a sense, the tendency of many modern commentators on the *Sermons on the Song of Songs* to overlook the violence of its representations testifies to Bernard's ultimate success in casting warfare and death as beautiful, salvific, desirable. Yet this very rhetoric exposes how devotional practice contituted just one of the universalizing *pelles* upon which Latin Christendom inscribed its own hegemony.

Epilogue: The Politics and Prosaics of Translation

While it would be difficult to assess the precise cultural work the *Sermons on the Song of Songs* performed in the launching of the Second Crusade, there can be little doubt that Bernard imputed extraordinary authority to his textual and hermeneutical performances. When he promises in sermon 27 to "throw light on the secret hidden by those skins that portray the beauty of the Bride," he may well have had in mind the whitened parchment on which the Song of Songs itself—not to mention his own hermeneutic—was written. As the author of the *Chanson de Roland*, Wolfram, and other writers were anxiously aware, the practice of writing necessarily involved the literal staining of skin with the "stigma" of blackness (thus a twelfth-century writer irreverently described the *cartae* of Pope Paschal II as "the skins of wethers blackened with ink and weighted with a little lump of lead"[67]). By refracting his conception of religious and ethnic difference through an extended meditation on the sacrificial homoerotics of Christian warfare, Bernard unmistakably located his own scriptive practice within the salvational ideology of crusading.

As the wide dissemination and influence of the *Sermons* suggest, however, Bernard's own attempts to interpellate and produce a crusading public can be only part of the story. I want to conclude by considering briefly an apparently isolated effort at the turn of the twelfth century to appropriate the *Sermons on the Song of Songs* into a political and social environment that was decidedly extra-monastic. MS Nantes Dobrée 5, which dates from the late twelfth or early thirteenth century, consists of French prose translations of three Bernardine works, including the first forty-four *Sermons on the Song of Songs*, *De diligendo Dei*, and the sermons on the *Missus est*, as well as several shorter homiletic works (all anonymous) most likely composed in the vernacular.[68] Because the *Sermons* (which occupy the manuscript's first twenty fascicles) conclude with sermon 44 and thus correspond to one of the widespread Latin redactions of the cycle, there is good reason to assume that they were originally translated as a discrete work and only later bound with the other texts in the manuscript.[69] While there is unfortunately no prologue revealing the identity of the translator, the patron of the translation, or even the reason for its existence, the manuscript was clearly produced for a secular audience.[70]

I would like to suggest that this translation of the *Sermons*, which appeared sometime between the departure of the Third Crusade and the return of the Fourth, may have been intended to heighten crusading sentiment among the French aristocracy—or at the very least may have been read and received as such. First, the simple fact that the *Sermons* were translated into French at this particular moment allied them even more closely than Bernard's original with the explicit crusading propagandism found in vernacular literatures. "Nigra sum sed formosa" in Bernard, for example, became "Ge sui noire, mais ge sui bele," a phrase echoic of the blackness of Muslims in the *chansons de geste*. Ecclesiastical injunctions to "prendre la croiz" would have been very familiar to those who would read in the vernacular *Sermons* that "la vergunge de la croiz est plaisanz" ("the ignominy of the cross is pleasing").[71] And Bernard's pronouncement that the Christian body is not a native home or residence, "mais loges de soldeor u hostez de trespassant" ("but a soldier's tent or pilgrim's hut") in which one must travel when "la noirors est de la Glis" ("blackness is on the Church"),[72] had already appeared in French when Villehardouin described the Fourth Crusade as "nostre pelerin" ("our pilgrimage") and recounted the "grant joie et mult grant pitié de cele croiz."[73] The lack of any unambiguous references to crusading in the translation, as in Bernard's original, would only have served to augment its rhetorical efficacy. As D. A. Trotter has demonstrated, Old French literature is characterized for the most part by just such a "lack of precision" in its employment of crusading terminology.[74]

Also intriguing are the specific time and place in which the translation of the *Sermons* appeared. As the few scholars who have written on the Nantes manuscript agree, its language shows distinctive traces of the Walloon dialect, which, along with paleographical evidence, allows it to be placed with a high degree of certainty in turn-of-the-century Flanders or northeastern France.[75] This historical and geographical specificity suggests that the suitability of the French *Sermons* as crusade propaganda was more than a product of the imagery the work shared with its literary counterparts.

Like the Second Crusade, the Third and Fourth Crusades were characterized by a high degree of Cistercian involvement, both in their instigation and in their popularization through preaching. The most prominent preacher of the Third Crusade was Henry of Albano, the abbot of Clairvaux from 1176 to 1177.[76] As papal legate in the early 1180s, Henry was highly regarded for his preaching against the Cathars in southern France—so much so, it appears, that the papacy itself practically fell into his lap. Rather than vying for the papal crown, however, Henry elected to preach the crusade. Accompanied by Baldwin IV of Hainault, he preached throughout northeastern France and Flanders, the precise regions in which the Nantes manuscript originated.[77] Next, in 1198, the legendary Fulk of Neuilly, after pleading unsuccessfully with the general chapter of the Cistercians for their help in preaching the Fourth Crusade, was granted by Innocent III the authority to compel "any black or white monks and any regular canons whom Fulk might choose to assist him in preaching the crusade";[78] after the turn of the century, the Cistercians themselves became more than willing participants. Cole suggests, in fact, that Martin, abbot of the Cistercian monastery of Pairis in the Alsace, may have been a more successful preacher of the Fourth Crusade than Fulk himself.[79] Given the general rise in vernacular preaching beginning in the late twelfth century,[80] it should come as no surprise that one of the most prized works of Cistercian predicatory literature was rendered into French just as the Cistercians themselves were becoming an ever more visible part of this trend.

Finally, the translator rendered Bernard's sermons into *prose*, not verse, and did so in northeastern France or Flanders during the reign of Philip Augustus (1179–1223), who returned from the Third Crusade in 1191. In her recent study of early French prose historiography, Gabrielle Spiegel has argued that the genre's emergence can be attributed in large part to an ongoing economic, political, and military conflict between the French crown and the French-speaking Flemish aristocracy in the years around 1200. As Spiegel argues, the "profound shift in the discursive practices of the French nobility" signaled by their patronage of vernacular prose translations represented "a form of ethical reassurance and political legitimation at a moment of social and political crisis," a moment in which the physical integrity and economic well-being of their domains were threatened.[81]

The one sub-genre of thirteenth-century prose historiography that

Spiegel's study does not treat (as she herself acknowledges) is the earliest corpus of French crusading chronicles (including Villehardouin's), all of which "emanate from the same northern French region . . . and discuss the crusading activities of the same group of northern and Flemish lords among whom the patronage of vernacular historiography was so marked."[82] Moreover, even the chronicles Spiegel does examine are pervaded with the ideology and imagery of crusading. By far the most popular example of the new prose historiography was the Pseudo-Turpin chronicle, originally a twelfth-century Latin work allegedly written by Turpin, the archbishop in the *Chanson de Roland*. Given the preponderance of moralizing exempla, theological speculation, and predicatory passages in the chronicle, Pseudo-Turpin is almost certainly a clerical work, an attempt to recruit the ever-popular *Chanson de Roland* into the service of twelfth-century ecclesiastical politics.[83] In the words of one of its translators, the Pseudo-Turpin chronicle recounts "the story of how the good emperor Charlemagne went to Spain to conquer the land over the Saracens" ("l'estoire si cum li bons empereires Karlemaines en ala en Espagnie por la terre conquerre sour les Sarasins").[84]

As one of the earliest translations from Latin into French prose, then, the *Sermons* in Nantes Dobrée 5, like the French versions of the Pseudo-Turpin chronicle, appeared during decades when the "militant insistence on prose" among the Flemish nobility was inextricably bound up with the ideology of crusading,[85] an ideology only reinforced by the Cistercians who actively propagated it in their preaching tours through the region. If this translation does indeed represent an attempt to appropriate one of the most influential and widely disseminated twelfth-century devotional texts into a robust vernacular culture of warfare and dominion, it could hardly have chosen a more suitable Latin original.

Notes

Earlier versions of this essay were presented in May of 1995 at the International Medieval Congress at Kalamazoo and at the University of Toronto symposium out of which this collection evolved. I would like to thank the symposium's organizers, Andrew Taylor and David Townsend, for their invitation to participate in the project and for their advice and encouragement at various stages. Comments by Rita Copeland, Carolyn Dinshaw, Jody Enders, Steven Kruger, Brian McGuire, Robert Stein, and the two anonymous readers for the press raised some challenging questions about my thesis, and I thank them for forcing me to rethink the essay's argument and organization.

1. A. G. Rigg, *A History of Anglo-Latin Literature, 1066–1422*, 1.

2. Robert Bartlett, "Colonial Aristocracies of the High Middle Ages."

3. Robert Bartlett, *The Making of Europe: Conquest, Colonization, and Cultural Change*, 292.

4. Ibid., *The Making of Europe*, 261. See also Robert Ignatius Burns, *Islam Under the Crusaders: Colonial Survival in the Thirteenth Century Kingdom of Valencia*.

5. Benedict Anderson, *Imagined Communities: Reflections on the Origin and Spread of Nationalism*, 21.

6. Bernard of Clairvaux, *Sermones super Cantica canticorum* 27.12, 162–63. All references to the *Sermones* will be to this edition and hereafter will be internal. I have relied on *On the Song of Songs I*, trans. Kilian Walsh; *On the Song of Songs II*, trans. Kilian Walsh; and *On the Song of Songs III*, trans. Kilian Walsh and Irene M. Edmonds, but with numerous modifications.

7. Augustine, *Confessions*, 13.15, trans. R. S. Pine-Coffin, 322. See Jesse Gellrich, *The Idea of the Book in the Middle Ages: Language Theory, Mythology, and Fiction*, 29–31, for a discussion of this imagery and its medieval afterlife.

8. I am borrowing the distinction between "audience" and "public" from Anne Middleton's influential essay "The Audience and Public of *Piers Plowman*."

9. John Sommerfeldt, "The Chimaera Revisited," 6.

10. Ibid., 13.

11. The classic formulation is Jean Leclercq, "S. Bernard et la théologie monastique du XIIe siècle"; see also Leclerq's *The Love of Learning and the Desire for God: A Study of Monastic Culture*, trans. Catherine Misrahi, esp. ch. 9.

12. Adriaan H. Bredero, "The Conflicting Interpretations of the Relevance of Bernard of Clairvaux to the History of His Own Time," 58. As I was preparing the final revision of this chapter, I came across Martha Newman's wonderful new book treating precisely this problem: *The Boundaries of Charity: Cistercian Culture and Ecclesiastical Reform, 1098–1180*. Focusing in particular on the Cistercian ideal of *caritas*, Newman argues that a spirit of public service and involvement was inherent in, rather than anathema to, the order's spirituality, and that *caritas* itself "described the bond that linked the monks within their communities but also the bond joining all of Christian society" (18). This chapter complements Newman's study in obvious ways by exploring the compatibility between Bernardine devotion and the ideology of crusading, perhaps the one significant aspect of twelfth-century Cistercian political involvement that Newman does not address at length.

13. Michael Casey, *Athirst for God: Spiritual Desire in Bernard of Clairvaux's Sermons on the Song of Songs*, 37.

14. For Everwin's original letter, see his *Epistolae*, PL 182, cols. 676–80.

15. See Gillian Evans, *The Mind of St. Bernard of Clairvaux*, 138–41, for a discussion of these sermons and their political context.

16. Jean Leclercq, "Were the Sermons on the Song of Songs Delivered in Chapter?" vii–xxx.

17. Leclercq, *Bernard of Clairvaux and the Cistercian Spirit*, 96.

18. Leclercq, "La littérature provoquée par les *Sermons sur les Cantiques*," 208–22.

19. Leclercq, *Bernard of Clairvaux and the Cistercian Spirit*, 96.

20. See chapter epilogue.

21. Introduction, *S. Bernardi Opera*, vol. 1, xix–xxxi.

22. The following account is based on John G. Rowe, "The Origins of the Second Crusade: Pope Eugenius III, Bernard of Clairvaux, and Louis VII of France," 79–89, which scrupulously sorts through the conflicting chronicle accounts; and Penny J. Cole, *The Preaching of the Crusades to the Holy Land, 1095–1270*, 37–43.

23. For the original account of Bernard at Vézelay, see Odo of Deuil, *De profectione Ludovici VII in orientem*, 8–10.

24. Leclercq is characteristic here: "Of the different affairs of the Church in which Bernard was involved between the beginning and the end of the *Sermons on the Song of Songs*, there is one of which he does not speak: the second crusade. And this silence without doubt helps restore to its relative importance this event whose place in Bernard's life certain historians have tended to exaggerate. It was, in reality, only a parenthesis, late and of short duration. Certainly, Bernard was grieved by the failure of this enterprise, . . . but he never lost his peace" ("Introduction," in Bernard of Clairvaux, *On the Song of Songs IV*, xvi).

25. Cole, *Preaching*, 41; see also Hans-Dietrich Kahl, "Crusade Eschatology as Seen by St. Bernard in the Years 1146–1148," 35.

26. For a convincing argument for this precise dating see David Carlson, "The Practical Theology of St. Bernard and the Date of the *De laude novae militiae*."

27. *De laude novae militiae* 5.10; *In Praise of the New Knighthood*, trans. Conrad Greenia, 143; citations of the translation hereafter are internal.

28. Cole, *Preaching*, 41.

29. James Kritzeck, *Peter the Venerable and Islam*, 45; for Peter's relationship with Bernard see esp. 43–46.

30. See E. Ann Matter, *The Voice of My Beloved: The Song of Songs in Western Medieval Christianity*, for a wide-ranging discussion of the variety of Song of Songs allegories and commentaries throughout the medieval period.

31. Caroline Walker Bynum, *Jesus as Mother: Studies in the Spirituality of the High Middle Ages*, 110–69.

32. Brian Patrick McGuire, *The Difficult Saint: Bernard of Clairvaux and His Tradition*, 32–33.

33. Caroline Walker Bynum, *The Resurrection of the Body in Western Christianity, 200–1336*, 165.

34. *De diligendo Deo* 11.31, p. 145; *On Loving God*, 122.

35. On devotional homoeroticism in premodern Christianity more generally, see especially E. Ann Matter, "Discourses of Desire: Sexuality and Christian Women's Visionary Narratives"; Bruce Holsinger, "The Flesh of the Voice: Embodiment and the Homoerotics of Devotion in the Music of Hildegard of Bingen (1098–1179)"; Richard Rambuss, "Pleasure and Devotion: The Body of Jesus and Seventeenth-Century Religious Lyric"; and Kathy Lavezzo, "Sobs and Sighs Between Women: The Homoerotics of Compassion in *The Book of Margery Kempe*."

36. Eve Kosofsky Sedgwick, *Between Men: English Literature and Male Homosocial Desire*, 18.

37. Anne McClintock, *Imperial Leather: Race, Gender, and Sexuality in the Colonial Contest*, 24.

38. *S. Bernardi Opera*, vol. 5, 349–53.

39. Citations from Bynum, *Resurrection*, 165.

40. Henry Louis Gates, Jr., "Introduction: Writing 'Race' and the Difference It Makes," 5.

41. Steven Kruger, "Conversion and Medieval Racial, Religious, and Sexual Categories," and John Friedman, *The Monstrous Races in Medieval Art and Thought*, 59–86.

42. bell hooks, *Black Looks: Race and Representation*, 30–31.

43. For a brief but compelling discussion of the racialized implications of early Christian Song of Songs imagery and its "assimilation to an ideal of European whiteness" in Western art and literature more generally, see Elizabeth McGrath, "The Black Andromeda," 6–7 and notes.

44. For similar imagery in Peter the Venerable's representations of Islam, see Giles Constable, "Petri Venerabilis sermones tres, esp. 244.

45. *Visio Tnugdali*, 35.

46. Hildegard of Bingen, *Scivias* 2.3, trans. Columba Hart and Jane Bishop, 169–73.

47. Ruth Mellinkoff, *Outcasts: Signs of Otherness in Northern European Art of the Late Middle Ages*, 1: 67, 157.

48. On the fraught relation between the *Roland* and the Crusades, see Matthew Bennett, "First Crusaders' Images of Muslims: The Influence of Vernacular Poetry?"; Samir Marzouki, "Islam et Musulmans dans la *Chanson de Roland*"; and Norman Daniel, *Heroes and Saracens: An Interpretation of the Chansons de Geste*.

49. *Chanson de Roland* 125, lines 1634–35.

50. Ibid., 144, lines 1932–34.

51. Marzouki, "Islam et musulmans," 112–13.

52. See Norman Daniel, *Heroes and Saracens*, 110–17, for a discussion of crusade *mentalité* in the *chansons*; see also Paul Bancourt, *Les musulmans dans les chansons de geste du cycle du roi*, 67–72; and, for a number of German examples, Jurgen Brummack, *Die Darstellung des Oriente in den deutschen Alexandergeschichten des Mittelalters*, 155–65.

53. *Maugis d'Aigremont*, ed. Ferdinand Castets, line 3131.

54. *Blancandin et l'Orgueilleuse d'Amour: Roman d'aventure du XIIIe siècle*, ed. Franklin P. Sweeter, 173.

55. Daniel, *Heroes and Saracens*, 209.

56. Cited in Daniel, *Heroes and Saracens*, 289 n.

57. Wolfram von Eschenbach, *Parzival*, trans. André Lefevere, 3.

58. Ibid., 9, 14.

59. Bancourt, "Les musulmans," 67.

60. Wolfram von Eschenbach, *Parzival*, 202.

61. Jerome, *Liber interpretationum hebr. nom.*, 30.

62. McGuire, *The Difficult Saint*, 144.

63. Louise O. Fradenburg, " 'Be not far from me': Psychoanalysis, Medieval Studies, and the Subject of Religion," 52–53.

64. M. Anselme Dimier, "Mourir à Clairvaux!"; but see McGuire (*The Difficult Saint*, 97), who suggests that this popularity may result more from Clairvaux's fame as a place specifically of burial.

65. Bernard McGinn, "Saint Bernard and Eschatology," 180–85; Kahl, "Cru-

sade Eschatology," esp. 36–37; D. H. Green, *The Millstätter Exodus: A Crusading Epic*, 234–41.

66. McClintock, *Imperial Leather*, 22.

67. Cited in Jesse Gellrich, *Discourse and Dominion in the Fourteenth Century: Oral Contexts of Writing in Philosophy, Politics, and Poetry*, 31.

68. For a complete description of this manuscript, see G. Durville, *Catalogue de la bibliothèque du Musée Thomas Dobrée*, vol. 1: *Manuscrits*, 223–61; and, more recently, Robert Allen Taylor, "Li Sermon saint Bernart sur les Cantikes," ix–xvi.

69. Taylor, "Li Sermon," xi; see Leclercq's introduction to *S. Bernardi Opera*, vol. 1, xxvi–xxxi.

70. Robert Taylor, "The Old French 'Cistercian' Translations," 77.

71. Sermon 25.41, ed. Taylor, "Li Sermon," 293.

72. Ibid., 26.6–7, p. 297.

73. Cited in D. A. Trotter, *Medieval French Literature and the Crusades (1100–1300)*, 58.

74. Ibid., 33.

75. Taylor, "Old French," 76–77; Albert Henry, "Saint Bernard traduit vers 1200 en pays wallon."

76. See Cole, *Preaching*, 65–71.

77. Ibid., 67.

78. Ibid., 87.

79. Ibid., 92–97. For a contemporary account of Martin's crusade preaching, see Gunther of Pairis, *Historia Constantinopolitana*, esp. cols. 226–28; on Gunther see Francis R. Swietek, "Gunther of Pairis and the *Historia Constantinopolitana*."

80. Michel Zink, *Prédication en langue romane avant 1300*.

81. Gabrielle M. Spiegel, *Romancing the Past: The Rise of Vernacular Prose Historiography in Thirteenth-Century France*, 54.

82. Ibid., 7. It may be more than serendipitous that one of the nobles centrally involved in the origins of this dispute, Baldwin V of Hainault (later Baldwin VIII, count of Flanders), was the son of the same Baldwin IV who accompanied Henry of Albano in his preaching tour through northeastern France and Flanders. One of the very first translations of the Pseudo-Turpin chronicle (see below) was executed at the request of Yolande, the sister of Baldwin V (ibid.,70).

83. See Eugene Vance, *Mervelous Signals: Poetics and Sign Theory in the Middle Ages*, 84, and Spiegel, *Romancing the Past*, 69.

84. Cited and translated in Jeffrey Kittay and Wlad Godzich, *The Emergence of Prose: An Essay in Prosaics*, xiii–xiv.

85. Spiegel, *Romancing the Past*, 54.

Bibliography

ABBREVIATIONS

AHDLMA   *Archives d'histoire doctrinale et littéraire du moyen âge*
CCCM   Corpus Christianorum, Continuatio Medievalis
CFS   Cistercian Fathers Series
CSS   Cistercian Studies Series
OLD   *Oxford Latin Dictionary*. Ed. P. G. W. Glare. Oxford: Clarendon Press, 1982.
PL   Patrologia Latina
PG   Patrologia Graeca
RMLW   Latham, R. E., ed. *Revised Medieval Latin Word-List*. London: Oxford University Press, 1980.
SPCK   Society for the Promotion of Christian Knowledge

PRIMARY SOURCES

Abelard, Peter. "Abelard's Letter of Consolation to a Friend (*Historia calamitatum*)." Ed. J. T. Muckle. *Mediaeval Studies* 12 (1950): 163–213.
———. "Abelard's Rule for Religious Women." Ed. T. P. McLaughlin. *Mediaeval Studies* 18 (1956): 241–92.
———. *Historia calamitatum*. Ed. Jacques Monfrin. Paris: J. Vrin, 1959.
———. *Peter Abaelards Philosophische Schriften I. Die Logica "Ingredientibus"*. Ed. Bernhard Geyer. Beiträge zur Geschichte der Philosophie des Mittelalters 21.3. Münster: Aschendorff, 1927.
———. *Peter Abelard: Letters IX–XIV*. Ed. Edmé Renno Smits. Groningen: Rijksuniversiteit te Groningen, 1983.
———. *Peter Abelard's Ethics*. Ed. and trans. D. E. Luscombe. Oxford: Clarendon Press, 1971.
———. *Petri Abaelardi: Opera theologia II. Theologia christiana, Theologia scholarium (recensiones breviores) etc*. CCCM 12. Ed. M. Buytaert. Turnholt: Brepols, 1969.
———. *Petri Abaelardi: Opera theologia III. Theologia "Summi boni," Theologia "Scholarium"*. CCCM 13. Ed. M. Buytaert and C. J. Mews. Turnholt: Brepols, 1987.
———. *Petrus Abaelardus: Dialectica*. 2nd ed. Ed. L. M. de Rijk. Assen: Van Gorcum, 1970.
Abelard, Peter and Heloise. "The Letter of Heloise on the Religious Life and Abelard's First Reply." Ed. J. T. Muckle. *Mediaeval Studies* 17 (1955): 240–81.

———. *The Letters of Abelard and Heloise*. Trans. Betty Radice. Harmondsworth: Penguin, 1974.

———.*The Letters of Abelard and Heloise*. Trans. C. K. Scott Moncrieff. New York: Cooper Square, 1974.

———. "The Personal Letters Between Abelard and Heloise." Ed. J. T. Muckle. *Mediaeval Studies* 15 (1953): 47–94.

Augustine. *Confessions*. Trans. R. S. Pine-Coffin. New York: Penguin, 1987.

———. *De opera monachorum*. PL 40, cols. 547–82.

———. *In Joannis evangelium*. PL 35, cols. 1379–1976.

Bede. *Bede's Ecclesiastical History of the English People*. Ed. Bertram Colgrave and R. A. B. Mynors. Oxford: Clarendon Press, 1969.

Benoit de Sainte-Maure. *Le Roman de Troie*. 6 vols. Ed. Léopold Constans. Paris: Fermin Didot, 1904–12.

Bernard of Clairvaux. *Sermones super Cantica canticorum*. *S. Bernardi Opera*, vol. 1. Ed. J. Leclercq, H. M. Rochais, and C.H. Talbot. Rome: Editiones Cisterciences, 1957.

———. *On the Song of Songs I*. Trans. Kilian Walsh, The Works of Bernard of Clairvaux, vol. 2. CFS 4. Spencer, Mass.: Cistercian Publications, 1971.

———. *On the Song of Songs II*. Trans. Kilian Walsh, The Works of Bernard of Clairvaux, vol. 3. CFS 7. Kalamazoo, Mich.: Cistercian Publications, 1976.

———. *On the Song of Songs III*. Trans. Kilian Walsh and Irene M. Edmonds. CFS 31. Kalamazoo, Mich.: Cistercian Publications, 1979.

———. *On the Song of Songs IV*. CFS 40. Trans. Irene Edmonds. Kalamazoo, Mich.: Cistercian Publications, 1980.

———. *De diligendo Deo*. *S. Bernardi Opera*, vol. 3. Ed. J. Leclercq and H. M. Rochais. Rome: Editiones Cistercienses, 1963.

———.*On Loving God*. In *Treatises II*. Trans. Robert Walton. The Works of Bernard of Clairvaux, vol. 5. CFS 13. Kalamazoo, Mich.: Cistercian Publications, 1974.

———. *Liber ad milites templi de laude novae militiae*. *S. Bernardi Opera*, vol. 3. Ed. J. Leclercq and H. M. Rochais. Rome: Editiones Cistercienses, 1977.

———. *In Praise of the New Knighthood*. In *Treatises III*. Trans. Conrad Greenia. The Works of Bernard of Clairvaux, vol. 7. CFS 19. Kalamazoo, Mich.: Cistercian Publications, 1977.

———. *Sermones II*. *S. Bernardi Opera*, vol. 5. Ed. J. Leclercq and H. Rochais. Rome: Editiones Cistercienses, 1968.

———. *Epistolae*. *S. Bernardi Opera*, vol. 8. Ed. J. Leclercq and H. Rochais. Rome: Editiones Cistercienses, 1977.

Bernard of Fontcaude. *Adversus Waldensium sectam liber*. PL 204, cols. 793–840.

Bernard Silvestris. *Cosmographia*. Ed. Peter Dronke. Leiden: E. J. Brill, 1978.

———. *The "Cosmographia" of Bernardus Silvestris*. Trans. Winthrop Wetherbee. New York: Columbia University Press, 1973.

Burchard of Worms. *Decretorum libri viginti*. PL 140, cols. 537–1058.

Chrétien de Troyes. *The Complete Romances of Chrétien de Troyes*. Trans. David Staines. Bloomington: Indiana University Press, 1990.

Christine de Pizan. *The Book of the City of Ladies*. Trans. Earl Jeffrey Richards. New York: Persea Books, 1982.

Chrysostom, John. *Homiliae in Joannem*. PG 59, cols. 1–482.

———. *Homilies on the Gospel of St. John and the Epistle to the Hebrews*. Select Library of the Nicene and Post-Nicene Fathers, vol. 14. Ed. Philip Schaff. 1889. Reprint, Grand Rapids, Mich.: Eerdmans, 1969.

Curtius (Quintus Curtius Rufus). *Historiae Alexandri Magni Macedonis*. In *Quintus Curtius*. 2 vols. Ed. and trans. John C. Rolfe. Loeb Classical Library. Cambridge, Mass.: Harvard University Press, 1962.

Eusebius. *Ecclesiastical History*. 2 vols. Vol. 1, ed. and trans. Kirsopp Lake. London: Heinemann, 1926.

Everwin, provost of the Steinfeld Premonstratensians. *Epistolae*. PL 182, cols. 676–80.

Gerald of Wales. *Gemma Ecclesiastica*. *Giraldi Cambrensis Opera* (Rolls Series 21), vol. 2. Ed. J. S. Brewer. London: Longman, Green, Longman, and Roberts, 1862.

Gibbon, R., ed. *Vita B. Gosvini*. *Recueil des historiens des Gaules et de la France*, vol. 14. Ed. Michel-Jean-Joseph Brial, 2nd ed. Léopold Delisle. Paris: Victor Palmé, 1877. 442–43.

Glossa Ordinaria. PL 114, cols. 9–752.

Godfrey of Disibodenberg and Theodoric of Echternach. *Vita sanctae Hildegardis*. Ed. Monika Klaes. CCCM 126. Turnholt: Brepols, 1993.

Gregory the Great. *Moralia in Job*. PL 75, cols. 499–1162.

Guibert of Gembloux. *Guiberti Gemblacensis Epistolae*. Ed. Albert Derolez. CCCM 66 and 66a. Turnholt: Brepols, 1988–89.

Gunther of Pairis. *Historia Constantinopolitana*. PL 212, cols. 221–56.

Heloise. See Abelard, Peter and Heloise

Hildegard of Bingen. *Analecta sancte Hildegardis opera spicilegio solesmensi parata*. *Analecta sacra*, vol 8. Ed. J. B. Pitra. Monte Cassino: Typis Sacri Montis Cassinensis, 1882.

———. *Briefwechsel*. Trans. Adelgundis Führkötter. Salzburg: Müller, 1965.

———. *Hildegardis Bingensis Epistolarium*. Ed. Lieven Van Acker. CCCM 91, 91a. Turnholt: Brepols, 1991, 1993.

———. *Hildegardis Liber vite meritorum*. Ed. Angela Carlevaris. CCCM 90. Turnholt: Brepols, 1995.

———. *The Book of the Rewards of Life*. Trans. Bruce W. Hozeski. New York: Garland, 1994.

——— *Hildegardis Scivias*. Ed. Adelgundis Führkötter and Angela Carlevaris. CCCM 43 and 43a. Turnholt: Brepols, 1978.

———. *Scivias*. Trans. Columba Hart and Jane Bishop. New York: Paulist Press, 1990.

———. *Liber divinorum operum simplicis hominis*. PL 197, cols. 739–1038.

———. "Saint Hildegard of Bingen and the *Vita sanctae Hildegardis*." Trans. Anna Silvas. *Tjurunga* 29 (1985): 4–25; 30 (1986): 32–41; 32 (1987): 46–59.

Honorius of Autun. *De sancta Maria Magdalena*. PL 172, cols. 979–82.

Jerome. *Commentarium in Epistolam ad Galatas libri tres*. PL 26, cols. 331–468.

———. *Epistolae*. PL 22, cols. 325–1284.

———. *Selected Letters of St. Jerome*. Trans. F. A. Wright. Cambridge, Mass.: Harvard University Press, 1963.

Pseudo-Jerome. *Epistola IX, Ad Paulum et Eustochium.* PL 30, cols. 122–42.

Pseudo-Jerome. *Epistola XIII, Virginitatis laus.* PL 30, cols. 163–76.

John of Salisbury. *Ioannis Saresberiensis Metalogicon.* Ed. J. B. Hall and K. S. B. Keats-Rohan. CCCM 98. Turnholt: Brepols, 1991.

——. *The Metalogicon of John of Salisbury: A Twelfth-Century Defense of the Verbal and Logical Arts of the Trivium.* Trans. Daniel D. McGarry. Berkeley: University of California Press, 1955.

Maugis d'Aigremont. Ed. Ferdinand Castets. Montpellier: Coulet, 1893.

Nock, A. D., and A.-J. Festugière, eds and trans. *Corpus Hermeticum.* 4 vols. Paris: Belles Lettres, 1945–54.

(Odo of Cluny). *In veneratione sanctae Mariae Magdalenae.* PL 133, cols. 713–21.

Odo of Deuil. *De profectione Ludovici VII in orientem.* Ed. and trans. Virginia Gingerick Berry. New York: Columbia University Press, 1948.

Origen. *Commentary on John.* PG 14, cols. 21–830.

——. "Origen on 1 Corinthians." Part 4. Ed. Claude Jenkins. *Journal of Theological Studies* 10 (1908–09): 29–51.

Ovid. *Amores, Medicamina faciei femineae, Ars amatoria, Remedia amoris.* Ed. E. J. Kenny. Oxford: Clarendon Press, 1961.

Peter the Venerable. *The Letters of Peter the Venerable.* Vol. 1. Cambridge, Mass.: Harvard University Press, 1967.

——. "Petri Venerabilis sermones tres." Ed. Giles Constable. *Revue Bénédictine* 64 (1954): 224–72.

Pritchard, R. Telfryn, ed. and trans. *The History of Alexander's Battles: Historia de preliis—The J1 Version.* Toronto: Pontifical Insitute of Mediaeval Studies, 1992.

Smith, Harold, trans. *Ante-Nicene Exegesis of the Gospels.* 4 vols. London: SPCK, 1926.

Sweetser, Franklin P., ed. *Blancandin et L'Orgueilleuse d' Amour: Roman d'aventure du XIIIe siècle.* Geneva: Librairie Droz, 1964.

Vita beatae Mariae Magdalenae. PL 112, cols. 1431–1508.

——. *The Life of Saint Mary Magdalene and of her Sister Saint Martha: A Medieval Biography.* Ed. and trans. David Mycoff. CSS 108. Kalamazoo, Mich.: Cistercian Publications, 1989.

Wagner, Albrecht, ed. *Visio Tnugdali.* Erlangen: A. Deichert, 1882.

Walter of Châtillon. *Galteri de Castellione Alexandreis.* Ed. Marvin Colker. Padua: Antenore, 1978.

——. *The Alexandreis.* Trans. R. Telfryn Pritchard. Toronto: Pontifical Insitute of Mediaeval Studies, 1986.

——. *The Alexandreis of Walter of Châtillon: A Twelfth-Century Epic.* Trans. David Townsend. Philadelphia: University of Pennsylvania Press, 1996.

——. *Moralisch-satirische Gedichte Walters von Châtillon.* Ed. Karl Strecker. Heidelberg: Carl Winter, 1929.

——. *Tractatus contra Judaeos.* PL 209, cols. 459–574.

William of St. Thierry. *Disputatio adversus Petrum Abaelardum.* PL 180, cols. 250–328.

William of St. Victor. "Le 'Contra quatuor labyrinthos Franciae' de Gauthier de Saint Victor." Ed. P. Glorieux. *Archives d'Histoire Doctrinale et Littéraire du Moyen Âge* 27 (1952): 187–335.

Wolfram von Eschenbach. *Parzival*. Trans. André Lefevere. New York: Continuum, 1991.

SECONDARY SOURCES

Adams, Parveen. "Of Female Bondage." In *Between Feminism and Psychoanalysis*, ed. Teresa Brennan. London and New York: Routledge, 1989. 247–65.

Adorno, Theodor. *The Authoritarian Personality*. New York: John Wiley, 1964.

Aers, David. *Community, Gender, and Individual Identity: English Writing, 1360–1430*. London and New York: Routledge, 1988.

Allen, Sister Prudence. *The Concept of Woman: The Aristotelian Revolution, 750 BC–AD 1250*. Montreal: Eden Press, 1985.

Anderson, Benedict. *Imagined Communities: Reflections on the Origin and Spread of Nationalism*. London: Verso, 1983.

Baldwin, John. *The Language of Sex: Five Voices from Northern France Around 1200*. Chicago: University of Chicago Press, 1994.

Bancourt, Paul. *Les musulmans dans les chansons de geste du cycle du roi*. 2 vols. Ph.D. diss. Université de Provence, 1982.

Barkan, Leonard. *Transuming Passion: Ganymede and the Erotics of Humanism*. Stanford, Calif.: Stanford University Press, 1991.

Bartky, Sandra Lee. *Femininity and Domination: Studies in the Phenomenology of Oppression*. London and New York: Routledge, 1990.

Bartlett, Anne C. "Commentary, Polemic, and Prophecy in Hildegard of Bingen's *Solutiones triginta octo quaestionum*." *Viator* 23 (1992): 153–65.

Bartlett, Robert. "Colonial Aristocracies of the High Middle Ages." In *Medieval Frontier Societies*, ed. Robert Bartlett and Angus Mackay. Oxford: Clarendon Press, 1989. 23–47.

———. *Gerald of Wales, 1146–1223*. Oxford: Clarendon Press, 1982.

———. *The Making of Europe: Conquest, Colonization, and Cultural Change*. London and New York: Routledge, 1992.

Belsey, Catherine. *Critical Practice*. London and New York: Routledge, 1980.

Benjamin, Jessica. *The Bonds of Love: Psychoanalysis, Feminism, and the Problem of Domination*. New York: Pantheon Books, 1988.

Bennett, Matthew. "First Crusaders' Images of Muslims: The Influence of Vernacular Poetry?" *Forum for Modern Language Studies* 22 (1986): 101–22.

Benton, John F. "Philology's Search for Abelard in the *Metamorphosis Goliae*." *Speculum* 50 (1975): 199–217.

Benton, John F. and Fiorelli Prosperetti Ercolli. "The Style of the 'Historia Calamitatum': A Preliminary Test of the Authenticity of the Correspondence Attributed to Abelard and Heloise." *Viator* 6 (1975): 59–86.

Bernheimer, Charles. "Penile Reference in Phallic Theory." *differences* 4, 1 (1992): 116–32.

Blamires, Alcuin. *The Case for Women in Medieval Culture*. Oxford: Clarendon Press, 1997.

———. "Women and Preaching in Medieval Orthodoxy, Heresy, and Saints' Lives." *Viator* 26 (1995): 135–52.

————. "Paradox in the Medieval Gender Doctrine of Head and Body." In *Medieval Theology and the Natural Body*, ed. Peter Biller and A. J. Minnis. York: York Medieval Press, 1997.

Blamires, Alcuin and C. W. Marx. "Woman Not to Preach: A Disputation in British Library MS Harley 31." *Journal of Medieval Latin* 3 (1993): 34–63.

Blamires, Alcuin, ed. with Karen Pratt and C. W. Marx. *Woman Defamed and Woman Defended: An Anthology of Medieval Texts*. Oxford: Clarendon Press, 1992.

Bonner, Stanley F. *Education in Ancient Rome from the Elder Cato to the Younger Pliny*. Berkeley: University of California Press, 1977.

Boswell, John. *Christianity, Social Tolerance, and Homosexuality: Gay People in Western Europe from the Beginning of the Christian Era to the Fourteenth Century*. Chicago: University of Chicago Press, 1980.

Bredero, Adriaan H. "The Conflicting Interpretations of the Relevance of Bernard of Clairvaux to the History of His Own Time." *Cîteaux. Commentarii Cistercienses* 31 (1980): 53–81.

Brooke, Christopher. *The Medieval Idea of Marriage*. Oxford: Oxford University Press, 1989.

Brown, Catherine. "*Muliebriter*: Doing Gender in the Letters of Heloise." In *Gender and Text in the Later Middle Ages*, ed. Jane Chance. Gainesville: University Press of Florida, 1996. 25–51.

Brummack, Jurgen. *Die Darstellung des Oriente in den deutschen Alexandergeschichten des Mittelalters*. Berlin: E. Schmidt, 1966.

Bullough, Vern L. "On Being a Male in the Middle Ages." In *Medieval Masculinites: Regarding Men in the Middle Ages*, ed. Clare A. Lees. Minneapolis: University of Minnesota Press, 1994. 31–45.

Burns, Robert Ignatius. *Islam Under the Crusaders: Colonial Survival in the Thirteenth-Century Kingdom of Valencia*. Princeton, N.J.: Princeton University Press, 1973.

Butler, Judith. *Gender Trouble: Feminism and the Subversion of Identity*. London and New York: Routledge, 1990.

Bynum, Caroline Walker. *Jesus as Mother: Studies in the Spirituality of the High Middle Ages*. Berkeley: University of California Press, 1982.

————. *The Resurrection of the Body in Western Christianity, 200–1336*. New York: Columbia University Press, 1995.

Califia, Pat. "Feminism and Sadomasochism." *Heresies* 12 (1981): 3–34.

————. "The Limits of the S/M Relationship." *Outlook* 15 (1992): 16–21.

Carlson, David. "The Practical Theology of St Bernard and the Date of the *De laude novae militiae*." In *Erudition at God's Service*, ed. John R. Sommerfeldt. Studies in Medieval Cistercian History 11. CSS 98. Kalamazoo, Mich.: Cistercian Publications 1987. 133–47.

Carmargo, Martin. *Ars dictaminis, ars dictandi*. Typologie des Sources du Moyen Âge Occidental 60. Turnholt: Brepols, 1991.

Carpenter, Jennifer and Sally-Beth MacLean, eds. *Power of the Weak: Studies on Medieval Women*. Urbana: University of Illinois Press, 1995.

Carruthers, Mary. *The Book of Memory: A Study of Memory in Medieval Culture*. Cambridge: Cambridge University Press, 1990.

Cary, George. *The Medieval Alexander*. Ed. D. J. A. Ross. Cambridge: Cambridge University Press, 1956.

Casey, Michael. *Athirst for God: Spiritual Desire in Bernard of Clairvaux's Sermons on the Song of Songs*. CSS 77. Kalamazoo, Mich.: Cistercian Publications, 1988.

Cerquiglini, Bernard. *Éloge de la variante: Histoire critique de la philologie*. Paris: Éditions du Seuil, 1989.

Chancer, Lynn S. *Sadomasochism in Everyday Life: The Dynamics of Power and Powerlessness*. New Brunswick, N.J.: Rutgers University Press, 1992.

Chenu, M. D. *Nature, Man, and Society in the Twelfth Century: Essays on New Theological Perspectives in the Latin West*. Trans. Jerome Taylor and Lester K. Little. Chicago: University of Chicago Press, 1968.

Cherewatuk, Karen and Ulrike Wiethaus, eds. *Dear Sister: Medieval Women and the Epistolary Genre*. Philadelphia: University of Pennsylvania Press, 1993.

Christensen, Heinrich. *Das Alexanderlied Walters von Châtillon*. Halle: Waisenhaus, 1905. Reprint, Hildesheim: Georg Olms, 1905.

Clark, Kenneth. *Civilisation: A Personal View*. London: British Broadcasting Corporation, 1970.

Coakley, John. Review of Hildegard of Bingen (*Epistolarium*, 1: I–XC. Ed. L. Van Acker. Turnholt.: Brepols, 1991). *Speculum* 68 (1993): 1132–33.

Cohen, Jeffrey Jerome and Bonnie Wheeler, eds. *Becoming Male in the Middle Ages*. New York: Garland, 1997.

Cole, Penny J. *The Preaching of the Crusades to the Holy Land, 1095–1270*. Cambridge, Mass.: Medieval Academy, 1991.

Constable, Giles. *Letters and Letter Collections*. Turnholt: Brepols, 1976.

Curtius, Ernst Robert. *European Literature and the Latin Middle Ages*. Trans. Willard R. Trask. Princeton, N.J.: Princeton University Press, 1973.

d'Alverny, Marie-Thérèse. "Alain de Lille et la *Theologia*." In *L'homme devant Dieu: Mélanges offerts au Père Henri de Lubac*. 3 vols. Paris: Aubier, 1964. Vol. 2, 111–28.

———. "Le symbolisme de la sagesse et le Christ de Saint Dunstan." *Bodleian Library Record* 5 (1954): 232–45.

Daniel, Norman. *Heroes and Saracens: An Interpretation of the Chansons de Geste*. Edinburgh: Edinburgh University Press, 1984.

Daniélou, Jean. *The Ministry of Women in the Early Church*. London: Faith Press, 1961.

DeCesare, R. *Glosse latine e antico-francese all' "Alexandreis" di Gautier de Châtillon*. Milan: Vita e Pensiero, 1951.

Deleuze, Gilles. *Coldness and Cruelty*. In *Masochism* (*Coldness and Cruelty* by Gilles Deleuze and *Venus in Furs* by Leopold von Sacher-Masoch). Trans. Jean McNeil. New York: Zone Books, 1991.

DeRijk, L. M. "Some New Evidence on Twelfth Century Logic: Alberic and the School of Mont Ste Geneviève (Montani)." *Vivarium* 4 (1966): 1–57.

Derolez, Albert. "Deux notes concernant Hildegarde de Bingen." *Scriptorium* 27 (1973): 291–95.

———. "The Genesis of Hildegard of Bingen's 'Liber divinorum operum.'" In *Texts and Manuscripts, essays presented to G. I. Lieftinck*, vol. 2, ed. J. P. Gumbert and M. J. M. DeHaan. Litterae Textuales. Amsterdam: A. L. Van Gendt, 1972.

Desmond, Marilyn. *Reading Dido: Gender, Textuality, and the Medieval Aeneid*.
Minneapolis: University of Minnesota Press, 1994.

Dimier, M. Anselme. "Mourir à Clairvaux!" *Collectanea ordinis Cisterciensis refor-matorum* 17 (1955): 272–85.

Dinshaw, Carolyn. *Chaucer's Sexual Poetics*. Madison: University of Wisconsin Press, 1989.

Dionisotti, A. Carlotta. "Walter of Châtillon and the Greeks." In *Latin Poetry and the Classical Tradition: Essays in Medieval and Renaissance Literature*, ed. Peter Godman and Oswyn Murray. Oxford: Clarendon Press, 1990. 73–96.

d'Olwer, Nicolau. "Sur la date de la *Dialectica* d'Abélard." *Revue du Moyen Âge Latin* 1 (1945): 375–90.

Dragonetti, Roger. *Le gai savoir dans la rhétorique courtoise*. Paris: Éditions du Seuil, 1982.

———. "Joufroi, Count of Poitiers and Lord of Cocaigne." *Yale French Studies* 67 (1984–85): 95–116.

Dronke, Peter. "Abelard and Heloise in Medieval Testimonies." Glasgow: Glasgow University Press, 1976. Reprint in *Intellectuals and Poets in Medieval Europe*. Storia e Letteratura, Raccolta di Studi e Testi, vol. 183. Rome: Edizioni di Storia e Letteratura, 1992. 248–94.

———. "Problemata Hildegardiana." *Mittellateinisches Jahrbuch* 16 (1981): 97–131.

———. "Thierry of Chartres." In *A History of Twelfth-Century Western Philosophy*, ed. Peter Dronke. Cambridge: Cambridge University Press, 1988. 358–85.

———. *Women Writers of the Middle Ages*. Cambridge: Cambridge University Press, 1984.

Duby, Georges. *The Chivalrous Society*. Trans. Cynthia Postan. London: Arnold, 1977.

———. *William Marshal: The Flower of Chivalry*. Trans. Richard Howard. London: Faber, 1986.

Durville, G. *Catalogue de la bibliothèque du Musée Thomas Dobrée*. Vol. 1 (Manu-scrits). Nantes: Musée Thomas Dobrée, 1904.

Dworkin, Andrea. *Pornography: Men Possessing Women*. New York: Perigree, 1979.

Eilberg-Schwartz, Howard. *God's Phallus and Other Problems for Men and Mono-theism*. Boston: Beacon Press, 1994.

Enders, Jody. *Rhetoric and the Origins of Medieval Drama*. Ithaca, N.Y.: Cornell University Press, 1971.

Evans, Gillian. *The Mind of St. Bernard of Clairvaux*. Oxford: Clarendon Press, 1983.

Farr, Susan. "The Art of Discipline: Creating Erotic Dramas of Play and Power." In *Coming to Power: Writings and Graphics on Lesbian S/M*. 3rd ed., ed. SAMOIS (lesbian/feminist S/M organization), 183–91. Boston: Alyson Publications, 1987: 183–91.

Ferguson, Chris. "Autobiography as Therapy: Guibert de Nogent, Peter Abelard, and the Making of Medieval Autobiography." *Journal of Medieval and Renais-sance Studies* 13 (1983): 187–212.

Ferrante, Joan. "The Education of Women in the Middle Ages in Theory, Fact, and Fantasy." In *Beyond Their Sex: Learned Women of the European Past*, ed. Patricia H. Labalme. New York: New York University Press, 1980. 9–42.

———. *Woman as Image in Medieval Literature*. New York: Columbia University Press, 1975.

Ferraro, Susan. "The Anguished Politics of Breast Cancer." *New York Times Magazine*, 15 August 1993.

Ferruolo, Stephen C. *The Origins of the University: The Schools of Paris and Their Critics, 1100–1215*. Stanford, Calif.: Stanford University Press, 1985.

Fetterley, Judith. *The Resisting Reader: A Feminist Approach to American Fiction*. Bloomington: Indiana University Press, 1978.

Fiorenza, Elizabeth Schüssler. *In Memory of Her: A Feminist Theological Reconstruction of Christian Origins*. New York: Crossroad, 1983.

Flanagan, Sabina. "Spiritualis Amicitia in a Twelfth-Century Convent? Hildegard of Bingen and Richardis of Stade." *Parergon* 29 (1981): 15–21.

Fradenburg, Louise O. "'Be not far from me': Psychoanalysis, Medieval Studies, and the Subject of Religion." *Exemplaria* 7 (1995): 41–54.

———. *City, Marriage, Tournament: Arts of Rule in Late Medieval Scotland*. Madison: University of Wisconsin Press, 1991.

———. "'Voice Memorial': Loss and Reparation in Chaucer's Poetry." *Exemplaria* 2 (1990): 169–202.

Freccero, Carla. "Notes of a Post-Sex Wars Theorizer." In *Conflicts in Feminism*, ed. Marianne Hirsch and Evelyn Fox Keller. London and New York: Routledge, 1990. 305–25.

Freud, Sigmund. "The Uncanny." Trans. James Sheridan. In *Standard Edition*, vol. 17. London: Hogarth Press, 1955. 219–56.

Friedman, John. *The Monstrous Races in Medieval Art and Thought*. Cambridge, Mass.: Harvard University Press, 1981.

Froula, Christine. "The Daughter's Seduction: Sexual Violence and Literary History." *Signs* 11 (1986): 621–44.

Gates, Henry Louis, Jr. "Introduction: Writing 'Race' and the Difference It Makes." In *"Race," Writing, and Difference*, ed. Henry Louis Gates, Jr., Chicago: University of Chicago Press, 1986. 1–20.

Gellrich, Jesse. *Discourse and Dominion in the Fourteenth Century: Oral Contexts of Writing in Philosophy, Politics, and Poetry*. Princeton, N.J.: Princeton University Press, 1995.

———. *The Idea of the Book in the Middle Ages: Language Theory, Mythology, and Fiction*. Ithaca, N.Y.: Cornell University Press, 1985.

Georgianna, Linda. "Any Corner of Heaven: Heloise's Critique of Monasticism." *Mediaeval Studies* 49 (1987): 221–53.

Gilson, Etienne. "La cosmogonie de Bernardus Silvestris." *AHDLMA* 3 (1928): 5–24.

Glorieux, P[alémon]. *La littérature quodlibétique de 1260 à 1320*. Le Saulchoir: Kain, 1925.

———. "Mauvaise action et mauvais travail: Le 'Contra quatuor labyrinthos Franciae.'" *Recherches de Théologie Ancienne et Médiévale* 21 (1954): 179–93.

Gold, Barbara K., Paul Allen Miller, and Charles Platter, eds. *Sex and Gender in Medieval and Renaissance Texts: The Latin Tradition*. Albany: State University of New York Press, 1996.

Golding, Sue. "Sexual Manners." *Public* 8 (1993): 61–68.

Goldman, James. *The Lion in Winter*. New York: Random House, 1966.

Gombocz, W. L. "Abaelardus Bedeutungslehre als Schlüssel zum Universaliens-problem." In *Petrus Abaelardus (1079–1142): Person, Werk und Wirkung*, ed. Rudolf Thomas et al. Trier: Paulinus-Verlag, 1980. 153–64.

Grabman, Martin. *Die Geschichte der scholastischen Methode: Nach den gedruckten und ungedruckten Quellen*. 2 vols., 1909–11. Darmstadt: Wissenschaftliche Buchge-sellschaft, 1957.

Green, D. H. *The Millstätter Exodus: A Crusading Epic*. Cambridge: Cambridge University Press, 1966.

Harich, Henriette. *Alexander Epicus: Studien zur Alexandreis Walters von Châtillon*. Graz: Verlag für die Technische Universität Graz, 1987.

Häring, Nikolaus M. *Commentaries on Boethius by Thierry of Chartres and His School*. Toronto: Pontifical Institute of Mediaeval Studies, 1971.

Haskins, Charles Homer. *The Renaissance of the Twelfth Century*. Cambridge, Mass.: Harvard University Press, 1927.

Henry, Desmond Paul. *The Logic of Saint Anselm*. Oxford: Clarendon Press, 1967.

Herwegen, Hildephonse. "Les collaborateurs de Sainte Hildegarde." *Revue Béné-dictine* 21 (1904): 192–203, 302–15, 381–403.

Hexter, Ralph. *Ovid and Medieval Schooling: Studies in Medieval School Commen-taries on Ovid's Ars amatoria, Epistulae ex Ponto, and Epistulae heroidum*. Mu-nich: Arbeo-Gesellschaft, 1986.

Holsinger, Bruce. "The Flesh of the Voice: Embodiment and the Homoerotics of Devotion in the Music of Hildegard of Bingen (1098–1179)." *Signs* 19 (1993): 92–125.

hooks, bell. *Black Looks: Race and Representation*. Boston: South End Press, 1992.

Huchet, Jean-Charles. "La voix d'Héloïse." *Romance Notes* 25 (1985): 271–87.

Irigaray, Luce. "This Sex Which Is Not One." Trans. Claudia Reeder. In *New French Feminisms: An Anthology*, ed. Elaine Marks and Isabelle de Courtivron. Am-herst: University of Massachusetts Press, 1980. 99–106.

Irvine, Martin. "Heloise and the Gendering of the Literate Subject." In *Criticism and Dissent in the Middle Ages*, ed. Rita Copeland. Cambridge: Cambridge University Press, 1996. 87–114.

Jaeger, C. S. "The Prologue to the 'Historia calamitatum' and the 'Authenticity Question.'" *Euphorion* 74 (1980): 1–25.

Jeffreys, Sheila. In *The Lesbian Heresy: A Feminist Perspective on the Lesbian Sexual Revolution*. London: Women's Press, 1994.

Jolivet, Jean. *Arts du langage et théologie chez Abélard*. Paris: J. Vrin, 1969.

———. "Les Principes féminins dans la *Cosmographia* de Bernard Silvestre." In *L'homme et son univers au moyen âge*, ed. Christian Wenin. Louvain: Éditions de L'Institut Supérieur de Philosophie, 1986. 296–305.

Jones, John. *Balliol College: A History, 1263–1939*. Oxford: Oxford University Press, 1988.

Jones, Nancy A. "By Woman's Tears Redeemed: Female Lament in St. Augus-tine's *Confessions* and the Correspondence of Abelard and Heloise." In *Sex and Gender in Medieval and Renaissance Texts: The Latin Tradition*, ed. Barbara K.

Gold, Paul Allen Miller, and Charles Platter. Albany: State University of New York Press, 1997. 15–39.

Kahl, Hans-Dietrich. "Crusade Eschatology as Seen by St. Bernard in the Years 1146 to 1148." In *The Second Crusade and the Cistercians*, ed. Michael Gervers. New York: St. Martin's Press, 1992. 35–47.

Kamuf, Peggy. *Fictions of Feminine Desire: Disclosures of Heloise*. Lincoln: University of Nebraska Press, 1982.

Keats-Rohan, K. S. B. "John of Salisbury and Education in Twelfth-Century Paris from the Account of His *Metalogicon*." *History of Universities* 6 (1986–87): 1–45.

Keen, Maurice. *Chivalry*. New Haven, Conn.: Yale University Press, 1984.

Kittay, Jeffrey and Wlad Godzich. *The Emergence of Prose: An Essay in Prosaics*. Minneapolis: University of Minnesota Press, 1987.

Knowles, David. *The Evolution of Medieval Thought*. New York: Random House, 1962.

Kritzeck, James. *Peter the Venerable and Islam*. Princeton, N.J.: Princeton University Press, 1964.

Kruger, Steven. "Conversion and Medieval Racial, Religious, and Sexual Categories." Paper presented at the Modern Language Association of America, Toronto, December 1994.

Küng, Guido. "Abélard et les vues actuelles sur la question des universaux." In *Abélard, le "Dialogue": La philosophie de la logique*, ed. Maurice de Gandillac et al. Actes du Colloque de Neuchâtel 16–17 novembre 1979. *Cahiers de la Revue de Théologie et de Philosophie* 6. Lausanne: Revue de Théologie et de Philosophie, 1981. 99–118.

Lacan, Jacques. "The Signification of the Phallus." In *Écrits: A Selection*. Trans. Alan Sheridan. New York: Norton, 1977. 281–91.

Lafferty, Maura Keyne. "Reading Latin Epic: Walter of Châtillon's *Alexandreis*." Ph. D. diss., University of Toronto, 1992.

Laplanche, Jean. *Life and Death in Psychoanlaysis*. Trans. Jeffrey Mehalman. Baltimore: Johns Hopkins University Press, 1976.

Laqueur, Thomas. *Making Sex: Body and Gender from the Greeks to Freud*. Cambridge, Mass.: Harvard University Press, 1990.

Laurie, Helen C. R. *The Making of Romance: Three Studies*. Geneva: Librarie Droz, 1991.

Lavezzo, Kathy. "Sobs and Sighs Between Women: The Homoerotics of Compassion in *The Book of Margery Kempe*." In *Premodern Sexualities*, ed. Louise Fradenburg and Carla Freccero. London and New York: Routledge, 1996. 175–98.

Leclercq, Jean. "S. Bernard et la théologie monastique du XIIe siècle." In *Saint Bernard théologien*, ed. Jean Leclercq. *Analecta Sacri Ordinis Cisterciensis* 9 (1953): 7–23.

———. "La littérature provoquée par les *Sermons sur les Cantiques*." *Revue Bénédictine* 64 (1954): 208–22.

———. *The Love of Learning and the Desire for God: A Study of Monastic Culture*. Trans. Catharine Misrahi. New York: Fordham University Press, 1961.

————. *Bernard of Clairvaux and the Cistercian Spirit*. Trans. Claire Lavoie. CSS 16. Kalamazoo, Mich.: Cistercian Publications, 1976.

————. "Were the Sermons on the Song of Songs Delivered in Chapter?" Introduction to *On the Song of Songs II*. Trans. Kilian Walsh, The Works of Bernard of Clairvaux, vol. 3. CFS 7. Kalamazoo, Mich.: Cistercian Publications, 1976.

Lees, Clare A., ed. *Medieval Masculinities: Regarding Men in the Middle Ages*. Minneapolis: University of Minnesota Press, 1994.

Lehmann, Chris. "Pat Churchill, Neurophilosopher." *Lingua Franca* 5 (March/April 1995).

Leupin, Alexandre. *Barbarolexis: Medieval Writing and Sexuality*. Trans. Kate M. Cooper. Cambridge, Mass.: Harvard University Press, 1989.

————."The Middle Ages, the Other." Trans. Frances Bartkowski. *Diacritics* 13 (Fall 1983): 22–31.

Lomperis, Linda. "From God's Book to the Play of the Text in *Cosmographia*." *Medievalia et Humanistica* n.s. 16 (1988): 51–71.

Lomperis, Linda and Sarah Stanbury, eds. *Feminist Approaches to the Body in Medieval Literature*. Philadelphia: University of Pennsylvania Press, 1993.

Luscombe, David E. "From Paris to the Paraclete: The Correspondence of Abelard and Heloise." *Proceedings of the British Academy* 74 (1988): 247–83.

————. *The School of Peter Abelard: The Influence of Abelard's Thought in the Early Scholastic Period*. London: Cambridge University Press, 1969.

Lutz, Cora E. *Schoolmasters of the Tenth Century*. Hamden, Conn.: Archon Books, 1977.

Manitius, Max. *Geschichte der lateinischen Literatur des Mittelalters*. Vol. 3. Munich: Beck, 1931.

Margherita, Gayle. "Originary Fantasies and Chaucer's Book of the Duchess." In *Feminist Approaches*, ed. Lomperis and Stanbury. 116–41.

Marzouki, Samir. "Islam et musulmans dans la *Chanson de Roland*." *Revue Tunisienne de Sciences Sociales* 13 (1976): 105–30.

Matter, E. Ann. "Discourses of Desire: Sexuality and Christian Women's Visionary Narratives." In *Homosexuality and Religion*, ed. Richard Hasbany. London: Haworth Press, 1989. 119–31.

————. *The Voice of My Beloved: The Song of Songs in Western Medieval Christianity*. Philadelphia: University of Pennsylvania Press, 1990.

McClintock, Anne. *Imperial Leather: Race, Gender, and Sexuality in the Colonial Contest*. London and New York: Routledge, 1995.

————. "Maid to Order: Commercial S/M and Gender Power." In *Dirty Looks: Women, Pornography, Power*, ed. Pamela Church Gibson and Roma Gibson. London: British Film Institute, 1993. 207–32.

McGinn, Bernard. "Saint Bernard and Eschatology." In *Bernard of Clairvaux: Studies Presented to Dom Jean Leclercq*, ed. M. Basil Pennington. CSS 23. Washington, D.C.: Cistercian Publications, 1973. 161–85.

McGrath, Elizabeth. "The Black Andromeda." *Journal of the Warburg and Courtauld Institutes* 55 (1992): 1–18.

McGuire, Brian Patrick. *The Difficult Saint: Bernard of Clairvaux and His Tradition*. CSS 126. Kalamazoo, Mich.: Cistercian Publications, 1991.

McLaughlin, Mary Martin. "Abelard as Autobiographer: The Motives and Meaning of His 'Story of Calamities.'" *Speculum* 42 (1967): 463–88.

———. "Peter Abelard and the Dignity of Women: Twelfth Century 'Feminism' in Theory and Practice." In *Pierre Abélard, Pierre le Vénérable: Les courants philosophiques, littéraires et artistiques en Occident au milieu du XIIe siècle*, ed. René Louis, Jean Jolivet, and Jean Châtillon. Paris: Éditions du Centre National de la Recherche Scientifique, 1975. 287–333.

McLeod, Glenda. "'Wholly Guilty, Wholly Innocent': Self Definition in Heloise's Letters to Abelard." In *Dear Sister: Medieval Women and the Epistolary Genre*, ed. Karen Cherewatuk and Ulrike Wiethaus. Philadelphia: University of Pennsylvania Press, 1993. 64–86.

McNamara, Jo Ann. "The *Herrenfrage*: The Restructuring of the Gender System, 1050–1150." In *Medieval Masculinites*, ed. Lees. 3–29.

Mellinkoff, Ruth. *Outcasts: Signs of Otherness in Northern European Art of the Late Middle Ages*. 2 vols. Berkeley: University of California Press, 1993.

Messer-Davidow, Ellen. "The Philosophical Bases of Feminist Literary Criticisms." *New Literary History* 19, 1 (1987): 63–103.

Mews, C. "On Dating the Works of Peter Abelard." *Archives d'Histoire Doctrinale et Littéraire du Moyen Âge* 52 (1985): 73–134.

Middleton, Anne. "The Audience and Public of *Piers Plowman*." In *Middle English Alliterative Poetry and Its Literary Background*, ed. David Lawton. Cambridge: D. S. Brewer, 1982. 101–54.

Minnis, A. J. *Medieval Theory of Authorship: Scholastic Literary Attitudes in the Later Middle Ages*. 2nd ed. Philadelphia: University of Pennsylvania Press, 1988.

Moore, R. I. *The Formation of a Persecuting Society: Power and Deviance in Western Europe, 950–1250*. Oxford: Basil Blackwell, 1987.

Morris, Colin. *The Discovery of the Individual, 1050–1200*. New York: Harper and Row, 1972.

Moulton, Janice. *The Organization of Language*. Cambridge: Cambridge University Press, 1981.

Murphy, James J. "The Teaching of Latin as a Second Language in the Twelfth Century." *Historiographica Linguistica* 7 (1980): 159–75.

Murray, Jacqueline and Konrad Eisenbichler, eds. *Desire and Discipline: Sex and Sexuality in the Pre-Modern West*. Toronto: University of Toronto Press, 1996.

Nadeau, Chantal. "Girls on a Wire Screen: Calvini's Cinema and Lesbian S/M." In *Sexy Bodies: The Strange Carnalities of Feminism*, ed. Elizabeth Grosz and Elspeth Probyn. London and New York: Routledge, 1995: 211–30.

Newman, Barbara. "Authority, Authenticity, and the Repression of Heloise." *Journal of Medieval and Renaissance Studies* 22 (1992): 121–57. Reprint in Newman, *From Virile Woman to WomanChrist*.

———. "Divine Power Made Perfect in Weakness: St. Hildegard on the Frail Sex." In *Medieval Religious Women*, vol. 2, *Peaceweavers*, ed. John A. Nichols and Lillian Thomas Shank. CSS 72. Kalamazoo, Mich.: Cistercian Publications, 1987. 103–22.

———. "Flaws in the Golden Bowl: Gender and Spiritual Formation in the Twelfth Century." *Traditio* 45 (1989–90): 111–46.

———. *From Virile Woman to WomanChrist: Studies in Medieval Religion and Literature*. Philadelphia: University of Pennsylvania Press, 1995.

———. *Sister of Wisdom: St. Hildegard's Theology of the Feminine*. Berkeley: University of California Press, 1987.

Newman, Martha. *The Boundaries of Charity: Cistercian Culture and Ecclesiastical Reform, 1098–1180*. Stanford, Calif.: Stanford University Press, 1996.

Nichols, Stephen G. "An Intellectual Anthropology of Marriage in the Middle Ages." In *The New Medievalism*, ed. Marina S. Brownlee, Kevin Brownlee, and Stephen G. Nichols. Baltimore: Johns Hopkins University Press, 1991. 70–95.

Nouvet, Claire. "The Discourse of the 'Whore': An Economy of Sacrifice." *Modern Language Notes* 105 (1990): 750–73.

Nye, Andrea. "A Woman's Thought or a Man's Discipline? The Letters of Abelard and Heloise." *Hypatia* 7 (1992): 1–22.

Ong, Walter J. "Latin and the Social Fabric." In *The Barbarian Within and Other Fugitive Essays and Studies*. New York: Macmillan, 1962. 206–19.

———. "Latin Language Study as a Renaisssance Puberty Rite." *Studies in Philology* 56 (1959): 103–24.

———. *Orality and Literacy: The Technologizing of the Word*. London and New York: Routledge, 1982.

———, ed. *Rhetoric, Romance, and Technology: Studies in the Interaction of Expression and Culture*. Ithaca, N.Y.: Cornell University Press, 1971.

Owen, D. D. R. *Eleanor of Aquitaine: Queen and Legend*. Oxford: Basil Blackwell, 1993.

Painter, Sidney. *William Marshal: Knight-Errant, Baron, and Regent of England*. 1933. Reprint, Toronto: University of Toronto Press in association with the Medieval Academy of America, 1982.

Parks, Ward. "Flyting and Fighting: Pathways in the Realization of the Epic Contest." *Neophilologus* 70 (1986): 292–306.

———. *Verbal Duelling in Heroic Narrative: The Homeric and Old English Traditions*. Princeton, N.J.: Princeton University Press, 1990.

Partner, Nancy F. "Did Mystics Have Sex?" In *Desire and Discipline: Sex and Sexuality in the Premodern West*, ed. Jacqueline Murray and Konrad Eisenbichler. Toronto: University of Toronto Press, 1996. 296–311.

———. "No Sex, No Gender." *Speculum* 68 (1993): 419–43.

Pfau, Marianne Richert. "Music and Text in Hildegard's Antiphons." In *Symphonia armonie celestium revelationum*, ed. and trans. Barbara Newman. Ithaca, N.Y.: Cornell University Press, 1988. 74–94.

Quilligan, Maureen. *The Allegory of Female Authority: Christine de Pizan's "Cité des Dames"*. Ithaca, N.Y.: Cornell University Press, 1991.

Raby, F. J. E. *A History of Secular Latin Poetry in the Middle Ages*. 2nd ed. 2 vols. Oxford: Clarendon Press, 1957.

Rambuss, Richard. "Pleasure and Devotion: The Body of Jesus and Seventeenth-Century Religious Lyric." In *Queering the Renaissance*, ed. Jonathan Goldberg. Durham, N.C.: Duke University Press, 1994. 253–79.

Rashdall, Hastings. *The Universities of Europe in the Middle Ages*. 2nd ed. Ed. F. M. Powicke and A. B. Emden. 3 vols. Oxford: Clarendon Press, 1936.

Rich, Ruby B. "Feminism and Sexuality in the 1980's." *Feminist Studies* 12 (1986): 525–61.

Riché, Pierre. *Les écoles et l'enseignement dans l'Occident chrétien de la fin du Ve siècle au milieu du XIe siècle.* Paris: Aubier Montaigne, 1979.

Rigg, A. G. *A History of Anglo-Latin Literature, 1066–1422.* Cambridge: Cambridge University Press, 1992.

Robertson, D. W., Jr. *Abelard and Heloise.* New York: Dial Press, 1972.

———. *A Preface to Chaucer: Studies in Medieval Perspectives.* Princeton, N.J.: Princeton University Press, 1963.

Rowe, John G. "The Origins of the Second Crusade: Pope Eugenius III, Bernard of Clairvaux, and Louis VII of France." In *The Second Crusade and the Cistercians,* ed. Michael Gervers. New York: St. Martin's Press, 1992. 79–89.

Rubin, Gayle. "Thinking Sex: Notes for a Radical Theory of the Politics of Sexuality." In *The Lesbian and Gay Studies Reader,* ed. Henry Abelove, Michèle Aina Barale, and David M. Halperin. London and New York: Routledge, 1993. 3–44.

———. "The Traffic in Women: Notes on the 'Political Economy' of Sex." In *Toward an Anthropology of Women,* ed. Rayna Reiter. New York and London: Monthly Review Press, 1975. 157–210.

Rudner, Delaynie. "The Censored Scar." *Gauntlet* 9 (1995): 12–39.

Said, Edward. *Orientalism.* New York: Pantheon, 1978.

Schrader, Marianna and Adelgundis Führkötter. *Die Echtheit des Schrifttums der heiligen Hildegard von Bingen.* Cologne: Böhlau, 1956.

Sedgwick, Eve Kosofsky. *Between Men: English Literature and Male Homosocial Desire.* New York: Columbia University Press, 1985.

Segal, Lynne. *Slow Motion: Changing Masculinities, Changing Men.* New Brunswick, N.J.: Rutgers University Press, 1990.

Seidler, Victor J. *Rediscovering Masculinity: Reason, Language and Sexuality.* London and New York: Routledge, 1989.

Sikes, J. G. *Peter Abailard.* Cambridge: Cambridge University Press, 1932.

Silvas, Anna. "Saint Hildegard of Bingen and the Vita Sanctae Hildegardis." *Tjurunga* 29 (1985): 4–25; 30 (1986): 32–41; 32 (1987): 46–59.

Silverman, Kaja. *Male Subjectivity at the Margins.* London and New York: Routledge, 1992.

Silverstein, Theodore. "The Fabulous Cosmogony of Bernard Silvestris." *Modern Philology* 46 (1948–49): 92–116.

Sinfield, Alan. *Cultural Politics—Queer Reading.* Philadelphia: University of Pennsylvania Press, 1994.

Solterer, Helen. "Figures of Female Militancy in Medieval France," *Signs* 16 (1991): 522–49.

———. *The Master and Minerva: Disputing Women in French Medieval Culture.* Berkeley: University of California Press, 1995.

Sommerfeldt, John. "The Chimaera Revisited." *Cîteaux: Commentarii Cistercienses* 38 (1987): 5–13.

Southern, R. W. *Medieval Humanism and Other Studies.* Oxford: Basil Blackwell, 1970.

Spiegel, Gabrielle M. "History, Historicism, and the Social Logic of the Text in the Middle Ages," *Speculum* 65 (1990): 59–86.

———. *Romancing the Past: The Rise of Vernacular Prose Historiography in Thirteenth-Century France*. Berkeley: University of California Press, 1993.

Stock, Brian. *Myth and Science in the Twelfth Century*. Princeton, N.J.: Princeton University Press, 1972.

Stone, Laurence. "History and Postmodernism, III." *Past and Present* 135 (1992): 189–94.

Swietek, Francis R. "Gunther of Pairis and the *Historia Constantinopolitana*." *Speculum* 53 (1978): 49–79.

Taylor, Robert. "The Old French 'Cistercian' Translations." In *Medieval Translators and Their Craft*, ed. Jeanette Beer. Kalamazoo, Mich.: Medieval Institute, 1989.

Taylor, Robert Allen. "Li Sermon saint Bernart sur les Cantikes." Ph.D. diss., University of Toronto, 1964.

Tepper, Sheri S. *The Gate to Women's Country*. New York: Doubleday, 1988.

Thomas, Richard F. *Lands and Peoples in Roman Poetry: The Ethnographical Tradition*. Cambridge: Cambridge Philological Society, 1982.

Thomas, Rudolf et al. eds. *Petrus Abaelardus (1079–1142): Person, Werk und Wirkung*. Trier: Paulinus-Verlag, 1980.

Thompson, Augustine. "The Debate on Universals Before Peter Abelard." *Journal of the History of Philsophy* 33 (1995): 409–29.

Tompkins, Jane. "A Short Course in Post-Structuralism." *College English* 50, 7 (1988): 733–47.

Townsend, David. "*Mihi barbaries incognita linguae*: Other Voices and Other Visions in Walter of Châtillon's *Alexandreis*." *Allegorica* 10 (1992): 21–37.

Trotter, D. A. *Medieval French Literature and the Crusades (1100–1300)*. Geneva: Librairie Droz, 1988.

Trudeau, Gary. "*And What Do We Have for the Witnesses, Johnnie?*" New York: Holt, Rinehart and Winston, 1975.

Tweedale, Martin M. *Abailard on Universals*. Amsterdam: North Holland Publishing, 1976.

———. "Abelard and the Culmination of the Old Logic." In *The Cambridge History of Later Medieval Pilosophy*, ed. Norman Kretzmann et al. Cambridge: Cambridge University Press, 1982. 143–57.

Vance, Eugene. *Mervelous Signals: Poetics and Sign Theory in the Middle Ages*. Lincoln: University of Nebraska Press, 1986.

von Bezold, Friedrich. *Das Fortleben der antiken Götter im mittelalterlichen Humanismus*. Bonn and Leipzig: Kurt Schroeder, 1922.

Waddell, Helen. *The Wandering Scholars*. London: Constable, 1949.

Ward, J. O. "The Date of the Commentary on Cicero's 'De Inventione' by Thierry of Chartres (ca. 1095–1160?) and the Cornifician Attack on the Liberal Arts." *Viator* 3 (1972): 219–37.

Weedon, Chris. *Feminist Practice and Poststructuralist Theory*. Oxford: Basil Blackwell, 1987.

Williams, John R. "William of the White Hands and Men of Letters." In *Anni-*

versary Essays in Mediaeval History by Students of Charles Homer Haskins, ed. Charles Holt Taylor. Boston: Houghton Mifflin, 1929. 365–87.

Wilson, Katharina and Elizabeth Makowski. *Wikked Wives and the Woes of Marriage: Misogamous Literature from Juvenal to Chaucer*. Albany: State University of New York Press, 1992.

Zink, Michel. *Prédication en langue romane avant 1300*. Paris: Éditions Honoré Champion, 1976.

Ziolkowski, Jan. "Cultural Diglossia and the Nature of Medieval Latin Literature." In *The Ballad and Oral Literature*, ed. Joseph Harris. Harvard English Studies 17. Cambridge, Mass.: Harvard University Press, 1991. 193–213.

Zumthor, Paul. *Essai de poétique médiévale*. Paris: Éditions du Seuil, 1972; *Toward a Medieval Poetics*. Trans. Philip Bennett. Minneapolis: University of Minnesota Press, 1992.

———. "Jonglerie et langage." *Poétique* 9 (1972): 321–36.

———. *Parler du moyen âge*. Paris: Éditions du Minuit, 1980.

Zwierlein, Otto. *Der prägende Einfluss des antiken Epos auf die "Alexandreis" des Walter von Châtillon*. Stuttgart: Steiner, 1987.

Contributors

ALCUIN BLAMIRES is Senior Lecturer at the University of Wales, Lampeter and is the editor of *Women Defamed and Women Defended: An Anthology of Medieval Texts* and the author of a number of articles on medieval gender studies.

MARILYNN DESMOND is Associate Professor of English and Comparative Literature at the State University of New York, Binghamton. She is the author of *Reading Dido: Gender, Textuality, and the Medieval Aeneid*.

CLAIRE FANGER holds her Ph.D. in Medieval Studies from the University of Toronto. She is the cotranslator, with Sian Echard, of *The Latin Verses in the Confessio Amantis: An Annotated Translation*.

JOAN FERRANTE is Professor of English and Comparative Literature at Columbia University. She has published extensively on Old French epic and romance and on Dante. Her work on questions of gender includes *Woman as Image in Medieval Literature, from the Twelfth Century to Dante* (1975) and her forthcoming study of Hildegard of Bingen.

BRUCE HOLSINGER is Assistant Professor of English at the University of Colorado at Boulder. He has written on the homoerotics of devotion in the works of Hildegard of Bingen and in the culture of early polyphonic music.

ANDREW TAYLOR is Assistant Professor of English at the University of Saskatchewan. He has published on medieval reading practice and minstrel performance and is a coeditor of *The Idea of the Vernacular: An Anthology of Middle English Literary Theory, 1280–1530*.

DAVID TOWNSEND is Associate Professor of Medieval Studies and English at the University of Toronto. He has translated the *Alexandreis* of Walter of Châtillon into English verse (University of Pennsylvania Press) and has published extensively on the interpretation of medieval Latin texts.

Index

Acknowledgments

Our first thanks go to the contributors to this volume and to all the participants in the 1995 conference at the University of Toronto where this project first took shape. Karla Mallette, Mary Catherine Davidson, and Lara Hinchberger helped organize the conference, and Rosemary Beattie provided invaluable guidance.

In preparing the collection we benefited from the attentive readings of the two anonymous reviewers for the University of Pennsylvania Press, whose suggestions made this a much stronger volume.

For their generous funding of the conference and their assistance with the costs of publication we thank the Social Sciences and Humanities Research Council of Canada; the Centre for Medieval Studies, the Departments of Classics and English, the Offices of the Provost, the Deans of the School of Graduate Studies and of the Faculty of Arts and Science, and the Vice-President for Research and International Relations at the University of Toronto; and the Office of the Dean of Arts and Science and the Publication Fund at the University of Saskatchewan.

Special thanks go to Claire Fanger, who prepared the index with efficiency and scholarly acumen.

Rob Norquay bore patiently the repeated appropriation of the dining room table.

Roberta Frank, director of the Centre for Medieval Studies at the University of Toronto, and Paul Reichardt, chair of the Department of Literature and Language at Northern Kentucky University, offered generous and wise counsel.

Finally, we thank the many friends and colleagues who wove the web of conversation, indefinable and essential, from which this collection emerges.